Ideas and Ideologies
General Editor:
Eugene Kamenka

Justice

Edited by Eugene Kamenka
and Alice Erh-Soon Tay

St. Martin's Press
New York

© Edward Arnold (Publishers) Ltd 1980

All rights reserved. For information write:
St Martin's Press, Inc., 175 Fifth Avenue, New York, N.Y. 10010
Printed in Great Britain
First published in the United States of America in 1980

ISBN 0-312-44945-3

Library of Congress Cataloging in Publication Data

Main entry under title:
Justice.

(Ideas and ideologies)
Papers presented at a symposium on theories of jus-
tice in and for the second half of the twentieth century
held during the Extraordinary World Congress of the
International Association for Philosophy of Law and
Social Philosophy, at the University of Sydney in
August 1977.
Includes index.
1. Justice—Congresses. I. Kamenka, Eugene.
II. Tay, Alice Erh-Soon. III. Internationale
Vereinigung für Rechts- und Sozialphilosophie.
IV. Series: Ideas and ideologies.

Library of Congress Cataloging in Publication Data

JC578.J86   340.1'1   79-22174
ISBN 0-312-44945-3

Contents

Introduction

The idea of justice, more than any idea yet discussed in this series, is a perennial one. Some, indeed, would call it eternal. However that may be, it is not an invention of the seventeenth or eighteenth or nineteenth century, let alone of the twentieth. In this field, the considerations urged by Plato and Aristotle, and even by Confucius and Lao-tse, do not strike us as belonging to an infinitely remote and irrelevant past or as dealing with problems that are simply not our own. Perhaps this is so because justice is a formal concept and because the great classical definitions of justice are remarkably 'open' in character (as one of our contributors puts it), leaving each age or social group to pour in its own content or make its own application. The second half of the twentieth century, certainly, has seen such a fundamental and continuing debate about the practical requirements of justice—about the relationships between ethical, legal and social justice, between justice and rights, between justice, freedom and equality. That debate, as a number of contributors to this volume argue, has been characterized by a tendency to blur or reject distinctions between formal justice and natural justice, lawyers' justice and social or ethical justice, justice itself and other ethical categories, in the attempt to find a universal solvent, a supreme principle of action.

With this modern debate in mind, the Organizing Committee of the Extraordinary World Congress of the International Association for Philosophy of Law and Social Philosophy, held in Sydney and Canberra in August 1977, arranged as part of its programme a public symposium on 'Theories of Justice in and for the Second Half of the Twentieth Century'. That symposium, held in the Assembly Hall of the Faculty of Law of the University of Sydney, had Professors Brian Barry, J. A. Passmore and Julius Stone as its principal speakers. It was preceded by working group discussions on justice led by the Honourable Mr Justice F. C. Hutley, Professor L. C. Holborow and

Mr C. Arnold. The papers read at that symposium, together with the paper presented to the discussion group by the Polish legal philosopher, Professor Wiesław Lang, form the nucleus of this volume. Its editors and readers owe much to the legal and social philosophers from thirty-odd countries who took part in the work of the Congress and to the principal donors who made that Congress possible. They include the Committee for Post-Graduate Studies in the Department of Law, University of Sydney; the Utah Foundation; the State of New South Wales; the Commonwealth of Australia; UNESCO; the Australian National University; the Australian Academy of the Humanities; the Faculty of Law, University of Western Australia; the University of New South Wales; the New South Wales Bar Association; the University of Newcastle; the Academy of the Social Sciences in Australia; the Australia–Japan Foundation; the Faculty of Law, University of Queensland; Edward Lumley & Sons Pty Ltd; and the Australasian Universities' Law Schools Association. Without their help, the Congress and this book, we believe, would have been a poorer thing.

The editors also owe much to the support of the Max-Planck-Gesellschaft and the German Academic Exchange Service (DAAD) and to the hospitality of Trinity College, Oxford and the Max-Planck-Institute for Foreign Private Law and Private International Law in Hamburg, on whose premises their own contributions were written and the editing of the volume completed. Miss Marion Pascoe of the Department of Jurisprudence in the University of Sydney has rendered them much help, in the research for their own contributions, in checking the manuscript and proofs and in compiling the index.

Hamburg, February 1979   Eugene Kamenka
                                                    Alice Erh-Soon Tay

I

What is justice?

Eugene Kamenka

I

Justice, it is often said, is an idea and an ideal. Like law and morality, it rests on the tension or contradiction between what is and what at least some men think ought to be. It represents or pre-supposes a criticism of an existing reality or state of affairs allegedly in the light of principles or an ideal end-state; it is in that sense said to be both transcendent and a guide to action and evaluation. Like law and morality and other social phenomena that claim transcendence, it has often been associated with and seen as dependent upon the transcendence worshipped in religion. Thus justice has been regarded as the will of God or the gods, of cosmic forces, providence or destiny, that govern, shape and censure, distort or annihilate the designs of men. That element of transcendence, though singled out in and elevated by religion, does not need to be explained in religious terms. Transcendence is the recognition of an empirical fact: that men and situations are part always of a wider situation in space and time, that social arrangements and designs are independent of and precede and outlast the will and designs of any given individual, and that such social and individual designs may be logically and empirically dependent upon things outside their direct and immediate control. It can also be the recognition of logical, empirical or psychological priority: that some propositions or demands are logically, empirically or psychologically more fundamental, more pervasive than others related to them, indeed presupposed by them. In this latter sense, people can and do speak of justice or morality transcending law. In the Greek concepts of *moira* and *diké*, in the emphasis on 'harmony' and 'yielding' common to Confucianism and Taoism, we have the further recognition that the internal conflicts between social activities, moral-ities and human designs can be pressed to the point where they lead to mutual self-destruction—the recognition, that is, that even such conflicts have their necessary or 'proper' bounds or limits. It is from that recognition that the connection of justice with harmony arises and it is from the same recognition that arguments for the necessity of justice and of a divine or human lawgiver take their empirical departure.

Anacharsis the Scythian, who came from the plains north of the Black Sea and lived some two centuries before Plato, is reputed to have said:

> Nature is almost always in opposition to the laws, because she labours for the happiness of the individual, without regard to other individuals who surround him, while the laws only direct their attention to the relations by which he is united to them and because Nature infinitely diversifies our character and inclinations, while it is the object of the laws to bring them back to unity.

This tension between conflict and cooperation, discord and harmony, to which Anacharsis refers, has formed the underlying theme of most moral and political philosophy. Ethical and political theorists have portrayed it in different guises, as the struggle between egotism and altruism, self-love and love of the state, civil society and the political state, evil and good, chaos and harmony, nature and civilization or (alternatively) civilization and nature. Much of their portrayal has been characterized by confusion, especially by the confusions of individualism, reducing the conflict of social traditions and moralities to questions of individual outlook or desire, and often by the false belief that either conflict or cooperation is fundamental, an expression of 'real' human nature whose opposite arises unnaturally, artificially, through distortion. Whatever the truth of this matter (social forces and traditions, I would argue, precede and shape any given individual, and conflict and cooperation are equally natural and often presuppose each other), the fundamental concern with conflict and cooperation as social categories brings justice into relation with law and morality, makes it a central concept in each of those fields. But the problem of justice cannot be resolved by recourse to the myth of a single, common underlying morality that we all share, to the conception that the danger of mutual self-destruction implies clear and demonstrable 'rules of the road', which assign to each type of activity its proper rules and limits, or to an idea or ideal of universality, whether inherent in man or reason or in the laws, in which all particulars are subsumed and reconciled. That, as we shall see, is why it is impossible to give a satisfactory grounding in logic or in fact to the conception of justice as more than a specific social tradition—as the alleged idea, ideal or principle that determines impartially and rationally the nature and limits of all rights and duties, all benefits and entitlements, in society.

The concept of justice, as a concept bringing into relation law and morality or moralities, has tended to slide between two poles. It has been seen as the faithful realization of existing law, the vindication of it against arbitrary infraction or disregard. This conception of justice rules out, as a contradiction in terms, the concept of an unjust law or an unjust legal system or procedure: it equates justice with conformity to law. Generalized to cover legal systems that differ or that change, it tends to put special emphasis on procedure, on the manner of reaching decisions, on principled, 'rule-governed' conduct and judgement, contrasting these with the arbitrary, self-willed despotic. Justice is treating parties equally, that is, according to a general rule, to law. This is a concept of justice that is especially strong, as Professor Tay shows below, at periods when the comparatively rational procedures of legal argument and determination are being exalted against the violence of self-help and the irrationalities of quasi-magical ritual, such as trial by ordeal. It is strong, again, as it was in the works of the very young Marx, when the internal ('rational') requirements of law and the subjects it deals with can be contrasted with despotism, or with the external and therefore, in relation to law, arbitrary requirements of religion, monarchy, censorship. At the other pole, justice has been regarded as the ideal element in all law, as the 'idea' which is the end of the law and in terms of which any existing set of laws or legal procedures is to be judged, so that there are just and unjust laws, and not only unjust applications. It is at this end that the concept of justice is not merely a moral concept but is in constant danger of being merged with and swallowed up by the whole of morality, losing any specific connotation or edge, becoming a shorthand for all the urgent and important demands which we elevate in the name of morality. Alternatively, justice in the wider sense may be presented as the central and organizing concept in morality, justice as the righteousness of the Old Testament. The problem of distinguishing justice from morality in general, and of recognizing that different sorts of attitudes and demands may call themselves demands for justice, while conflicting with each other, is one to which both Professor Passmore and Professor Stone address themselves in this volume.

Justice, says Aristotle, consists in treating equals equally and unequals unequally, in proportion to their inequality. Justice, say the *Institutes* of Justinian, with the economy and sense of the systematic characteristic of the lawyer, 'is the set and constant purpose to give every man his due'. The connection of justice with equality and proportion has been elevated ever since as its central and specific feature. Aristotle, extremely perceptively, recognized that the equality implied in justice could be arithmetical, based on identity, or geometrical, based on maintaining the same proportion: justice based on arithmetical equality he called *corrective* or *commutative* justice; it was, for him, the justice of the judge, to be used in imposing punishment and making orders for compensation to be paid. For these purposes all men were to be treated equally, impartially. (Aquinas, later, regarded such justice as the justice that governs contracts and exchange, justice between individuals as individuals.) Justice based on geometrical equality, on giving to each according to his merit or desert, Aristotle called *distributive* justice, concerned with allocating benefits. Such justice, for him, was the proper business of the legislator. It should be applied in determining political rights, honours and the distribution of wealth. Aquinas, later, and a whole series of social natural law theorists from Grotius to Leibniz and Wolff, emphasized distributive justice as being concerned with the creation and maintenance of a harmonious social whole, bringing about a synthesis between society and the individual, ultimately by reconciling in the *justitia communis* commutative, distributive and universal principles, but putting emphasis not on subjective rights but upon an objective social equilibrium. It is this final reconciliation of the different kinds of justice in the *justitia communis* which returns to a third sense of justice in Aristotle, justice as a moving equilibrium seeking to reconcile the conflicting demands of distributive and commutative justice. The problem of recognizing and resolving that tension is not only the subject of the whole of this volume, but the main burden of all argument about justice today, though those seriously concerned with law know full well that in its operations commutative and distributive justice cannot be sharply distinguished. We can distinguish, however, a much more specific and coherent tradition, centred on the concept of impartiality and the requirements of corrective justice, from the broader concern with distributive justice or universal justice, with its conflict over 'merits' and the fundamental basis of 'entitlement' and its consequent importation into the theory of justice of all the conflicts that surround social and moral policy generally.

II

Let us look first at justice in the narrow sense—if not as conformity to existing law, then at least as a concept intimately connected with law and legal morality and traditions rather than with morality generally. Sociological analysts of actual legal systems have tended to stress that law performs three different if perhaps related and relatable functions in society.[1]

1. Law seeks to establish and maintain what even Lenin called

---

[1] In what follows in this section, I have drawn on material Alice Tay and I have written jointly for A. E. S. Tay and E. Kamenka (eds), *Law-Making in Australia* (London and Melbourne, 1979), pp. 26 and 31–4 and in our 'Beyond the French Revolution: Communist Socialism and the Concept of Law', *University of Toronto Law Journal* XXI (1971), pp. 109–40.

certain simple fundamental rules of living together. Lenin and many others have thought that these were known to all ages and were something which, in the proper conditions, all rational persons of goodwill could agree upon. In fact, it is not easy to separate these so-called basic requirements of social life from historically specific conceptions of social aims and social goods and of particular social orders, with their fundamental constitutions, class and power structures, social and moral conceptions and taboos, protected by legal or customary sanctions with a degree of implied and actual force.

2. Law provides principles and procedures for conflict resolution between individuals and groups within a society, at least in so far as those individuals and groups accept a version or aspect of a common social order that includes submission to law.

3. To varying degrees at various times and in different places, law both guarantees and protects existing productive relationships and ways of distributing resources and provides the means for active intervention by the sovereign or state, for whatever reasons or at whatever behest, to actualize new principles and policies for resource allocation and to enforce and supervise the carrying out of these.

These three functions of law—the peace-keeping and social harmonizing function, the conflict-resolution function and the resource-allocation function—have all been recognized in and given varying emphasis by different theories or alleged types of justice. The peace-keeping and social harmonizing function is much emphasized, as we might expect, in theories of justice that elevate its connection with the social organism or whole, with determining the 'proper' place of individuals, activities and institutions in a structured totality free of destructive conflicts. Such a view of justice is especially strong in traditional, pre-modern, organic, pre-capitalist societies (communities), characterized by the German sociologist, Ferdinand Tönnies, as *Gemeinschaft* societies.[2] In the *Gemeinschaft* type of social regulation, punishment and resolution of disputes, the emphasis is on law and regulation as expressing the will, internalized norms and traditions of an organic community, within which every individual member is part of a social family. Here there tends to be no sharp distinction, if there is any formal distinction at all, between the private and the public, between the civil wrong and the criminal offence,

---

[2] In his *Gemeinschaft und Gesellschaft (Community and Association)*, first published in 1887, and appearing in numerous revised editions until his death in 1936. There are now two English translations, based on the text of later editions. See also E. Kamenka, 'Gemeinschaft and Gesellschaft', *Political Science* (NZ) XVII (1965), pp. 3–12, for a fuller discussion of the different types of wills and attitudes to the separation of means and ends involved in the distinction between *Gemeinschaft* and *Gesellschaft*.

between politics, justice and administration, between political issues, legal issues and moral issues. There is little emphasis on the abstract, formal criteria of justice. The person at the bar of judgement is there, in principle, as a whole man, bringing with him his status, his occupation and his environment, all of his history and his social relations. He is not there as an abstract right-and-duty-bearing individual, as just a party to the contract or as owing a specific and limited duty to another. Justice is thus substantive, directed to a particular case in a particular social context and not to the establishing of a general rule or precedent. Its symbols are the seal and the pillory. The formalisms of procedure in this type of justice, which can be considerable, are linked with magical taboo notions, are emotive in content and concrete in formulation; they are not based on abstract rationalistic concepts of justice and procedure. The almost over-whelming strength of this *Gemeinschaft* strain in traditional Chinese legal practice, with its emphasis on the emperor and the magistrate as the father of his people, and in popular Chinese concepts of the political order, justice, morality and the place of the individual in society, is widely recognized; it was very much the medieval world-picture in Europe, it was also characteristic of proceedings before the early English jury and in the Russian peasant *mir*, especially as envisaged in the *sudebnik* of Ivan III in 1497; it remains characteristic of aspects of justice in communist societies, with their emphasis on the general social behaviour of the accused.

The *Gemeinschaft*, for Tönnies and for me, is not a description of an actual existing society in all its aspects: it describes a dominant or strong *Moment* (in the Hegelian sense) of a society; it is a Weberian ideal type, linking actual institutions and historical ideologies or perceptions on which they rest and which they mould and showing how these presuppose and tend toward a particular view of man and society and the relations between them. There are in any society countervailing trends to the dominant world-view, institutions that do not fit, beliefs that do not square—sometimes very powerful or important institutions or beliefs. The king's common law in feudal England was one such institution that, in certain respects, quite fundamentally did not square and stood in contradiction with baronial justice. So were elements of Roman private law (as opposed to Roman public law) in the Republic, the Principate and the Empire, even if the concept of *ius* was backed by the *Gemeinschaft* philosophy of the Stoics. For the *Gemeinschaft* as *Gemeinschaft* does not have, as we have seen, a specific legal tradition. It brings together law, justice and morality and fuses them with politics and administration. The countervailing trends—Roman law, for example, and even the Greek codes—are strikingly the product of commerce and cities, of the need to provide for justice between citizen and foreigner, those inside the

Gemeinschaft and those outside it, and of class struggles within the *Gemeinschaft* in which the lower classes demanded guarantees and settled procedures in place of the patrician conception of justice as custom, *their* customs.

The *Gemeinschaft* conception of justice, then, in its general assumptions or trend is a particular conception of justice rather than a universal one, though it has universal pretensions. It elevates social harmony and subordinates both conflict resolution and resource allocation to a conception of the total social order. In doing so, it does not simply neglect conflict resolution or resource allocation: it takes a different view of them, emphasizing a sharp dichotomy of reconciliation or total outlawry in conflict, elevating status, 'merit' and such concepts as the just price in resource allocation. But it is true that the *Gemeinschaft* conception of justice is above all the conception of the *justitia communis*, in which universal principles of justice and both commutative and distributive justice are reconciled as mere parts of the whole and in which law, too, is seen as only an instrument. The content of this *justitia communis* tends to be provided by custom, tradition and a conception of a religiously sanctified order, in modern conditions, by social ideology and its policies. Behind them, of course, lurk historical accident, power and interest. In so far as the *Gemeinschaft* conception of justice may be said to have contributed something comparatively timeless to the conception of justice, or to display a common feature with other conceptions of justice, it has done so by elevating in its moral conceptions of justice the element of reciprocity —of rights and privileges involving duties as a moral and not a logical matter. (This is what Confucius does in taking the five relationships —governor and governed, parents and children, elder brother and younger brother, husband and wife, friends—as models for the social order.) The *Gemeinschaft* is not clear, in fact, it is systematically unclear, about what is often taken to be a fundamental characteristic or even definition of justice in modern positivist thought—justice as action according to rule. It elevates the situational ethic against the ethic of rules and principles.

Today, there is in many quarters considerable enthusiasm for a new secular *Gemeinschaft*—an organic community in which all persons and all activities are seen and judged as part of an organic whole, but without recourse to status, structured hierarchies or religious or customary taboos. The evidence so far is that status, structure, hierarchy and a strong quasi-religious ideology meant to provide social direction and cohesion emerge quickly when the experiment is on a national scale; but again the conception of justice that is elevated (if one is elevated at all) is that of the *justitia communis*, with its discounting of law and legal rights, its belief that justice is not to be seen as primarily or distinctively a legal matter, as application of rules, but as a matter of assessing ('understanding') the total man and the total situation.

To the traditional *Gemeinschaft*, Tönnies counterposed the modern commercial, politically pluralist and democratic society, the *Gesellschaft*. The *Gesellschaft* type of law and legal regulation is in all respects the very opposite of the *Gemeinschaft* type. It arises out of the growth of individualism and of the protest against the status society and the fixed locality; it is linked with social and geographical mobility, with cities, commerce, and the rise of the bourgeoisie. It assumes a society based on external, mechanical as opposed to organic solidarity, made up of atomic individuals and private interests, each in principle equivalent to the other, capable of agreeing on common means while maintaining their diverse ends. It emphasizes formal procedure, impartiality, adjudicative justice, precise legal provisions and definitions, and the rationality and predictability of legal administration. It is oriented to the precise definition of the rights and duties of the individual through a sharpening of the point at issue and not to the day-to-day *ad hoc* maintenance of social harmony, community traditions and organic solidarity; it reduces the public interest to another, only *sometimes* overriding, private interest. It distinguishes sharply between law and administration, between the public and the private, the legal and the moral, between the civil obligation and the criminal offence. Its model for all law is contract and the *quid pro quo* associated with commercial exchange, which also demands rationality and predictability. It has difficulty in dealing with the state or state instrumentalities, with corporations, social interests and the administrative requirements of social planning or a process of production, unless it reduces them to the interests of a 'party' to the proceedings, confronting another 'party' on the basis of formal equivalence and legal interchangeability. The American constitution and the Bill of Rights and the French Declaration of the Rights of Man and the Citizen are the fundamental ideological documents of the *Gesellschaft* type of law, which reached the peak of its development in the judicial attitudes of nineteenth-century England and of German Civilians. It is enshrined, at least in part, in the concept of the *Rechtsstaat* and the rule of law, that is, of a specifically legal conception of the foundations and core of the operation of justice in society. It is at home with the social contract theory of society, with individualism and abstract rights. This view again elevates a specific, historically shaped conception of justice, closely linked with individualism and a specific legal tradition, grounded in the private law of the Romans and focusing on law and justice as conflict resolution according to broad general principles and rules applying to all persons in that situation. But while this view of justice too elevates one particular function, that of conflict resolution, it has its characteristic views of the social-ordering and resource-allocation function. It assimilates the former, as far as possible, to the minimum framework necessary for orderly and effective individual pursuits, that is, to the rules of the road or the basic regulations of buying and selling necessary to make a market possible. Resource allocation it leaves to the efforts of individual enterprise, at least in principle. (In fact, of course, no society has been a pure *Gesellschaft* and no relations or institutions have ever been based solely on the cash nexus or individual interest.) But the *Gesellschaft* conception of law and justice is especially suspicious of the attempt to derive these from the social whole; it sees the state as resting on law and serving the pluralism of private interests, rather than imposing a superior and independent universal interest or justice.

The fundamental character and presuppositions of this *Gesellschaft* conception of law and justice, of justice as based on the juridical element in human affairs, have been delineated sharply and well by one of its strongest but also most perceptive critics, the Soviet Marxist legal theorist E. B. Pashukanis, doyen of Soviet legal science in the late 1920s and early 1930s, 'disgraced' in the mid-1930s and a victim of Stalin's terror a year or two later.

Shallow Marxists, especially those engaged in political propaganda rather than thinking, have assiduously enough promoted the view, later also espoused by the more jurimetric American 'realists', that systems of law and legal traditions are not an independent social force but merely ideologies or tools, reflecting or 'rationalizing' the will of the Sovereign, the judge or the interests of a ruling class, having no character or shape of their own. In his *The General Theory of Law and Marxism*, first published in Moscow by the Socialist Academy in 1924, Pashukanis argued the contrary and presented what is essentially a radical and thoroughgoing critique of any attempt to treat law as mere class ideology or to speak of a proletarian system of law replacing a bourgeois system. The point on which any analysis of *law* must concentrate, he argued, is that not all rules or norms are *legal* rules or norms and not all social relationships are *legal* relationships. While most Marxists before him had taken the element of state compulsion to be the characteristic or defining element of law, Pashukanis insisted that army regulations, rules binding the members of an order or priesthood, or the authoritarian prescriptions of a family head or elder, for example, do not constitute or become *law* if or because they are sanctioned by authority, be it even the authority of the state. They are not law and do not have the form of law because they are based on relations of domination and submission, because they involve obedience to rules rather than the determination of rights.

What is characteristic of *law* and constitutes the 'essence' or formal quality of law, according to Pashukanis, is the conception of a juridical subject confronting other juridical subjects on the basis of equality and 'equivalence'. Law is thus characteristically adjudicative and is thereby distinguished from administration; its essence is involved and revealed in the conception of *contract* rather than that of decree. The categories and principles characteristic of law presuppose the legal subject as an individual acting 'freely' in his relations with other 'free' individuals and having rights as well as duties. Such legal subjects must, in law, be abstracted from their social context and reduced to legal individuality and abstract equality, so that even the state can appear in litigation only as another individual subject having rights and duties vis-à-vis the citizen in the same way that the citizen has rights and duties vis-à-vis it.

In line with this, Pashukanis attempted to show how the contractual model in fact dominates all areas of law—public law, with its conception of the social contract and the rights of the citizen; criminal law, which makes the wrongdoer 'pay' for his crime according to a scale of fixed penalties; matrimonial and family law, which dissolves familial relationships into a system of reciprocal rights and duties. Here Pashukanis is much closer than Lenin or Reisner—or Vyshinsky and even contemporary Soviet legal theorists—to Marx's fundamental critique of 'abstract' law and 'abstract' bourgeois justice as proclaiming a formal equality which, in the concrete social situation of class societies, amounts to real *in*equality. 'The "Republic of the Market" ', Pashukanis wrote in the preface to the second Russian edition of his *General Theory of Law and Marxism*, 'conceals the "Despotism of the Factory".'

Pashukanis went on to argue that many Marxist writers, in treating law as ideology and emphasizing the elements of state compulsion and hypocritically concealed class interest, fail to notice the much more direct connection between law and the economic structure of society. The fundamental presupposition of law, that is, the principle of the juridical subject (involving the formal principle of freedom and equality, autonomy of the person, and so on), is not, he argued, merely a hypocritical tool used by the bourgeoisie to enslave the proletariat; it is a real, active principle embodied in bourgeois society once it breaks free from the feudal-patriarchal order. Further, the victory of the law is not merely an ideological process, but a real, material one— a 'judicializing' of human relationships which accompanies the development of a commodity and money economy (in Europe, of capitalism), and which involves the overthrow of serfdom and the separation of political power from society as a particular, *partial* power. Thus, law is not just the 'ideology' of the bourgeoisie, but a reflection of the assumptions of commodity exchange: it reflects and secures the conditions necessary for the barter and exchange of products on which commodity production (that is, production for a market) is built.

Legal categories, for Pashukanis then, are a precise parallel to the similarly 'abstract' economic categories of commodity-producing societies—value, capital, labour, rent—which are fundamental to bourgeois economics and economies (and to all commodity-producing economies), but which lose their medium of existence in societies not oriented to exchange where, for example, production is for use. Just as the bourgeois economy is the most highly developed and most abstract form of commodity production, so bourgeois law is the most highly developed and abstract form of law and legal relations. The juridic subject is the abstract goods-possessor elevated to the heavens; the legal relations he enters into correspond to his commercial relations in the market place, express them, and safeguard the conditions of their existence. Thus, according to Pashukanis, law in the proper sense develops around the activities of barter and trade, finds its initial strongholds in cities, comes into conflict with patriarchal relations of formal domination and submission, and finally reaches its apogee in bourgeois society.

In socialist society, however, where production is no longer for exchange, Pashukanis held, the categories of law will become as irrelevant, and be as fatally undermined, as the categories of market economics. Policy, economic planning, and administration replace law. The concept of the juridical subject becomes as inapposite as it would be in a primitive commune, an army, or a work-team. It gives way to the socio-economic norm.

Just as the *Gesellschaft* view of law and justice elevates the conflict-resolution function and the commutative conception of justice, so Pashukanis's conception of administration and social policy replacing law elevates the resource-allocation function and the distributive view of justice. It is perhaps the most urgently demanded view of justice today and it stands, as Pashukanis well recognized, in some quite fundamental tensions with the *Gesellschaft* view of justice, though there is no lack of theorists who try to create logical links from one to the other by way of the requirements of human equality, 'real' autonomy, and so on. But in Western democratic societies, at least, there is a widespread recognition that some of the basic achievements of the concept of justice enshrined in the Western legal tradition are not to be simply swept away, that social policy, social regulation and consequent state and bureaucratic-administrative power must be kept in check by ideals, principles and procedures derived from Western private law and the basically corrective, adjudicative conception of justice. There is also a widespread feeling, however, reflected in much legal reform in recent years, that this adjudicative form of law and justice cannot cope, in a satisfactory way, with new or increasingly urgent social requirements and demands—with the increasing interdependence of individuals accompanied by great inequalities of power, with the need for large-scale planning and mass administration, with the attempt to maintain consensus or workable relations in areas of major social conflict, such as industrial relations, with the need to right past wrongs (a procedure, Chairman Mao tells us, that requires us to exceed the proper limits). These, as everyone knows, are the antinomies of justice and the contradictions of our time. They constitute the social and moral crisis of liberation and the basis of decreasing respect, in many circles, for its interpretation of justice. The primary difficulty of the bureaucratic-administrative view of justice—its fundamental antinomy—is that the equality it often claims to promote is at the same time most seriously undermined by the way in which its distributive aims require ever more complex regulations and systems of distribution that *distinguish* between citizens and their activities in terms of social policies and social consequences, that substitute status-rights for general and pervasive rights.

III

The legally based judgement of justice, once it has been divorced from religious incantation and the reading of omens and has become a professional pursuit and a specific social tradition, presents itself as above all an intellectual activity. It may involve, or be furthered by, 'empathy'—the immediate ability of stepping into another's shoes, feeling as he or she feels, knowing how he or she would act. There are those who believe that the sentiment of justice and the sentiments of morality would not exist if it were not for this human capacity to identify with others, to share their sorrows and their pains, or at least find them relevant to one's own condition. But in the actual exercise of the judgement of justice both sympathy and empathy and the ability to see like Solomon into another's heart or to devise tests to ascertain its condition are part of the search for truth, for a correct specification of the problem, and not a substitute for it. Otherwise, there would be no distinction between justice on the one hand and mercy and loving kindness, what the Christians call charity, on the other. Aristotle distinguished *justice* in all its types from *equity*, which is the judge's thorough appreciation of the concrete case and its individualizing features. Justice requires the ability to generalize, though not without the complexity of the concrete; it requires us to see the case or various features of it as instances or types of events. If we were not able to do that, we would not be able to use words to describe the case or to argue toward or explain a decision. At the same time, justice cannot be in principle wordless, the justice of the soul or the emotions: it must describe and classify, subsume under or bring within general principles and rules. That is what is implied in treating like cases alike.

An attempt to elucidate the requirements of justice in this narrower sense, on the basis of logic, of the requirements of communication and rational discourse (of which the judgement of justice is part), has been made by some modern theorists such as Professor Ilmar Tammelo. Successful communication, the conditions of discourse, requires that words be used invariantly, in the same sense to cover the same events, that inconsistency and contradiction be avoided, that lies be not told and relevant facts be not concealed, that people say what they mean, that there be no arbitrary, self-willed, unpredictable change of concepts or meaning and no unexplained exclusions. These are therefore among the foundations of justice as in intellectual activity. Treating the same situation in the same way, which is the precise counterpart of using words invariantly, is what is meant by the equality and impartiality of (commutative) justice. The technical and the formal languages of the law may create a barrier between the layman and the lawyer and thus impede the public recognition that justice is done. But on this account, when effectively framed, these languages make a vital contribution to justice. Those who find it prudent or honourable to regulate a large part of their activities in concrete detail by the requirements of law come to depend on these languages, to make their activities describable in them, to recognize that their activities are of a type and, as such, legal or illegal, just or unjust. (The two latter characterizations need not be identical, of course, but in most legal systems and in the English law of equity in particular there is specific provision for considering whether an action is just or unjust rather than legal or illegal.)

Any detailed consideration of actual traditions and conceptions of justice in its narrower sense in given societies, however, will force us to recognize elements that go beyond this internal logic or ethic or rational intellectual activity. A concern for equality, human dignity, material well-being, individual autonomy and social goods would all readily be listed by many people today as necessary requirements for a judge to do any kind of justice, however narrow its sense. Yet if we think of the Inquisition, in the scrupulous concern that at least some of its officers and judges had for the souls of men and the well-being of the community, as they saw it, do we want to say that the Inquisition was unjust, or rather that it was deluded or immoral or simply had a different morality coupled with the empirically false belief that torture produces truth? And how many more facets of justice in its narrow sense that many men elevate today—the right in serious matters to be represented by counsel, to have notice and details of the charges made against one, to have officials state the powers under which they act and have them act within those powers, to take just a few—are not the most patent results rather than the underlying principles of a long and specific historical development in the constitutional and legal fields?

There is no way, I personally believe, in which general principles of justice, any more than general principles of morality, can be derived from the common unhistorical sentiments of mankind or from the dictates of reason, dictates that are supposed to but cannot move us to action. Yet the judgement of justice, even in its narrowest legal sense, requires step after step, evaluation and choice and finally a decision that tells people what to do. What then is justice and how sound are its claims to respectability?

Justice, it seems to me, is not so much an idea or an ideal as an activity and a tradition—a way of doing things, not an end-state. To say this is not to say, narrowly, that justice is simply a set of procedures, a question of form and not of substance. That is neither my point nor my belief. Nor is it enough to say that justice is simply action according to law, the recognition of rules and the framing of rules of recognition. Justice involves and must involve concrete evaluation, consideration of factual situations, belief and disbelief of testimony, selection of principles and descriptions, ordering of preferences and interests. It would be nonsense to call such an activity purely formal, not concerned with substance, or to say that it can be exhaustively covered by pre-existing rules. But justice as an activity, I believe, derives its special nature as a means of evaluating and resolving conflicts from its intellectual character. Justice is the intellectual consideration and resolution of conflict by an impartial and disinterested third party whose judgement the parties or their social niveau in principle accept. As an intellectual activity, the activity and judgement of justice carry with them the ethic of discourse and enquiry—the careful, impartial, disinterested examination of claims and of the nature of the matter; the consideration of consequences, in the situation, for the parties and for the society around them and the rules by which it lives; the assessment of the strength and authenticity of competing interests and demands, of public interest, moral sentiment and customary expectations; and the relation of all this to a systematic, coherent and comparatively predictable set of social rules capable of accommodating the existing complexity of interests and the likelihood of significant social change. Because in this, as in all serious intellectual enquiry, there are so many issues at stake, so many interests and considerations to be weighed, there is no general set of principles, no brief handbook of justice any more than there is a set of principles or a handbook for writing a biography or the history of a revolution. There are, of course, canons, stated or implied in considerable complexity in sophisticated legal systems and exemplified in the operation of such systems. But in the end, the doing of justice, like all intellectual activity, is an art in the sense that it calls for judgement, for creative imagination, for the ability to see or forge unsuspected connections. This is why I have used Professor Stone's phrase 'the judgement of justice' and why I agree with him that there is, in most judgement, a creative leap. This is not because, in my view at least, a judgement can never be deduced from premises. Sound judgements can be so deduced from, or furnished with, suitable premises. It is in the construction of those complex chains of premises, in choosing at a particular point to introduce one premise rather than another, and doing this over and over again by redescribing, redefining, making new connections, that the creativity of the judgement of justice lies. (Heuristic or persuasive reasoning, I believe, is simply logical reasoning with some—suspect—premises missing.) Creativity does not need to be exercised all the time: much of justice, after all, is and needs to be routinely predictable. But just as I believe that some countries have greater literatures than others or greater literatures at one time than another, so it seems to me that some countries have better justice and a better tradition of justice than others or at one time than another.

There is, however, a second sense in which there is a leap to judgement, and here justice, where not based on the application of existing legal norms, is no longer a purely intellectual activity in the sense of being grounded only in the ethic of enquiry and argument. I accept, roughly and not in all its details or choice of language, the analysis of normative moral arguments put forward in C. L. Stevenson's *Ethics and Language*, carrying on the great work of David Hume. Analysis reveals in every evaluation an ultimately irreducible pro or con attitude or evaluative standard. This is socially produced and is in that sense not mere arbitrary subjectivity; it is also normally backed by reasons, which take account of facts, including the calculation of consequences, and which may deduce a particular pro attitude from other pro attitudes or strive to give it a place in a system of pro attitudes by analogy, contrariety and all sorts of other looser logical relations. But in the end there is no way of showing a pro attitude which is ultimate for the purposes of a particular argument to be wrong or mistaken; one can only counter it with a different attitude. No competent judge, I believe, is for one moment unaware of the fact that he cannot derive all the pro attitudes necessary for judgement from justice itself, from the internal logic of justice as an activity and its intellectual requirements. Leaving aside the special ethic of discourse, the machinery of justice is an amoral machinery which gets its moral inputs from outside—from the norms elevated by the legislator, when he goes, as he constantly does, beyond making provisions for the mechanics of the activity of justice; from the moral sentiments, expectations and demands of the community, or the sections of the

community, that are especially relevant or weigh especially heavily
with the judge; from public policy, convenience, the judge's conception of social interest, and so on. The manner in which these norms
are fed into the machinery is not mechanical: there is constant interaction, balancing of criteria for selection, mixing of internal and
external requirements. But justice as reason by itself cannot deliver
the judgement. This is why many writers—Professor Edmond Cahn,
for instance—have argued that justice as the actual handing down of
judgement requires both reason and emotion, both a tradition of
formal justice and a pro attitude. Some have sought a systematized
pro attitude in a *sense* of justice, allegedly common to all mankind.
Professor Cahn, like the negative utilitarians who find the concept of
suffering a more workable moral criterion than the concept of
pleasure, gives primacy to the sense of injustice. That there are such
senses, such ready sentiments among men, I have no doubt. But I
cannot see them as anything but historical products, complex and
shifting, not the foundation for justice and morality, but the products
of whole systems of moral and legal attitudes and beliefs. They may be
necessary for the successful operation of a tradition of justice in a
society and the machinery associated with it, but they grow up
together with it and in interaction with it and a wider social climate.
Thus, I would say that the (socially shaped) concept of justice pre-
cedes and shapes the allegedly 'primitive' concept of fairness—a concept that differs in different periods and societies and reflects more
general views about justice. What is true is that outrage produces
legislative reform more frequently than the reception of new philosophical principles.

My emphasis on justice as an intellectual activity—as the process
of weighing and balancing symbolized by the scales of justice, but as
a process which involves detailed consideration of matters of substance that cannot be subsumed under simple rules of procedure—
raises difficulties about the concept of a just decision as opposed to
the concept of reaching a decision justly. It seems to me that the
concept of a just decision can never be based on reason: it can only be
based on an existing set of norms, human expectations or (always
limited) social consensus. All of these shift. But in fact, we speak of
a just decision not only in a context but often also loosely. When we are
not praising a decision for its intellectual virtues—for the care and
reasoned argument, impartiality and perceptiveness, that went into it
or its conformity with a system of expectations and attitudes—we may
be admiring features that do not belong strictly to justice. Consider
the statesmanship and showmanship of King Solomon, producing his
sword to cut the baby in two and thus not only discovering the comparative strength of the rival claimants' love, previously unknown,
perhaps even to the parties themselves, but publicly discomfiting

and discrediting one of the claimants (though even here much of the admiration is for the intellectual means). Statesmanship—the capacity to make the parties find new bases for cooperation or to force the parties to realize the untenability of one or both of their positions— is not the same as doing justice, even if it may lead to the same result. We tend to think of it as characteristic of arbitration and as involving skills of persuasion, negotiation and the glossing over and obscuring of issues from which subsequent or present disagreement might arise. The much extolled face-to-face justice of *Gemeinschaft* institutions, with its emphasis on saving the face of both parties and enabling them to live together, or the alternative insistence on their common prostration before and subservience to a higher belief, interest or ideology, is similarly not what, in this narrower sense, we mean by justice— even if in specific kinds of social situations, other things like mutual dependence or common ideology being given, it may resolve disputes just as effectively. When we speak of a 'just' decision *sensu strictu*, it seems to me, we do so with reference to a *system* of procedures, attitudes and beliefs. Such a system is not normally a system of black-letter law: the positivist treatment of law as the will of the sovereign or as a system of commands that are self-contained is simply wrong, as Professor Tay shows below. Law itself makes provision for reference to external beliefs, expectations and moral attitudes. It is in reference to such an entire system, incorporating social expectations, that a decision is just. But while justice as an activity can carry with it an ethic and a tradition that is in principle capable of coherent development on a firm foundation, the 'just' decision is always relative. There is, in that sense, no absolute justice.

Justice, it is rightly said, presupposes conflict: there is no problem of justice, and no conception of it, where there are no conflicts. But some of the fascination that the problem of justice has had for moral philosophers is connected with what one might call the tragic dimension of the term, the fact that conflicts can be and often are between what we see as deserving causes or equally rightful claims that cannot both be satisfied. Thus, philosophers have seen that the values they extol, the ideals they commend to us, can and do conflict with each other and that justice, both as a philosophical abstraction and as a concrete activity, is constantly faced with striking a balance between incompatible goals and even with having recourse to conflicting criteria. These are the antinomies of justice. They are not the result of poor reasoning or inadequate grasp of a theoretical concept: they are part of the human condition. It is perhaps as well that justice is blind. It may hurt too much to see. But on my account, it should be portrayed with a lens and protected in its integrity by a certain hardness of heart, rather than blindness. Justice, after all, is not the only virtue and it would be as well if it left some room and autonomy for the others, concentrating on its own proper business rather than playing God and defining the whole human condition. In that respect, the *Gesellschaft* conception of justice is more specific and coherent than either the *Gemeinschaft* or the bureaucratic-administrative conceptions of justice, which rest on but do not critically examine much wider moral claims.

IV

Justice as rational, intellectual decision—characteristically seeking to resolve strongly competing claims that do not individually indulge in the rational activity of seeing themselves as part of a wider whole, with its own requirements—has often been seen, especially in former days, as concerned, above all, with the social whole and the 'proper' place within it of individuals, their activities and their demands, thus leading to justice in its wider sense. For religious thinkers like Augustine, and for the many who have lamented that the wicked flourish like the green bay tree, perfect justice was possible only in another place and the just society on earth was an ideal toward which man (or some men) strove without attaining it. The difficulty lay in describing such a society without giving patent evidence of time-boundedness and partiality. Neither Plato's Republic nor Aquinas's rather hierarchical conception of the just society would immediately strike all men as the sort of social organization that reason itself commands: establishing and demonstrating the alleged demands of practical reason has been one of the most contested and ultimately profitless philosophical activities of all time. The philosophical assumptions on which it depends—that an 'ought' can be derived from an 'is', or that human desires and needs can be brought to a common measure, reconciled in a *summum bonum* or common good of society—are more than suspect: they have been exposed time and again in the history of thought. Any given social arrangement, any elevation of specific principles of harmony and balance, of giving men their 'deserts' and proper place, as Marx saw, will suit some and not others and can be considered fair or unfair, just or unjust in a broader sense, only in the light of given historical expectations that have changed and will no doubt continue to change with remarkable rapidity, elevating some concerns at the expense of others, remedying one felt inequity to produce new and unexpected ones. For the last two hundred years, initially in Western societies, there has been a major elevation, in the name of justice, of individual rights, counterposed to the concern for shared belief, tractability and collective responsibility and to the emphasis on duty that characterized the governor's concern for a stable social whole. That movement is still not at an end: it has burst into many areas, the school, the family, the workplace, only very recently. But it is already confronted, to some extent, by other concerns, as the contributions of Professors Barry and Lang and of Drs Feher and Heller to this volume show. Such concerns in advanced industrial societies are with environment and conservation and have produced an attack on man's aggressive and acquisitive relationship with nature, including plants and animals. In socialist societies seeking to overcome economic backwardness the concern is with promoting production, inculcating labour discipline and social discipline generally and stimulating enterprise, skill and conscientious and imaginative contribution to work in societies that lack all these; for critical Marxists the concern is with developing new, and not merely satisfying old, 'needs' or capacities, to produce the man 'rich in needs'.

There have been and still are those, of course, who believe in the society of perfect justice, or rather in the society that requires no justice and loses all conception of it because it knows no significant social conflict or inequality, as a coming society in this world. Karl Marx was among their number and it is characteristic of that line of thought that it envisages the total withering away of state and law, of those institutions that gain their social respect from the extent to which they resolve conflicts, provide the bases for order and cooperation and concern themselves with both commutative and distributive justice, in a formal, rule-bound and systematic way. No society has yet attained that condition. Societies without states—tribal groups or chieftain societies—are not societies without coercion, rules and observances and procedures for judgement and the imposition of punishment or compensation. Contemporary socialist societies governed by Marxist-Leninist parties deny, of course, that they have yet attained true communism, but it is not easy for the uncommitted observer to discern in their elevation of ever more complex legal and administrative functions a trend toward the withering away of state and law. For the Marxian vision of the ultimate society of true communism is more than the conception of a society in which all production, distribution and exchange is under state or some form of social control. It is a vision of a society in which the category of particularity has been overcome, in which all men display a truly general will that stands in total rational and cooperative union with the wills of other men, in which the very possibility of endemic or systemic conflict has been removed. To that extent, it belongs with Augustine's City of God and not with the historical world of conflict and cooperation, universality and particularity that we live in. It is a vision in which justice as a specific concern allegedly has no function and is therefore given no place. Marx, of course, is not the only thinker to believe that private property and money are the sole grounds on which social division and self-interest can arise and that conflict can therefore be comparatively easily, even if not immediately, abolished by confiscatory action at an appropriate stage of history. Nevertheless, he was clearly wrong. That there are now Marxists, with their own experience of socialist societies to back them, who think more subtly than this, the contribution of Drs Feher and Heller does much to remind us. But it is interesting and revealing that the 'official position' in Marxist-Leninist societies today, with their insistence that systemic social injustice has already disappeared in their countries, should put no emphasis in its legal theory for socialist countries on the concept of justice. It elevates instead the characteristically bureaucratic-administrative conception of socialist legality, that is, of obedience to formal rules.

V

'Justice', John Stuart Mill wrote in his *Utilitarianism*, 'is a name for certain classes of moral rules, which concern the essentials of human well-being more clearly, and are therefore of more absolute obligation than any other rules for the guidance of life'. This is the broader—indeed for an individualist society, the broadest—conception of justice as the principle of social organization and the regulation of individual claims and entitlements. John Stuart Mill himself, of course, was an individualist, believing in a separation between private and public spheres and in the maximum cultivation of individual autonomy and private rights compatible with human welfare as established by the principle of utility. But the principle of utility itself, taken alone as elevating an objective standard of welfare, tends to displace both justice and the concept of rights from any centrality or ultimacy in moral reasoning. Principles of justice from outside utilitarianism may be brought in to facilitate the logically difficult passage from each man seeking his individual welfare or utility to each man having a duty to further the greatest happiness of the greatest number. Certainly, that passage from the one to the many and from description to advocacy cannot be justified within utilitarianism. But once it has been elevated into a principle or policy, the importance of justice, as of rights, drops off, to be replaced by the bureaucratic-administrative conception of a science of legislation and a rational calculation of the 'proper' distribution of benefits. That is exactly what E. B. Pashukanis had in mind, except that he preferred 'principles of construction' and 'socio-technical norms' to 'the science of legislation'. His conscious and unconscious followers are alive and active in many countries and in many fields in any particular country. They see themselves as bearers not of a particular interest or moral tradition but as the representatives of reason and 'the science of society'.

The celebrated definition of the requirements of justice given by the great eighteenth-century philosopher, Immanuel Kant—act externally so that the free exercise of your personal will (*Willkür*) could be brought under a general law together with the freedom of everyone—consummates the separation between law and justice on the one hand, as concerned only with external behaviour, and morality on the other, as concerned with the inner life. It also consummates the individualism of Hobbes and Pufendorf; it sees justice as concerned simply with the problem of harmonizing individual wills by giving them the maximum liberty compatible with similar liberty for others —a view again to be made famous by John Stuart Mill. But Kant's central moral concept was autonomy, not utility. In connection with justice, as with morality, Kant was also giving a special logical twist to the concept of equality through applying his famous test of practical rationality, the principle of universalizability—that what I claim a right to do must not logically be dependent on denying others that right. The sentiment is clear to many, if not almost all, who are concerned with justice in modern individualistic societies. (It would have seemed odd and perhaps still does seem odd in many other societies not wedded to equality.) It is usually taken to be a 'formal' principle and one of the chief difficulties with it, indeed, is that any reasonably cunning or intelligent person can define or characterize the particular agent or action in a theoretically general but practically so restricted way as to promote all forms of discrimination and factually arbitrary distinction without violating the principle. Yet we cannot apply the principle without limiting its range at all.

As Professor Stone says below, the principle is either too broad or too narrow. At best, psychologically rather than logically, the influence of the Kantian criterion—and it has been enormously influential—has been to create a presumption against distinctions between people in respect of legal and moral obligations. If we wish to use rules to distinguish between one group and another, one person and another, one situation and another—to move from arithmetical to geometrical equality—we are asked to give 'good reasons', to show how the discriminations we make are morally or in terms of justice, relevant. This view is a very common one indeed, today: it is almost, in Western democratic societies, the ideology of our time, put with force and conviction as, for example, in S. I. Benn's and R. S. Peters's *Social Principles and the Democratic State*, and providing, consciously or unconsciously, most of the argument behind the concept of social justice—the creation of a state of affairs in which all persons, as far as possible, are ends and not means, entitled to respect for their autonomy and the maximum possible equality, as moral beings, with all others. It is on the basis of the Kantian philosophy generally, rather than on the basis of his specific and not especially interesting philosophy of law, that commutative and distributive justice are most commonly seen today as equally necessary parts of justice. For with the discrediting of doctrines of the social whole, contemporary talk about justice is normally individualist in nature and those socialists who reject individualism are more inclined, like Marx himself, to use the categories of fraternity, equality, rationality or universality and not that of justice.

John Stuart Mill and Immanuel Kant are the two great moral philosophers in Western democratic societies who speak to our time and who are most commonly brought together, in varying mixtures, to produce the social philosophies and conceptions of total, social or distributive justice of our day. (In this respect, as providing the moral foundations of social philosophy, Marxism is not a serious independent competitor. This is shown by the vacillations of contemporary Marxists between elevating welfare and the rational control of the process of production, distribution and exchange for the benefit of mankind, on the one hand, and elevating of the free autonomous individual who acts rationally and universalizably in socialist humanism, on the other hand. Rule utilitarianism, by contrast—perhaps the most commonly held form of utilitarianism today, at least among philosophers—weds Kantian conceptions and concerns with the principle of utility to emphasize the utility of rules and principles rather than individual actions.)

Professor H. L. A. Hart, dealing with the question of justice and morality much more analytically than I have done here, believes that the idea of justice 'consists of two parts: a uniform or constant feature, summarized in the precept "Treat like cases alike" and a shifting or varying criterion used in determining when, for any given purpose, cases are alike or different.'[3] In modern times, as he rightly says, the principle that *prima facie* human beings are entitled to be treated alike has become so widespread that discrimination on ground of colour and race, when it occurs, is almost always defended on the basis that those discriminated against allegedly have not yet developed certain essential human attributes. We have moved, or many of us have moved, from the principle of treating like cases alike, and people in certain situations or respects equally, to a presumption that people should be treated equally and actually *be* equal in all respects, though the latter proposition is certainly still the subject of widespread dispute, symbolized for a period, in the divergent assumptions that underlie John Rawls's *A Theory of Justice* and Robert Nozick's *Anarchy, State and Utopia*. In the existence of 'higher' principles of justice or reason or morality that enable us to resolve that conflict as

---

[3] H. L. A. Hart, *The Concept of Law* (Oxford, 1961), p. 156.

a matter of truth or logic, I do not believe.[4] For, as Professor Hart also argues, when, and on what rules or criteria, we are to draw distinctions for the purposes of justice is not a matter to be solved within a timeless theory of justice or morality which, for the serious critic, quickly dissolves into shifting and competing moralities. In order to discriminate among those intelligently, one has to argue, to consider consequences and other matters of fact and logical relations between moral propositions or beliefs, as both Rawls and Nozick and many ideologists do. But in the end one is promoting a morality, a particular arrangement of society and view of life and not analysing rationally and dispassionately the concept of justice. For concepts of justice, as I have striven to argue, do not merely address themselves to different problems: they conflict, just as lives and principles conflict, and they are not resolvable into a total conflictless and coherent theory of justice in general which all rational beings must accept.

To say with W. H. Auden,

> Yet law-abiding scholars write:
> Law is neither wrong nor right,
> Law is only crimes
> Punished by places and by times,

is not to bring out a fatal paradox or inconsistency in moral scepticism: it is simply to recognize the earthly and human character of moralities, theories of justice and institutions of law, and thereby to strengthen rather than weaken an appreciation of what they stand for and what they stand against. To be morally, legally and politically adult is to pursue, defend and revise one's claims without having to believe that the design of the universe requires them to be met and that those opposing them are less than human. If one does want greater security than this, a reliance on logic as opposed to *Weltanschauungen* and emotive appeal, then one has to rest content with what Chaïm Perelman, in a very strict sense, has called 'formal justice'—the application of the same norm to all members of what is considered to be the one

---

[4] The attempt to make 'fairness' such a criterion by treating it as more fundamental than, or independent of, the total concept of justice that can be erected on its foundations is interestingly untranslatable into most languages, for example German, Russian and Chinese, where the only way of rendering the childish and therefore allegedly primitive plea, 'that is unfair', is to use the words 'that is unjust' (*ungerecht, nespravedlivo, pu kong ping*—the last, the normal Chinese term for unjust or unfair used by the people, interestingly having for its literal meaning 'against public harmony'). The function of fairness or of equality in such theories is to link the somewhat more settled principles of corrective justice with those of distributive justice in a common and allegedly meanary theory. In fact, the required concreteness and bases for discrimination can be got out of the notions of fairness and equality only by smuggling these in under the guise of explicating what everyone would accept or come to see if he thought about it, that is, by appealing to socially and historically conditioned expectations masquerading as timeless truths.

category for the purposes of application of that norm. The definition of the category—so crucial to the actual judgement of justice— Perelman and I agree in seeing as relative or emotive, in the sense of depending on shifting and conflicting *Weltanschauungen*, on innumerable conceptions of what Perelman calls 'concrete' justice and what less able theorists often see as 'real' justice. Choosing between them is man's work, not God's; it is best done when there is room and time to think, and a tradition to think in.

2

Civil justice
and its rivals

J. A. Passmore

First of all, we need to be reasonably confident that we are talking about justice, not about the closely related but still quite distinct concepts of liberty, equality, humanity. So let us take as our point of departure an Aristotelian definition which has preserved its vitality over the centuries—a good ground for believing that it accurately formulates our intuitions. That is the definition of justice as 'treating equals equally and unequals unequally, but in proportion to their relevant differences'.

Aristotle's definition, we at once observe, is exceptionally 'open' in character, open in respect to the meaning of 'equals', 'proportion', 'relevant differences'. Compare it, in this respect, with the definition of an isosceles triangle as a triangle in which two of the sides are equal. That, too, defines by reference to equality. But we have only to take out a ruler to determine whether the equality condition is satisfied in any particular case, and hence whether a particular triangle is indeed isosceles. There is no such measuring device which will enable us to determine what persons are to be counted as equal, in what equal treatment consists, or what counts as a 'relevant difference'. Admittedly, Aristotle himself makes some attempt to geometrize the concept of equal treatment, relating it to the theory of proportions. But it is widely agreed that this part of his argument not only is, but was bound to be, a failure.

Of much more permanent interest is Aristotle's observation that in Athens the fundamental dispute was about what differences were relevant in justifying unequal treatment or, as he puts the matter, about who had 'merit'. Some Athenians said that all free citizens should be treated equally, others that men of good birth, men of property, or men of excellence should be given preferential treatment. Aristotle's definition left controversy on this point open: it did nothing to settle it. That is precisely why it has survived. Had Aristotle defined justice as 'treating all Athenian citizens equally and foreigners in proportion to their status', it would not have lasted beyond his own time. As his definition now stands, Aristotle supplied a framework which later generations could fill out with their special views about who ought to be accounted equal and who, if any one, ought to be given preferential treatment.

The leading tendency of the nineteenth-century liberal-democratic movement was greatly to reduce in number the kinds of difference which could relevantly be called upon to justify preferential treatment, the kinds of difference, that is, which constituted 'merit'. The abolition of slavery and serfdom, the religious emancipation acts, the introduction of universal suffrage were all of them directed against claims to possess 'merit'. Socialist and fascist totalitarian societies tried to reverse that tendency. They set up new forms of 'merit'. The possession of such characteristics as having working-class parents, belonging to a particular political party, being Aryan were, in one totalitarian society or another, taken to justify preferential treatment. But in liberal-democratic societies the process of reducing the number of grounds of 'merit' continued during the twentieth century. Being white, being male, being heterosexual have successively lost ground as 'merits'.

The ideal toward which this particular political movement was directed—let us call it the ideal of *civil justice*—can be expressed, if very roughly, as follows: except by way of punishment or as a result of incapacity, no person ought to be excluded from participation in any form of desirable activity unless there is, of necessity, competition for entrance to it, when the more competent ought always to be preferred to the less competent. ('Competent' has here to be understood in a broad sense: it means the demonstrable ability to engage in the activity in question in a manner which will sustain and advance it.) The only 'merit' civil justice admits, then, is competence; competence, and competence alone, justifies preferential treatment. Admittedly, as the concessive clauses make plain, individuals can be excluded from participation in desirable activities as a punishment. Such exclusion, indeed, is the only form of punishment, apart from fines, which is still practised in societies which reject corporal punishment. Admittedly, too, the very young, the insane, the seriously handicapped are often excluded *en masse* as incapable, from the application of civil justice. But these exclusions are all to be thought of as, at least in principle, temporary, as lasting only until the young grow older, the insane regain their sanity, the handicapped are cured, the criminal is released. And even so, the tendency has been to enlarge the range of activities in which such partially excluded persons can participate. Out-patient care for the insane, the lowering of the voting age, week-end imprisonment, workshops for the handicapped, all have this effect.

The Stoic-Christian ideal, most familiar perhaps from the Epistle to the Galatians—'a world in which there is neither Jew nor Greek, there is neither bond nor free, there is neither male nor female'—is, from the standpoint of civil justice, as fully satisfied as natural differences permit in a world in which there are no slaves and in which anti-discrimination laws ensure that all forms of civil life are open on exactly the same terms to Jews and to Greeks, to males and to females. Love and mercy, of course, go beyond justice. But civil justice requires no more than treatment which is proportionate to competence. And it protects against the partiality of love and the uncertainties of mercy.

Why pick on superior competence as a 'merit'? Is this not quite as arbitrary as deciding that those who are white or male or Gentile or Protestant or wealthy should be preferentially selected? There is on the face of it at least one excellent reason why such a decision, unlike the decision to permit, say, only white males to become doctors, is not purely arbitrary. Desirable activities will, if the principle of civil justice is accepted, be conducted at the highest possible level. This consideration, admittedly, carries no weight with the more intransigent critics of civil justice. It does not really matter, some of them will say, whether a society contains the best possible doctors, humanists, industrialists, artists, scientists, technologists. An ideal society will be one which enables all its members to express themselves in whatever form of activity they desire to engage. If the effect is that the sopranos in the opera company bray like asses and the baritones squeak like mice, that is of no importance. Or at least it is of no importance as compared with the moral iniquity of allowing any exception whatsoever to the principle that everybody ought in all circumstances to have precisely the same right to participate in every form of desirable activity (not merely the same right to *compete for* participation).

All judgements of quality, some critics of the competence criterion would add, are in any case subjective. There is no way of giving any sense to the phrase, 'conducting desirable activities at the highest possible standards', which does not make of it an arbitrary judgement of preference—quite improper, then, as a test of 'merit'. In practice, to make so-called 'competence' a test is to prefer those who pander to the tastes of the ruling elite.

Such arguments are particularly characteristic of the second half of the twentieth century, at least in liberal-democratic societies. Science, the humanities, scholarship, education, technical inventiveness, education, medicine, law have all been brought into question by discontented bourgeois intellectuals. (To this particular form of intellectual treason the socialist societies have not succumbed.) I have tried to defend these activities elsewhere;[1] I shall not attempt to do so now. But such critics serve an important function in reminding us that the competence test, if it is to be anything more than arbitrary, must rest on a certain assumption: that it is essential for certain forms of activity to be conducted at the highest possible level and that this is sometimes possible only if participation in them is restricted. The onus of proof is always on those who insist on the need for a competence test. For *in general* civil justice will demand that participation in every form of desirable activity be equally open to everybody who wishes to participate in it.

One might wish to add, as a second defence of civil justice, that those who work hard *deserve* to be preferred to the lazy and the casual. Unfortunately, the concept of desert has been brought into disrepute by its association with the patronizing phrase, 'the deserving poor'. But what makes that phrase so objectionable is its association with charity. Charity ought to pay no attention to desert. So Hamlet can properly rebuke a Polonius who promises to 'use the players according to their desert'. 'Use them', he says, 'after your own honour and dignity: the less they deserve, the more merit is in your bounty.' If charity is in question, then certainly the less deserving the recipient, 'the more merit is in your bounty'. Charity moves well beyond the bounds of what Hume called the 'mean and cautious' virtue of justice.

A second argument against desert does not admit of this reply. It finds expression in Hamlet's rhetorical question, 'use every man after his desert, and who shall 'scape a whipping?' That is the voice of Augustinian Christianity, and the lesson of many of the parables; *every* human being is so undeserving that to prefer one to another on the ground of desert is a total absurdity. In a more secular age, the argument, rather, is that human beings are so moulded by circumstances over which they have no control—parental hostilities or the social environment into which they are born—that to speak of any individual as being peculiarly 'deserving' is totally unrealistic. And, certainly, for anybody to describe *himself* as 'deserving' is a peculiarly distasteful kind of Pharisaism, not least when it comes from those who proclaim themselves to be 'self-made'. We are none of us self-made: we are what we are partly as the result of a long series of 'graces' bestowed on us by others. We are none of us, either, in a position to 'throw the first stone', if doing so entails that we are ourselves without serious moral defect. But the fact remains that in a given situation some people are in fact more deserving than others.

Justice has to decide between people as they are, not between

---

[1] Most generally in the last two chapters of *The Perfectibility of Man*, in relation to science in *Science and Its Critics* and *Man's Responsibility for Nature*, and in relation to education and art in forthcoming books on *The Philosophy of Teaching* and *The Seriousness of the Arts*.

people as they might have been. Had a person's past history been different, he might not have embarked upon a particular contract; had it been different, he might not have been as devoted as he now is to a particular form of activity. But all of this is irrelevant, from the standpoint of justice, to the question whether he deserves to win a case based on the contract or to win preferment for his devotion. That some people, as they now are, are more deserving than others, is something we take for granted whenever we complain of an appointment to a position, let us say, that it is unjust.

Suppose, for example, as a result of the lottery favoured by some of the critics of civil justice, a competent person fails to get entrance to a university; the lottery winner is lazy, only intermittently interested, quite devoid of the instinct of workmanship in the form appropriate to the activity in which he is engaged, unwilling to submit to the discipline of training. The lottery is fairly conducted, but is the outcome just? To say of an appointment that it was justly decided, since it went to the candidate who deserved to win, will arouse no comment. But suppose we were to say that it was justly decided, because it went to the candidate who most needed the job? Wouldn't that be a complete misuse of the concept of justice? Out of humanity, a selection committee might prefer the candidate who is most in need. But it should not then pretend that it is acting justly. And something similar is true of 'the appointment was justly decided, because it went to the candidate who won the lottery for it'. Lotteries —'tossing-up'—may have to be called upon when there is no rational way of deciding, as when identical twins enter a beauty contest. But when there are grounds for deciding, to have recourse to a lottery is unjust.

A rather different question is whether civil justice as an ideal has now run out of steam, its mission, at least in liberal-democratic countries, accomplished. I think not. In its name, we can still demand radical changes. Those who reach a certain age, for example, are, in many cases, excluded *as a class*, whatever their competence, from participating in certain forms of desirable activity. This is inconsistent with the principles of civil justice. So, too, I should say, is the exclusion of workers from participation in the management of industrial enterprises if this is based solely on the ground that they are not the owners of capital. The supposition that the possession of property constitutes a 'merit' is inconsistent with the principles of civil justice, however much it may have appealed to Athenian property owners.

An even more fundamental question is whether the ideal of civil justice is compatible with the restrictions on immigration which almost every society now imposes. On the face of it, being a foreigner ought not to count as a demerit; we certainly cannot justify preference for citizens as we justified preference for competence. Foreigners, as a class, are as capable as citizens of carrying on activities at a high level and as deserving of selection to do so. I shall look at this case in a little more detail, not only because it raises a significant moral problem which almost every country in the world has at some time to face, but because it introduces us to a very different concept of justice.

Of course, if the competence of a migrant is in *undesirable* activities, civil justice does not demand his admission. There can be controversies about what activities are desirable, as there can be controversies about what counts as competence. These controversies an appeal to civil justice cannot, of itself, settle. But very obviously a country is not obliged to admit a member of the Mafia who intends to set up a kidnapping enterprise, however competent he may be.

On the other hand, merely to urge that the immigrant will put out of a job some member of the society to which he proposes to migrate is not sufficient to justify an exception to the principles of civil justice. Such displacements are a characteristic effect of any application of the principles of civil justice. Freed slaves can put citizens out of work; the entry into the civil service of competent graduates can put 'men of good family' out of work; women can put men out of work; the continued employment of those who have reached retiring age can put the young out of work. In the long run, the entry of competent persons into a country or into a form of activity will, there is good reason to hope, create work. But if we take account only of immediate effects—we cannot be fully confident about the remote effects—and adopt the principle that civil justice should be set aside whenever, as a consequence of its application, somebody might lose his job, it would very rarely *not* be set aside. (It is obvious that restrictions imposed by unions, industrial or professional, which rest on such principles as 'last on, first off', or preference for unionists, or promotion by seniority, are wholly incompatible with the principles of civil justice.)

A more radical defence of immigration restrictions would directly challenge my assumption that being a foreigner does not count as a demerit—an assumption which Plato and Aristotle would certainly have dismissed as absurd. This challenge often rests on such arguments as the following: the members of a single society have implicitly or explicitly entered into a contract one with another, a contract to accept certain obligations, to assume certain responsibilities. A foreigner is not a party to the contract and hence has no *right* to take part in the desirable activities of the society. If he is admitted to a country this is an act of grace, not of justice, somewhat as in Christian theology grace, not justice, takes us to heaven.

There are two possible ways of reading this argument: the first as a restriction on civil justice, the second as appealing to a different ideal of justice. On the first reading, I have suggested, the argument cannot be sustained. To restrict the application of civil justice to citizens is incompatible with its spirit and destroys the defence constructed against its enemies, namely that it assists in the maintenance and development of desirable activities at the highest level and gives preference to the deserving.

What about the second reading? Let us call the alternative ideal in question 'communal justice'. Roughly, it can be expressed thus: communal justice consists in fulfilling those obligations, and recognizing those rights, which flow out of one's membership of a particular community. Its connections are with fraternity—in a somewhat formal sense—rather than with liberty. Very frequently, it is invoked not only to justify restrictions on the participatory rights of immigrants or foreign residents but even to justify the exclusion from full participation in a society of those who hold particular religious views, belong to certain international organizations, or are members of a particular social class. For such persons, so it is argued, cannot *really* accept the communal system of obligations and rights; they cannot exhibit the degree of devotion which Hegel took to be essential to community membership. Their Jewishness, their Roman Catholicism, their communism, their membership of a multi-national organization, their bourgeois origins, makes that impossible. 'Equals', on this interpretation, means 'equally devoted as members of a society' and only to such persons is equal treatment to be extended. It makes a 'relevant difference' that a person is an 'outsider'.

In essence, then, communal justice and civil justice stand in total opposition to one another. That is why the proponents of civil justice cannot safely appeal to communal justice in order to justify immigration restrictions. One could, indeed, write the history of liberal democracy as a history of the strengthening of the concept of civil justice so as to exclude the reservations, in the name of communal justice, which at first applied to it. (Correspondingly, one could write the history of totalitarianism as the reactionary destruction of civil justice in the name of communal justice.)

No doubt, one cannot plausibly deny that the satisfaction of some of the conditions which the proponents of 'communal justice' emphasize is a necessary condition for the survival of any community, part of the definition, we might even say, of what it means to constitute a single community. Some degree of willingness to co-operate and to compromise, to think in terms of interests other than one's own immediate interests, to accept obligations, is as essential to the continued existence of a community where civil justice generally prevails as it is to a totalitarian tyranny. Plato was right enough: in this communal sense of justice, which was broadly his, there must be some degree of justice even in a band of thieves. But for that very reason, communal solidarity is not the distinguishing characteristic of a just society. And if it be replied that the just society is the one in which communal justice is realized to the highest degree, whereas in a band of thieves it is realized only in a low degree, then we should be obliged to conclude that a totalitarian society is the most just of all societies.

Then, since we have set up defences of immigration restrictions only to break them down, are we obliged to conclude that the ideal of civil justice can be fully implemented only in a world in which there are no national boundaries, in an internationally governed 'one world', a world in which, quite literally, there will be 'neither Greek nor Jew'? That conclusion has often been drawn. Yet we may well hesitate before accepting it.

For national diversity, however much we may detest some of its manifestations, is important for much the same reasons as ecological diversity. It keeps alive cultural stocks which may need from time to time to be reintroduced into cultures in which they have become attenuated, as the Arabs kept alive Greek science and philosophy. It provides a diversity of cultures within which new ideas can hope to find a niche not elsewhere available for them, as new ideas about freedom sprung up among northern tribes. It provides refuges—for some of us the ideal of a world government from which there is no refuge except suicide is the horror of horrors. In other words, it assists in the conservation, the development, the renovation of desirable activities. For such diversity a high price must no doubt be paid, as is also true in the ecological case. There are cultures, as there are kinds of living being, which we should prefer to be without; refuge can be offered to terrorists, as well as to anti-totalitarian dissidents; a diversified world is not likely to be an entirely peaceful one. But the alternative is a stagnantly conformist world, with that sort of boxed-up uniformity which the 'international style' of architecture so drearily foreshadows.

At the same time, this argument does not carry us as far as its proponents often suppose. For, again as in the ecological case, diversity *within* a society is as important as diversity *between* societies. If the preservation of national differences is desirable, this does not mean that each national culture should be preserved, as far as possible, in the manner of a specimen in a museum. It was *migrants* who carried science to Athens, as later to Italy. Ethnic diversity can bring new life to a society which has begun to petrify. The most that can be concluded is that there are circumstances in which a society can properly impose restrictions on those who wish to immigrate into it, not in the name of civil justice, let alone in the name of communal justice, but because its existence as a society in which certain sorts of desirable activity flourish will otherwise be destroyed. It need not surprise us that the principle of civil justice can sometimes be outweighed by other considerations. We justified the competence test by saying that its application served to ensure that the desirable activities of a community are carried on at the highest level. If in 'one world' those activities would be subject to threat, that can very properly lead us to reject 'one world' as an ideal even if, within such a world, the requirements of civil justice could, in principle, be more fully satisfied. Variety and liberty have their claims, as well as justice.

Other cruxes for the proponent of civil justice can be approached in a similar fashion. So one might justify the sending back of graduating students to their own country, rather than allowing them to participate in the activities of their host country, on the ground that desirable activities need to be widely spread if their maintenance is to be safeguarded. One can justify, even, the exclusion of those whose allegiance is to some other country from certain forms of desirable activity, for example, from certain forms of government service, on the grounds that to admit them would threaten the continued existence of those desirable activities. In all such cases, however, the path is an easier one for the proponent of communal justice; the proponent of civil justice grows steadily more uneasy as rights of participation are, by such arguments, whittled away. We should regard them, at the very least, with suspicion, accept them only reluctantly.

One easy way out of the dilemmas into which we can be led by an allegiance to principles of civil justice is to reject that concept entirely in favour of *formal* justice. Justice, it is then argued, is simply a matter of the application of law. A society can pass whatever laws it chooses to pass, including laws which exclude immigrants. Questions of injustice arise only if it fails to apply those laws— which may themselves be discriminatory—in an impartial fashion. In every other context, an appeal to justice is merely a political demand, with no moral force.

The concept of impartiality lies at the centre of formal justice exactly as does the concept of liberty at the centre of civil justice and the concept of fraternity at the centre of communal justice. Justice is represented as blind and as holding a pair of scales in order to indicate that fact. It is blind to differences between persons, except those which are relevant in law; it weighs their case without regard to such differences. Formal justice gives preferential treatment to those who have a better case in law: that is the sole 'merit' it admits. Although legal systems exhibit its workings most perspicuously, we can extend the concept of formal justice to cover any situations in which there is a set of rules or fixed conventions for dealing with persons impartially. If a child is indignant at being treated unjustly in a classroom, or a passenger in a bus queue, or a university student in an examination, his appeal is to formal justice.

It would considerably simplify our enquiry if we could bring ourself to believe that all justice is formal justice. But I find it impossible to persuade myself that there is no such thing as an unjust law, that only the application of a law can be unjust. This would have such consequences as that a law excluding Roman Catholics from entry into the universities is in itself neither just nor unjust, injustice arising only if the law is so administered as to discriminate *between* Roman Catholics or to count as Roman Catholics persons who are clearly not of that faith.

Neither should it be supposed that all our intellectual problems would then be over, that justice would simply consist in the application, according to fixed rules, of laws which are so precisely framed as wholly to determine the judge's decision. There are legal systems which do everything they can to achieve this ideal; there are particular laws which we might safely programme a computer to apply. But application, interpretation, are by no means entirely straightforward notions; neither is impartiality. In the twentieth century, we have become peculiarly sensitive to the difficulties inherent in them, sometimes to the extent of denying that there can be any such thing as impartiality, or the straightforward interpretation of a law, or the simple application of it to particular cases. Indeed, the whole concept of formal justice is sometimes attacked as a mere sham, with the aid of which particular social groups maintain and strengthen their control over other social groups.

There are two distinct questions here: whether formal justice is *by its very nature* a mere facade for the arbitrary exercise of power, or whether in *a particular society*, as one way in which that society reveals itself to be defective, it is so used by those who control that society. I shall consider only the first, the more fundamental, of these hypotheses. Revolutionaries, taking it to be true, have sometimes set out with a fixed determination to destroy all lawyers and to replace systems of law with a system in which each case would be separately considered, decided not in the light of laws but in terms of 'general social welfare' or 'social justice'. But they have soon abandoned their original intentions. The schoolboy testifies to the value of formal justice when he describes a teacher as 'a brute, but a just brute' or finds most intolerable the teacher whose decisions display 'favouritism' and the pupil who seeks that favouritism.

As between two brutes, indeed, the brute whose judgements are in some measure based on explicit principles is superior to the brute whose actions are entirely arbitrary. That is not to say much in favour of formal justice but it is to say something. Even more obviously than civil justice, formal justice protects, to pick up my earlier phrase, against the partiality of love ('favouritism') and the uncertainties of mercy. The only alternative to systems of formal justice is the world of Kafka's *The Trial*, in which human beings are found guilty by judges whose decisions they can in no way anticipate. 'Where mystery begins, justice ends,' so Edmund Burke once wrote. (And nothing could be more mysterious than the workings of a system which makes no regular use of laws, rules, regulations.) Not to have any idea where one stands, to be wholly subject to the changing whims of autocracy, this is the worst of all situations, destructive of any sort of human dignity. Even in those systems which allow the judge considerable liberty in, let us say, determining a sentence, the judge's discretion is not unbounded. It is subject to appeal, it has to be supported by reference to general principles of some sort. Granting that judicial judgements are not so closely determined by law as the more perfervid defenders of formal law have sometimes pretended, allowing, too, that particular judges are not always models of impartiality and that within any particular social system the direction of their partiality can be largely anticipated, systems of formal justice are still very different from arbitrary exercises of power. It is in respect to formal justice that the dictum 'let justice be done, though the heavens fall' has its greatest plausibility.

In itself, formal justice is not a rival to civil justice. Indeed, the tests of competence on which civil justice relies have to be administered in the spirit of formal justice. Formal justice may have to determine, furthermore, how civil justice applies in a particular case, as on the other side the principle of civil justice ought to govern the selection of judges. It is only when each claims to be the *sole* form of justice that they can be represented as being rivals.

The case of social justice is very different. Social justice, in all its forms, departs from the principles of civil justice at one central point: it recognizes a 'merit' other than competence, the 'merit' of being disadvantaged. Crudely speaking, it is the reverse image of that older view, already familiar to Aristotle, that the possession of property justifies preferential treatment; not possessing property, according to the proponents of social justice, constitutes a 'merit'. If, however, such proponents now prefer to speak in terms of the 'disadvantaged' rather than the poor, this choice of language is not just another exemplification of the contemporary passion for euphemism (as illustrated by that absurd phrase, 'the underprivileged'). It concentrates attention on the fundamental point at issue: that some persons are so confined by their socio-economic circumstances as to be unable either to participate, except in a very limited fashion, in the desirable activities of the community or to demonstrate their competence. This can be as true of women, even when they are not poor, as of the poor.

In its most moderate form—let us then call it *facilitatory* social justice—the advocates of social justice do not reject outright the leading assumptions of civil justice. They do not deny either that some forms of activity are particularly desirable or that when a process of selection is inevitable, competence is the proper criterion. But they go beyond civil justice by demanding that a society should take positive steps to *facilitate* the wider participation of its members in desirable activities and the selection of the potentially most competent persons in any competitive situation. Such facilitation takes the form of so modifying the socio-economic circumstances which disadvantage particular individuals that those circumstances no longer act as a shackle.

If I call this the 'most moderate' form of social justice, I do not mean to imply that its proponents are necessarily, in their political allegiances, 'moderates'. They may argue, indeed, that social justice, even in this moderate sense, cannot be fully achieved by any means other than a violent revolution. The moderation attaches only to their ideal, not to the means which they are prepared to adopt in order to realize it. The ideal is 'moderate' only in so far as, in contrast with other ideals of social justice, it represents the minimal departure from civil justice, demanding preferential treatment for the disadvantaged only in the process of preparing themselves for selection, not at the stage of selection itself.

There is, indeed, a natural step from 'the law ought to be open to everyone', understood in terms of civil justice, to 'the law ought to be open to everyone', understood in terms of facilitatory social justice—as meaning, that is, that nobody ought to be prevented by his socio-economic circumstances from defending his rights at law. For the formal right, it can plausibly be argued, is empty so long as law is in practice open only to the wealthy. And an easy step, too, from 'the universities ought to be open to everyone', understood as meaning that nobody should be excluded for being of a particular sex, colour, religion or political affiliation to 'the universities ought to be open to everyone', meaning that nobody should be excluded because he cannot afford to attend a university. Any good reason one can offer for making the universities accessible, as they were gradually made accessible in the last century to Dissenters, Jews, women, is, on the face of it, an equally good reason for making them accessible to the financially disadvantaged. If civil justice is defended on the ground that it is fundamentally important for the desirable activities of the community to be conducted at the highest possible level, then one can rightly argue that some of the disadvantaged are just as competent to undertake university studies, given the necessary financial assistance, as are the advantaged. As for desert, who could deny that those disadvantaged persons who nevertheless succeed in displaying their superior competence are 'deserving'?

These arguments have proved convincing, if to varying degrees, in every liberal-democratic society as well as in socialist societies. Although, as I remarked, poverty is not the only form of disadvantage, facilitatory social justice for a long time concentrated its attention on reducing the effects of poverty. Poverty is the most *immediately visible* of all disadvantages, especially in societies in which great importance is attached to the accumulation of wealth. The disadvantages suffered by women, in contrast, are manifested mainly in their absence from places in which, by social tradition, they are in any case not expected to be. (Even in the case of blacks, Ellison called his novel on black Americans *The Invisible Man*.) So facilitatory social justice naturally assumed such forms as scholarships, free education, which gradually extended its range from the elementary school to the graduate school, and legal aid. All of these give preference to the disadvantaged either directly, through means-tests, or indirectly, in so far as they are financed by progressive income-tax. And they facilitate access to law, broader participation, the capacity to demonstrate competence.

Welfare schemes, national health schemes, pension schemes can be justified in the same terms: they are necessary if the disadvantaged are to live any but a very restricted kind of life. (I am here defending such schemes in terms of justice. They can also be defended, of course, in terms of simple humanity, as relieving misery. But the two lines of defence ought not to be confused. The relief of misery does not, of itself, fall within the province of justice.) No doubt some few individuals deliberately choose to be poor, precisely on the ground that poverty is a necessary condition for engaging in certain types of desirable activity, just as they may choose not to marry. But there is a broad connection between economic security, a degree of health, and the capacity to participate, a connection sufficient to justify the general presumption that such schemes will facilitate, even if they are by no means sufficient to ensure, wider opportunities to participate or to display competence.

When it comes to forms of disadvantage other than poverty, the liberal-democratic proponent of social justice finds it harder to know how to act. These disadvantages may arise out of irrational fears—a fear of, let us say, women or of blacks—or out of social traditions, such traditions as that 'woman's place is in the home', 'the blacks are innately inferior', traditions so powerful as to influence even those who are disadvantaged by them. Such applications of civil justice as laws against discrimination in employment attempt, no doubt, to diminish the force of these forms of disadvantage. But civil justice, so it is commonly argued, by no means suffices. Crèches, 'busing', fall into the category of facilitatory social justice rather than of civil justice. And dissatisfaction remains; somehow these social devices never quite achieve their hoped-for ends. Such dissatisfaction does much to explain the appeal of more radical forms of social justice.

Not unnaturally, too, some of the problems we encountered in relation to civil justice recur in relation to facilitatory social justice. Why, for example, should its application stop short at national boundaries? Can—in justice as distinct from humanity—disadvantaged countries properly be left to improve the participatory opportunities of their own disadvantaged citizens? Why should the principle that being disadvantaged constitutes a 'merit' be less than universal in its application? These are not merely questions a philosopher might think up as an intellectual exercise: they are seriously raised by the developing countries. Many countries, nowadays, will admit only migrants who can display their competence, not 'the poor and the hungry'; in respect to migrants, then, they have not made the transition from civil to facilitatory social justice—and not surprisingly, seeing that the economic and social costs of opening those doors more widely are overwhelming.

Even within the boundaries of a particular country, facilitatory social justice has its obvious economic costs and its more disputable social costs. Economic costs can rise to a point at which, by cutting into the surplus available for investment, they seriously threaten the continued existence of the community as a centre of diverse desirable activities. Social costs can have a similar effect. It is natural to be suspicious of those who tell us that welfare schemes can weaken the spirit of enterprise, can increase the power of the state to a degree which seriously threatens individual liberty, can end up by destroying justice itself. For these sentiments so often issue from the mouths of those who in fact care for nothing except the maintenance of their own power and privilege. But they cannot be lightly dismissed.

The consequence does not follow, however, that the attempt to secure facilitatory social justice ought to be abandoned, as too costly, too dangerous. The need, rather, is to explore new forms of social institution which will satisfy the demands of facilitatory social justice without strengthening the power of the state. Whether such institutions can be created, what form they can take—these are now, for such liberal–democratic countries as are not content to creep into totalitarianism, questions which they cannot afford to set aside as 'too hard'. If it turns out that the claims of facilitatory social justice can be fully satisfied only in a society in which liberty is destroyed, then some of us would be prepared to conclude: let social justice not be done. And we would say this the more confidently because we have good reason for believing that in such a society both civil and formal justice would rapidly be destroyed.

The criticisms of facilitatory social justice to which I have so far alluded would commonly be denominated 'conservative', especially in those countries, like the United States, in which their proper denomination 'liberal' has, however absurdly, come to be synonymous with 'socialist'. But radical reformers have rejected facilitatory social justice with no less vigour, if now on the ground that it fails to satisfy the claims of justice rather than because it can be pushed to such extremes as to destroy liberty.

Since facilitatory social justice remains faithful to the spirit of civil justice, so too it does not reject formal justice. Its advocates demand that the disadvantaged should be given opportunities to prepare themselves adequately for the processes of selection. But, as we have already pointed out, they do not demand that they be preferred *at the point of selection*; selection itself should, they freely grant, be strictly governed by rules, rules designed to secure impartiality.

The more radical proponents of social justice lay it down, on the contrary, that even when a disadvantaged person is, according to a formal interpretation of the rules of selection, inferior to an 'advantaged' competitor, the disadvantaged person can justly be preferred. This is on the ground that his disadvantages flow from past discriminations, for which he can justly demand reparation. Let us therefore speak of the ideal to which such advocates appeal as *reparative* social justice.

To illustrate its workings, consider a concrete case. A black and a white student apply for admission to a medical school and hence to the medical profession. As a result of properly administered selective tests, the black applicant is marginally excluded, the white applicant is marginally selected. The standards are high. There is no suggestion, then, that the black applicant is incompetent; simply, he does not do as well in the selective tests as the white applicant. In such circumstances, so the proponents of reparative social justice argue, it can be just to select the black applicant.

On what possible grounds? Several have been suggested, varying in the degree to which they are consistent with the principle of civil justice:

1. for all his inferiority in the selection tests, the black may make the better doctor;
2. gross injustice has been done to blacks in the past; now, by way of reparation, the old discriminations should be reversed;
3. by preferring the black candidate, the medical school would be making a contribution to the emergence of a more equal society;
4. it is a clear proof of injustice that blacks are not represented in medical schools in proportion to their numbers in the community; blacks may justly be preferred until that point is reached.

Each of these arguments raises large issues. Inevitably I can consider them only in a summary fashion. On the first point, the mere fact that the excluded black applicant *might* make a better doctor than the selected white applicant is insufficient to establish that the black applicant can justly be preferred. Tests of competence being what they are, so might any of the marginally excluded applicants, black or white, make better doctors than the marginally selected candidates, black or white. The imperfection of our selective tests could plausibly be regarded as a good ground for selecting the black student only if we were to discover that marginally selected black students regularly made better doctors than marginally selected white students. Then it would be a natural inference that marginally excluded black students were likely to be, in fact, more competent than marginally selected white students, that the selective processes were in some way biased against them. In such circumstances, one might well conclude, civil justice would not only permit but demand that the black applicant be preferred.

An alternative line of reasoning is that the tests are designed to measure general competence. Marginally excluded black applicants would in fact, the argument then runs, be better at curing certain disadvantaged ethnic groups than are marginally selected white doctors. So they ought to be preferred, on the principle of facilitatory social justice, in order to improve the socio-economic conditions of the disadvantaged. And such a preference is not incompatible with the principle of civil justice. For in relation to the desirable activity of improving the health of disadvantaged persons, the black applicant will in fact be the more competent.

To satisfy the principle of civil justice, those claims have not merely to be, as propounded, plausible but, what is much harder, have to be shown to hold good. If this can be done, then certainly we do not have to appeal to a special principle of reparative justice in order to justify our giving preference to the marginally excluded black student. Civil justice does not demand that the selective processes take any particular form, provided only that they do not discriminate on grounds other than competence. But it would demand clear evidence that any particular black falls into the class of those marginally excluded blacks against whom the tests are biased. (If, for example, the black has wealthy parents, this might not be true.)

Here formal justice steps into the picture, as ever a necessary concomitant to civil justice. Is there any way, it would ask, of formalizing as a set of rules, capable of impartial administration, the considerations which might properly lead us to prefer the marginally excluded black student? In principle, certainly, tests might be devised and built into the selection process, which would reflect the applicant's capacity to cope with disadvantaged patients or which would discount such superiority in examination achievement as derives from advantageous scholarly and socio-economic circumstances. But such tests are in practice hard to come by. And if we set formal justice aside, if we are content to argue, 'there is some reason for believing that marginally excluded black students as a class may make more competent doctors than either marginally selected or marginally excluded white students as a class, so let us prefer this particular black applicant', we leave the way open to panic-stricken preferential treatment in favour of whatever disadvantaged political groups are in the strongest position to exert political pressure. (Has anyone really considered whether the special considerations which apply to marginally excluded black applicants do not also apply to marginally excluded Polish applicants?) In short, from the standpoint of justice, we can easily find ourselves exactly where we once were, when civil and formal justice were abrogated in order to discriminate in favour of white Anglo-Saxon middle-class Protestant candidates, on the alleged ground that they 'really make better doctors' because they are more 'socially acceptable'.

To counter this analogy, the proponents of social justice are forced into a more radical line of reasoning which cuts clean across the principle of civil justice. This is obviously true of the second ground I distinguished: that since blacks have been discriminated against in the past, selective processes should now discriminate in their favour. 'Being discriminated against in the past' is, on this view, to count as a 'merit'. There is no longer the slightest suggestion that the effect of preferring the black applicant will be to sustain desirable activities at their highest level, that such marginally excluded black applicants are really more competent than marginally selected white candidates. Civil justice is quite openly set aside in favour of reparative justice, an attenuated form of retributive justice.

In its simplest and most plausible form, reparative justice rests on a principle which runs somewhat as follows: 'if X has injured Y, Y is entitled to demand reparation from X.' Thus stated, the principle has no application in the present instance. The white applicant has done no injury to the black applicant. Why should *he* be called upon to make reparation by being excluded? Indeed, if he is excluded, it is he, on this principle of reparation, who could properly claim compensation from the selectors as having been injured by them.

Let us look then, for a broader way of stating the principle of reparation. Perhaps as follows: 'if Y has a responsibility for protecting X, he ought to compensate X for injuries X suffers as a result of his neglect.' So, in certain communities, the state compensates victims of criminal assaults. And this might be justified on the ground that the state has failed in its general duty to protect its citizens against such assaults. Workers' compensation acts operate on the same general principle, although the application of 'responsibility to protect' is sometimes carried so far—as when workmen are compensated for injuries sustained on the way to and from work—as to suggest the operation of another, even more far-reaching, principle: 'if anybody is injured, *somebody* ought to compensate him.'

But the proponent of reparative social justice need not appeal to so far-reaching a principle. (Taken seriously, it would immobilize any social change. Even an increase in taxation injures *somebody*.) He might rest his case, rather, on the contention that discrimination is not merely an injury but an injustice, for which the state must bear responsibility, as having a duty to protect against injustice, and for which therefore it must make reparation.

But what sort of reparation? From certain points of view, facilitatory social justice can be thought of as reparative. But it makes reparation in a manner which does not infringe the principle of civil justice. How, in contrast, can it be just to compel X, a particular white applicant, to take the brunt of a civil injustice merely because the state ought to make reparation? (Consider our moral objections to the taking, and shooting, of randomly selected hostages as reparation for the activities of the Resistance.) One might try to construct, in defence, an argument of the following sort: 'injustice in selection is so serious a form of injustice that it demands reparation in the form of preference in selection.' But this argument, fully set out as 'civil injustice in so serious a form of injustice that it demands compensation in the form of committing acts of civil injustice', contains the same moral absurdity as: 'killing is so terrible a crime that the killer must be killed.' That the state, rather than an individual, is the agent of reparation, does not affect the moral quality of the act. That is to say nothing of the additional complication in the present case that the applicant to whom the injustice is to be done—unlike the killer who is killed—did not himself commit any injustice to the black applicant. The analogy, indeed, is with 'killing is so terrible a crime that whenever it occurs *someone* must be killed'—a morally still more primitive principle.

At this point, however, the proponents of reparative social justice may have recourse to another familiar principle, the principle of hereditary responsibility. It is exemplified in such doctrines as that we all justly suffer for being the children of Adam, or that Jehovah can justly visit the sins of the parents on the third or fourth generations. Outside the Judaeo-Christian tradition we meet it in Horace's 'guiltless though you are, you must expiate the sins of your fathers.' But a leading tendency of moral thinking over the last two centuries has been to reject the principle of hereditary responsibility as being clearly unjust, to deny that 'being so-and-so's son' constitutes either a 'merit' or a 'demerit'. And surely it would be morally retrogressive to take any other view.

An intermediate form of the principle is somewhat more plausible. It would run something like this: 'if Y has profited from doing an injury to X, and Z has inherited these profits, he can be called upon to compensate X.' But, even if this general principle be accepted, in the instance being considered it need not be at all true that the white applicant has inherited profits from his father's discrimination against blacks; he may, indeed, be a new immigrant to the country from, let us say, Iceland.

To be broad enough to justify the preference for the black over the white applicant, the principle of reparation would have to be stated, indeed, not in genetic terms but in terms of social inheritance, by reference to classes: 'everybody who belongs to a class which has in the past been discriminated against can now justly be preferred.' But in so general a form this principle is clearly untenable. Who doesn't belong to a class which has at some time become discriminated against? (whites in Japan; Anglo-Saxons by Normans; Protestants in Roman Catholic states.) Yet if we try to make the principle more specific, by substituting for 'any member of a class which has in the past been discriminated against' such phrases as, let us say, 'any member of the class of black persons', 'any woman', 'any member of the working class', we are simply being racist, or sexist, or classist, abandoning, in other words, the central concepts of civil justice. We are offering no general grounds whatsoever for supposing 'black', 'female', 'member of the working class' to be peculiarly relevant differences. In short, we are being unprincipled, the essence of injustice.

What about the third argument, that preferring the black applicant is a step toward a more equal society? If the presumption is that injustice can properly be done to an innocent bystander—in this case the white student—provided only that this will facilitate the emergence of a more equal society, this is once again an abrogation of justice, the morality of the terrorist. No doubt an attempt will be made to gloss over this fact by arguing that a more equal society is, automatically, a juster society, so that the injustice to individuals is in the cause of the final triumph of justice. But even leaving aside the appalling implications of such an argument, we can point out in reply that a more equal society is not necessarily a juster society, if it ignores relevant differences. (Compare with our society a society in which nobody, of whatever age, sex, health, interest or capacity is permitted to engage in any activity except agricultural labour.) Justice demands no more than that all *irrelevant* differences be ignored. Egalitarianism is a particular social ideal, neither more nor less just than that other social ideal which permits inequalities, based on relevant differences, in the interests of liberty and diversity. Whether absolute equality is desirable and, if so, what sort of equality, is quite a different question from whether justice, and if so, justice of what sort, is desirable. It was that enthusiast for justice, Proudhon, who wrote that 'the theory of a peaceful equality, founded on fraternity and sacrifice, is only a counterfeit of the Catholic doctrine of the goods and pleasures of this world, the principle of beggary, the panegyric of misery.'

Egalitarianism may rest its case, however, on there *not being any relevant differences*, appearances to the contrary arising out of past discrimination. That is the assumption which underlies the fourth argument in favour of preferring the black student, that an injustice has obviously been done, and must now be repaired, if the percentage of black medical students is not proportionate to their numbers in the community. So, it is concluded, black applicants must be preferred until that point has been reached. As I suggested earlier, this view arises in part out of discontent with the fact that applications of facilitatory social justice, and especially the widening of educational opportunities, have not altered, to anything like the degree anticipated, the percentage of blacks, or of women, in the occupations which intellectuals think of as being particularly desirable. The explanation that this is because only a few members of the disadvantaged groups either want to, or are able to, engage in these activities, such intellectuals find quite unbearable.

Their argument has a metaphysical foundation: it rests on what I shall call *the principle of cosmic justice*. It cannot be true, on this principle, that abilities are genetically determined. Any appearance to the contrary must be explained as the effects of social injustices. The world, as distinct from social organization, is fair; it would not be fair if people were unequally endowed; therefore people are not unequally endowed.

Traditional Christianity sought to explain divergencies from 'cosmic justice' by arguing, first, that as a result of Adam's Fall the world is (justly) not as it ought to be; secondly, that God's justice works in such mysterious (non-formal) ways that we are simply in no position to determine that anything in the world is unjustly as it is; thirdly, that any apparent injustices will be compensated for ('reparative justice') in a world to come. With the rise in secularism and with it the concepts of civil and formal justice, the force of these arguments was weakened. Retributive justice—invoked in the case of Adam's Fall —has come to be largely dismissed as not justice at all but only revenge. As against divine mysteriousness, justice, so it is argued, must not only be done, but must be seen to be done. Compensation in a remote future is discountable as too doubtful a prospect and, in any case, no excuse for creating distinctions in the first place.

But the old feeling, to which the Christian explanations are a response, still persists. What differs is that social injustices, rather than Adam's sin, are now appealed to in order to explain the existence of what appear to be natural differences in competence. So if, for example, Jews figure largely in university appointments, this can only be, on such a view, because they have been unjustly advantaged. The percentage of Jews selected as professors can, therefore, justly be reduced, even if, by ordinary selective criteria, they are the best applicants. (One must in fairness add that the proponents of this view sometimes argue that the disproportionate representation of Jews in universities is the result of unjust discrimination against Jews in those other fields in which they are disproportionately under-represented. But the immediate effect of the argument, all the same, is that in respect to participation in a form of activity to which they have been singularly devoted Jews can properly be discriminated against in favour of blacks.) In other words, reparative social justice demands the overturning of a principle which was for so long fought for, and with such difficulty achieved, in the name of civil justice. And demands it even at the cost of a sharp decline in standards of achievement.

I hesitate to discuss the issue any further. For there is no surer way of winning for oneself the reputation of being a reactionary of the most flagrant sort than by arguing that there can be genetic distinctions of a sort which are not the product of disease—when they would be in principle remediable by medical science—and which give a person advantages which are not the product of social injustice. One can easily understand why to propose any view of this kind has come to be regarded as the blasphemy of blasphemies, which one must shout down, cannot permit to be promulgated, a sin against the Holy Ghost. For the doctrine of genetic differences has often been used in the past, and is still being used, to justify manifest injustices and to lend a pseudo-theoretical foundation to tyrannies of the most appalling kind. Nobody who lived through the Nazi regime could fail to be conscious of this fact. And the Nazi treatment of Jews and Slavs is only one instance. The discriminations against the etas in Japan, the aborigines in Australia, the untouchables in India, the blacks in South Africa and the United States, are no less notable examples of unjust appeals to genetic differences. They are unjust, because we can be quite confident that there is no 'racial' group which does not contain some members who are more competent than some members of other groups even in those forms of desirable activity which do not form part of their native culture. Some Australian whites are exceptionally competent boomerang-throwers; some Australian aborigines are exceptionally competent senators. We can readily agree, too, that many tests of competence which profess to point only to genetic differences in fact fail to do so. (I argued as much in relation to intelligence tests over forty years ago.) We can accept it as a maxim, even, that genetic differences should be appealed to in order to explain difference of achievement only in the last resort.

These considerations entitle us to protest against any attempt to rule out blacks, or women, as incompetent *en masse* to enter any particular occupation. But they are not strong enough to justify the conclusion that the principles of social justice must be set aside in order to ensure that social groups are represented in proportion to their numbers in any form of desirable activity, that otherwise some injustice is being done.

For all I know, mathematical abilities may be equally distributed between men and women; the percentage of blacks who, with changing socio-economic circumstances, would make good philosophers may be greater than the percentage of whites who are good philosophers. I want only to insist, first, that it is an empirical question whether this is so: there is no *a priori* reason why it should be so; and secondly, as I argued previously, that justice has to take account of the differences which are presented for its decisions. That under changing circumstances these differences might not exist is not a consideration justice can take into account, although, of course, humanity can and does do so. If the question is who is to be selected as a professor of mathematics, the fact that social traditions disadvantage women who might otherwise have been good mathematicians, or that a competing candidate was advantaged by having had a mathematical parent, is a totally inadequate reason for preferring a woman candidate to a thus-advantaged male candidate.

Let me add, finally, that if we do agree that there are genetic differences in ability, this does not imply that we should complacently admit as much and stop at this point. The principle of facilitatory justice will demand that we do what we can to facilitate the entry of the genetically less able into desirable activities; where that is impossible, compassion comes into play.

About an even more radical form of social justice, *levelling* social justice, I have already had a little to say. Its leading presumption is that, in the interests of justice, the very concept of competence must be rejected, that an undergraduate education, let us say, must be open to all comers. For why, its proponents ask, should anyone have a greater right than anyone else to participate in any desirable activities? To this, there is an obvious reply: the activities in question will simply vanish if the entering students are not adequately prepared to engage in them. (This happened when universities were open only to the incompetent, lazy, bigoted, 'gilded youth'.) The promised land of the university will turn out to be nothing more than just another high school, or even an elementary school, while the desirable activities in which the students hoped to participate retreat to the graduate school or, beyond that, to post-doctoral fellowships. The prospects held out by levelling social justice are, in short, completely fraudulent. An examination in which nobody fails, a high distinction which everybody is awarded, a degree which everybody obtains—none of these then has the selective function it previously had. And on the principle of ecological niches, some other, less just, method of selection will take its place. Why, in any case, should we permit egalitarianism to masquerade as justice?

Perhaps I should add a word or two about what I shall call the *minimalist* theory of social justice. This is the principle that X can justly be given preferential treatment as compared with Y only when it is to the advantage of the most disadvantaged members of the community to do so. Briefly, my objection to this is a double one. First, that it is not a principle we can practically apply. It cannot in general be shown that subsidizing X but not Y to engage in a piece of scientific research is to the advantage of the most disadvantaged members even of the community in which that subsidizing takes place. It is, of course, easy to make such claims as that research into the structure of matter will relieve poverty, or cure cancer, but very hard to sustain them. Secondly, minimalist social justice assumes that 'being peculiarly disadvantaged' is in the long run the only 'merit'. ('Being a better scientist' is not, on this view, in itself a 'merit'; a greatly inferior scientist can justly be preferred if it would be to the advantage of the most disadvantaged to do so.) And this is an assumption which, I should argue, could only result in the emergence of a society in which no life-plans could be sustained, in which diversity would be so restricted that liberty would become meaningless. But to establish as much is a task I cannot now undertake. (If I read the situation aright, communist China has just now abandoned an experiment in minimalist social justice, perceiving the spiritual impoverishment in which it results.)

There is a great deal more that ought to be said in order to strengthen the case I have tried to construct for the maintenance and development of the principle of civil justice. But let me end with a set of very general observations and questions:

1.   Are we not trying to pack too much into the concept of justice and the correlative concept of rights? The question whether it is *wrong* to act in certain ways is not the same question as whether it is *unjust* so to act. Compassion, consideration, respect for others, generosity, mercy, love—none of these is reducible to justice. But much popular discussion of contemporary moral issues runs them together.

2.   Are we demanding too much of ourselves morally? Over two millennia ago the neo-Platonist Porphyry argued that human civilization would collapse if men were to try to extend justice to animals.

There is a growing tendency in our times to demand 'justice' not only for animals but even for all living things. At the same time, the demands made upon us, in the name of justice, on behalf of future generations have now reached unprecedented proportions, not to mention the demands made on behalf of prisoners, the insane and the inhabitants of the multitude of developing societies. Are we not liable, faced with such excessive moral demands, to fall back into a narrow self-concern, as the only practical policy? Or to suffer a moral collapse into a Marxism which limits our problems by laying it down that we need to take into account, only, how our actions bear upon the future victory of a particular class?

3.   Are we sacrificing too much to the ideal of justice or what we suppose to be justice? Every age tends to generate its own species of moral fanaticism, to set up a particular good as the sole good: charity, obedience, liberty, progress, happiness have all filled that position at one time or another. Is it really true – what is sometimes presumed to be a 'primary intuition'—that laws and institutions no matter how efficient and well arranged must be reformed or abolished if they are unjust? That an institution is 'efficient' is certainly not a sufficient reason for maintaining it in existence. A concentration camp can be efficient. But what if it be efficient in preserving, generating or developing some important good, even although it is unjustly organized? It is always a defect in an institution that it is unjust. Nevertheless an institution can, in the name of justice, be made futile, because it can no longer preserve the good it used to preserve. That it contains injustices is not a *demonstration* that it ought to be reformed or destroyed. It will often be the case, fortunately, that an institution will be better adapted toward preserving and developing the good if it is so reformed as to be more justly organized. But it *need not be.*

We have lost confidence, I have already suggested, in our capacity to distinguish. We have lost confidence that Mozart is a better composer than the creator of the latest pop-song, lost confidence that it is better to think rationally and critically than to succumb to occultism, lost confidence that public life is anything more than a display room for egoistic opportunities. So we have nothing to fall back upon but egalitarianism. But unless we are prepared to make distinctions and recognize their legitimacy as justifying unequal treatment, we cannot stop short of a wholly uniform society. Then we shall be free of problems about what constitutes equality and what constitutes equal treatment. Everyone will be equal before the law because no lawyer will be cleverer than any other lawyer. Everybody will have the same opportunities because no one's parents, no one's teachers, no one's friends, will be more competent than anyone else's. Everyone will hold the same views and work within the same artistic bounds because no one will be more imaginative than anyone else. But only tyranny, and even then imperfectly, could produce such a result.

3

Justice as reciprocity[1]

Brian Barry

I Introduction

What, if anything, do rich nations owe to poor ones? What, if anything, does the present generation owe those who are to come after it? In the last few years, we have seen an enormous increase in the salience of these questions. The poor countries have a comfortable majority in the General Assembly of the United Nations and have established in UNCTAD a permanent international organization dedicated to furthering their interests. The spectacular success of OPEC has forcibly drawn attention to the extent to which the prices of raw materials are subject to economic power and thus brought commodity prices more explicitly into the political arena. The east-west theme of cold war confrontation that ran through the third quarter of the century is being replaced in the final quarter by the north-south theme of confrontation between rich and poor nations.[2] At the same time, a new understanding of the complex interrelations that make life possible on earth has made us more aware of the way in which quite minor alterations of the ecological balance may have catastrophic long-run consequences. The interests of our remote descendants have started to figure explicitly in debates on the disposal of nuclear waste and the proposal to ban fluorocarbon aerosol propellants. Moreover,

[1] This chapter, originally presented as a paper at the opening symposium of the World Congress on Philosophy of Law and Social Philosophy, was prepared at the Center for Advanced Study in the Behavioral Sciences, Stanford, California, where the comments of Robert Simon were especially helpful. The present version is extensively revised and about half the material is completely new. I have benefited from reactions at the Congress to the original version of the paper and comments at seminars in a number of universities in Australia and New Zealand which I visited in August and September 1977.

[2] See, for an analysis of the changing character of international politics, Robert O. Keohane and Joseph S. Nye, *Power and Interdependence: World Politics In Transition* (Boston, 1977).

the literature of 'limits to growth', 'spaceship earth' and so on has served to emphasize the fact that, however sanguine one might be about new discoveries of raw materials and substitutes, resources are finite and we cannot therefore avoid facing the fact that the more we use the less there will be left for our descendants.

Most of us have only the haziest ideas about what justice requires in these cases. Even worse, we feel that the framework within which we normally think about justice—the framework that serves us well enough for thinking about relations among contemporaries in the same society—fails to give us a grip on these problems of international and intergenerational justice. In this chapter I shall explore them by setting out this framework of everyday thought, seeing exactly how international and intergenerational justice relate to it and then arguing that there is another conception of justice, also deeply rooted in our common ideas, that provides a key to the problems of justice between countries and between generations.

The framework within which we ordinarily discuss questions of justice among contemporaries who are members of the same society is, I suggest, that of justice as reciprocity. Every society of which I have read has some notion as to the rightness of meeting reasonable expectations that a favour will be returned, of pulling one's weight in cooperative enterprises, of keeping agreements that provide for mutual benefits, and so on.[3] Thus, Marcel Mauss, in his classic *The Gift*, 'stresses that there is a universally recognized obligation to reciprocate gifts which have been accepted', while A. R. Radcliffe-Brown 'assumed a principle of reciprocity which he called "the principle of equivalent return". This he held was expressed in the *lex talionis*, in the principle of indemnification for injury, and in the principle that those who give benefits should receive equivalent benefits.'[4]

Again, the most significant recent work of political philosophy, *A Theory of Justice* by John Rawls,[5] is built around the notion of justice as reciprocity. It has been said correctly that 'it is the contractualist conception of equality as reciprocity that is at the root of Rawls's interpretation of justice.'[6] The essence of justice as reciprocity for Rawls is what in his article 'Justice as Fairness' he called the duty

---

[3] See Alvin W. Gouldner, 'The Norm of Reciprocity', *American Sociological Review* 25 (1960), pp. 161–78 and 'Reciprocity and Autonomy in Functional Theory', in N. J. Demerath III and Richard A. Peterson (eds), *System, Change, and Conflict* (New York, 1967) pp. 141–69.

[4] Quotations from Gouldner, 'Reciprocity and Autonomy', p. 150, nn. 17 and 18. The first refers to Marcel Mauss, *The Gift* (Glencoe, Ill., 1954), the second to a Chicago University seminar of 1937, 'The Nature of a Theoretical Nature Science of Society'.

[5] John Rawls, *A Theory of Justice* (Cambridge, Mass., 1971).

[6] John W. Chapman, *Nomos* VI, edited by Carl J. Friedrich and John W. Chapman (New York, 1963), pp. 147–69 at p. 149.

of fair play: 'the obligation which participants who have knowingly accepted the benefits of their common practice owe to each other to act in accordance with it when their performance falls due'.[7] 'Fair play' in this sense is an important part of justice as reciprocity but we have many other usages involving the concepts of fairness which we employ to assess the extent to which reciprocity is being satisfied or violated. Thus, we speak of a fair exchange, when the values of the things exchanged are equivalent, and of a fair offer as a proposal for a fair exchange. We speak of fair compensation, when the value of the compensation matches the loss sustained. And we speak of fairness not only in relation to the way in which the burdens of a common enterprise are distributed but also in relation to the way in which the benefits are distributed. Other things being equal, if one person puts more into an activity yielding a common benefit, it is considered fair that he should get more out.[8]

The first half of this chapter will be devoted to the further analysis of justice as reciprocity. I shall look at justice as reciprocity under three heads. The first is justice as requital, that is to say making a fair return for benefits received (section II). The second is justice as fidelity, that is to say, carrying out one's side of a bargain voluntarily entered into (section III). The third is justice as mutual aid, that is to say, playing one's part in a practice of helping those in need (section IV).

The second half of the chapter will be concerned with the limitations of justice as reciprocity, even when its bounds are drawn quite widely, as in my discussion. After pointing out these limitations in relation to justice between countries (section V) and justice between generations (section VI), I shall put forward another conception of justice—justice as equal opportunity (section VII). In conclusion (section VIII) I shall sketch in the implications of this conception for justice between nations and justice between generations.

---

[7] John Rawls, 'Justice as Fairness', reprinted in P. Laslett and W. G. Runciman (eds), *Philosophy, Politics and Society*, second series (Oxford, 1962), pp. 132–57 at p. 146.

[8] See George Caspar Homans, *Social Behavior: Its Elementary Forms* (New York, 1961), chapter 12, for an exposition of the view that 'men are alike in holding the notion of proportionality between investment and profit that lies at the heart of distributive justice' (p. 246). Homans explicitly equates distributive justice and fair exchange: 'Fair exchange, or distributive justice in the relations among men, is realized when the profit, or reward less cost, of each man is directly proportional to his investments' (p. 264). See Elaine Walster and G. William Walster, 'Equity and Social Justice', *Journal of Social Issues* 31 (1975), pp. 21–43 for a review of the small-group literature subsequent to *Social Behavior*.

II Justice as requital

I intend under this heading to include a mixed bag, united only by the general idea of *quid pro quo*. Thus, I include fair dealing in explicit trading situations and the more diffuse notion of making an adequate return contained in the notion that 'one good turn deserves another.' The converse of this, for bad turns, is that anyone who harms another should provide compensation or suffer punishment. I include Rawls's duty of fair play, which calls on those who have enjoyed, or stand to enjoy, a public good to be willing to contribute to the cost of providing it. (In 'Justice as Fairness' Rawls gave the examples of taxes for the provision of government services and of trade union dues.)[9] The converse of the 'anti-free rider' principle is that anyone who contributes especially effectively to the provision of a collective benefit is in fairness entitled to be rewarded more highly by the (other) recipients of the benefit. Clearly, justice as requital could be analysed in much more detail, and the types of justice as requital roughly distinguished here could be further developed. But for my present purpose, it is enough if I have pointed in an unambiguous way to a conception of justice that is at least in some forms non-controversial and universal.[10]

III Justice as fidelity

This is the aspect of justice that was for Hobbes the whole of it: 'that men perform their covenants made'. The connection between fidelity and reciprocity is obvious, so much so that it is not surprising to find the part taken for the whole and all of justice as reciprocity reduced to contractual relations. Thus, Hobbes takes up two aspects of what I have been calling justice as requital: commutative justice as 'equality of value of the things contracted for' and distributive justice as 'the distribution of equal benefit, to men of equal merit'. And he disposes of them as criteria of justice by arguing, against the first, that 'the just value, is that which [the contractors] be contented to give', and, against the second, that 'merit ... is not due by justice; but is rewarded of grace only.'[11] This, however, simply presupposes the

[9] Rawls, 'Justice as Fairness', p. 146. The inadequacy of voluntary contributions as a way of supporting the cost of public goods is argued in Mancur Olson, Jr, *The Logic of Collective Action* (Cambridge, Mass., 1965). For a sophisticated formal analysis which explores the question under what circumstances cooperative behaviour can be maintained without coercion, see Michael Taylor, *Anarchy and Cooperation* (London, 1967).

[10] For a discussion of some of the ramifications of justice as requital and the difficulties that arise in applying it, see Robert E. Goodin, *The Politics of Rational Man* (London, 1976), chapters 6 and 7.

[11] Thomas Hobbes, *Leviathan*, chapter 15, Everyman edn (New York, 1950), pp. 124.

definition of 'justice' that Hobbes has already given, in terms of keeping convenant.

Charles Fried has expressed the Hobbesian position on the first as follows:

> The plausibility of [mutual promising] as showing the kind of practice which must be considered just depends on this—that the sacrifices which are made by each individual are by hypothesis less than the gain to that individual. Furthermore, we need not determine whether any individual has in fact received full value, and more, for his sacrifice, since as the practice is defined, it is the individual himself who approves the exchange.[12]

Consider a case such as one reads of now and then, of somebody who digs out a picture or a stamp collection that has been gathering dust in the attic and sells it to a dealer at a fraction of its market value. The dealer has not used force or fraud and was under no legal obligation to supply information as to the true value of the object purchased. And the object was clearly less valuable to the seller at the time of the sale than the money he was offered for it, otherwise he would not have chose to sell. Yet there is surely a perfectly clear sense in which this deal is unfair: the profit from the transaction is too unequally divided between the parties. Notice that we may say that a morally scrupulous dealer would not have taken unfair advantage of the seller's inexperience in this way without committing ourselves to the view that the law should void the contract or even to the view that the dealer had violated a duty. Yet the basis of our judgement that the dealer would have been more admirable if he had behaved differently is surely not that he would have shown himself generous or benevolent but that he would have shown sensitivity to the requirements of fairness.

Thus we can, and do, say intelligibly that a contract is unfair between the parties because the value of the things exchanged is unequal, although it is still a contract. And we do, quite rightly, say that it is unfair if men of equal merit are treated differently, even if the giving of a reward is a matter of grace. The parable of the labourer in the vineyard (Matthew 20.i–xvi) illustrates the point. That the lord of the vineyard gave more than the customary rate to those who had worked less than a full stint was a matter of 'grace' in Hobbes's terminology, and the lord's reply to one who had 'borne the burden and heat of the day'—'Friend, I do thee no wrong; didst not thou agree with me for a penny?'—is undeniably to the point. But there is surely also a genuine issue of fairness embodied in the complaint, 'these last have wrought but one hour, and thou hast made them

---

[12] Charles Fried, 'Justice and Liberty', *Nomos* VI, pp. 126–46 at p. 133.

equal to us.' Indeed, unless it is assumed that there is a natural sentiment of fairness—equal pay for equal work—that is being flouted, the
parable loses its force which is, I take it, to emphasize the difference
between the grace of God and human justice.

Hobbes had an ulterior political motive, of course, in denying that
there were alternative criteria of justice: he did not want to provide
any excuses for non-performance of covenants since that might
weaken the absolute claims of the sovereign. But it is quite consistent
to say that a contract you entered into is unfair in that it does not
exchange equal values or give a greater return for a greater contribution but that it would be unfair not to carry out your side of a bargain
freely agreed to.

A quite different ulterior political motive has led Robert Nozick, in
Anarchy, State, and Utopia, to deprecate the Rawlsian duty of 'fair
play'. Nozick's fear is that it will license any group of people to create
a duty to contribute to some common enterprise simply by providing
unasked-for benefits. 'One cannot, whatever one's purposes, just act
so as to give people benefits and then demand (or seize) payment.
Nor can a group of people do this.'[13] He therefore wants to insist
that there must be actual consent before it is legitimate to coerce
people to contribute to a common good. Once again, the implication is
that justice as reciprocity is reduced to contractual relations.

Characteristically, Nozick does not bother to offer any arguments,
and rests the burden of his case on an eccentric example involving a
public address system and 'some of the people in your neighbourhood'
who put down everybody's name on a list to broadcast over it for a
day [pp. 93–5]. It is indeed doubtful whether the case as stated gives
rise to a duty to broadcast, still less that it gives the others a right to
coerce you to do so (though I do think that as a matter of decency you
should give advance notice of your intention not to perform). However, it is far from clear that the case as stated falls under Rawls's
principle of fair play. For Rawls defined the duty of fair play by saying
that 'a person is required to do his part as defined by the rules of
an institution when two conditions are met: first the institution is
just (or fair) . . . and second, one has voluntarily accepted the benefits
of the arrangement or taken advantage of the opportunities it offers to
further one's interests.'[14] Nozick's case may, I think, be defective as a
counter-example on all three possible counts: it does not constitute an
example of an 'institution' for the purpose of the principle; it is not
just for 'some people' in the neighbourhood to arrogate to themselves

[13] Robert Nozick, *Anarchy, State, and Utopia* (New York, 1974), p. 95.
[14] Rawls, *Theory of Justice*, pp. 111–12. I am indebted to the comments on Nozick's
example in Thomas Scanlon, 'Nozick on Rights, Liberty, and Property', *Philosophy
and Public Affairs* 6 (1976), 3–25 at pp. 15–17.

the right to direct the use others make of their time; and listening to the public address system is scarcely voluntary.

If we turn to the real-life analogue of Nozick's example, it seems clear to me that the American public television stations have a good case for appealing (as they do) to the sense of fairness of those 'free riders' who choose to watch but do not contribute to the expenses of running the service. And I would add that considerations of fairness legitimate (if they do not require) that public television should be supported by a compulsory levy on the owners of television sets, as it is in many countries. It may be argued, of course, that this is unfair because some will be forced to contribute who do not watch public television or (in a country where there is no commercial television) would prefer having commercial television rather than paying for a licence. But to anyone except a fanatic the issue presents itself as a choice between the unfairness of permitting 'free riders' and the unfairness of collecting from non-beneficiaries, and there is no reason why the judgement should always go the same way. Let us leave aside the question of enforcement, however. The crucial point for present purposes is the simple one that the public television stations do have a legitimate claim in terms of fairness against those who benefit from the programmes but fail to contribute—a claim that Nozick's thesis would render unintelligible.[15]

The Rawlsian duty of fair play, as I noted above, requires that the benefits should have been accepted voluntarily. However, the general anti-free-rider principle is not limited in this way. It is unfair to enjoy the benefits of a practice without doing your part, even if you could not avoid enjoying these benefits. For example, if you live in an area where only smokeless fuel is permitted to be burned, you cannot help breathing cleaner air, having to wash curtains less often and so on, but that does not in any way diminish your obligation to play your part and burn only smokeless fuel. Similarly, if other visitors to some remote beauty spot obey the rule that they should take their litter out with them, you cannot help enjoying the absence of litter, but again that would not make it any less unfair for you to leave yours behind.

Nozick's nightmare of people arbitrarily being able to impose obligations of fairness on you by doing you favours fails to take account of the fact that it takes more to create a practice (or in Rawls's terms an institution) than a few people getting together and starting to provide benefit for others. One of the main purposes of law is to

[15] For an analysis of the implications for the provision of public goods of a morality favouring each person who benefits giving his 'fair share' of the costs, see Russell Hardin, 'The Contractarian Provision of Public Goods', *Papers of the Peace Science Society (International)* 22 (1977). Hardin notes the importance of setting a standard 'Membership fee' to create a 'uniquely prominent, relatively fair solution for cost-sharing'.

define practices and thus create well-defined duties of fairness. The threat of criminal penalties is not very important as a motive for compliance with rules against domestic air pollution or littering. The law is, however, significant as a coordinating device, defining a standard of conduct that it would be fair for all to adhere to, provided others do. Nozick's idea that, if a random collection of self-appointed do-gooders cannot create obligations of fairness, then neither can a public authority, entirely misses the point.

'The law', Paul Freund has said, 'is addicted to the device of finding "implied" contracts as a way out of novel problems, and of assimilating relations—such as public utility and customer—to a contractual mold.'[16] No doubt there are good technical reasons for this device, but in general the argument against trying to cram all cases of reciprocity into contract is an extension of that deployed by David Hume against the use of a fictitious 'original contract' to underwrite political obligation. If the real point is that of reciprocal advantage, nothing is gained by going through an extra loop and saying that the obligation derives from the fact that it would have been worth contracting had the occasion arisen.[17]

I have criticized the reduction of requital to fidelity. Rawls, in *A Theory of Justice*, goes in the other direction. He says that 'the principle of fidelity is but a special case of the principle of fairness applied to the social practice of promising' and that 'the obligation to keep a promise is a consequence of the principle of fairness' [pp. 344, 346]. If he meant simply that the principle of fidelity and the principle of fair play both derive from justice as reciprocity this would be unexceptionable. But to assimilate them, as Rawls does, results in slighting the significance of voluntary agreement.

In the case of practices where participation is not optional, Rawls says (reasonably enough) that the duty of fair play comes into operation to require performance only when the practice is itself just in the way in which it distributes benefits and burdens. He tries to extend this to promising, by saying that the principle of fairness makes the carrying out of promises obligatory only where the practice of promising is itself just. An example of an unjust practice of promising would be one in which people were 'bound by words uttered while asleep,

[16] Paul A. Freund, 'Social Justice and the Law', in *On Law and Justice* (Cambridge, Mass., 1968), pp. 82–107 at p. 84.

[17] Freund's remarks on the history of Roman and English contract law seem to me to suggest that the notion of justice as fidelity was a development out of that of justice as requital. According to Freund, the generalized notion of a contract arose in Roman law from 'either a delivery of a thing in expectation of a performance ... or ... the performance of an act in expectation of counterperformance' (p. 84), while in English law 'the elements of both *quid pro quo* and reliance entered into its inheritance' (p. 85). It is worth noting that these are precisely the bases of an enforceable duty of fair play ridiculed by Nozick.

or extorted by force' [*Theory of Justice*, p. 345]. This is of course right, but it does not establish what Rawls wants. For the analogy of a particular non-voluntary practice is not the general practice of promising but 'a particular pattern of transactions' established by a set of mutual promises [p. 346]. And the point is that justice as fidelity requires performance even if the 'small-scale scheme of cooperation' established by this set of mutual promises violates justice as requital in the way in which it distributes benefits and burdens among the participants. This is, of course, simply to reiterate that justice as requital and justice as fidelity are independent derivations from the generic notion of justice as reciprocity, and may on occasion conflict.

IV Justice as mutual aid

Consider, to begin with, an ordinary case of voluntary insurance—against fire, theft or accident, for example. If we look at the operation of the scheme within a certain slice of time, and overlook the contractual basis of the arrangements, we see a large number of fortunate citizens, who have not had fires (and so on) in the period, each paying in money which is dispensed to the small number who have been unfortunate. Simply observing the pattern of transfers we could not distinguish the insurance company from a charitable institution, appealing to the generosity of the fortunate to give succour to the unfortunate. What makes the difference is, of course, reciprocity. Even the most coldly calculating egoist will, if he is rational and risk-averse, willingly pay insurance premiums because only by doing so can he establish a claim to compensation for unlikely but potentially devastating contingencies.

Private insurance is, as I have said, based on contractual relationships. In as far as it exhibits reciprocity, it is the kind dealt with in my remarks on justice as fidelity. The exchange is simply of a regular premium for a right to be paid in some contingency. The reason for beginning my discussion of justice as mutual aid with it is that it illustrates how, even in a society made up of devotees of Ayn Rand, there would be continuous redistribution from the fortunate to the unfortunate—on a purely voluntary basis. In what follows I shall argue that the insurance model can be extended to (a) a non-contractual practice of mutual aid and (b) a non-voluntary system of redistribution.

Imagine a small community a hundred miles from the nearest town. Each family possesses a car, but cars are, of course, liable to break down. To meet this contingency a two-part practice has developed: anyone who is going into town anyway shoud be prepared to give a ride to a person whose car is not in use, even at some minor inconvenience of scheduling, picking up, setting down, and so on; and in case of genuine emergency anyone for whom it is not unduly inconvenient should be prepared to make a special trip into town. This practice would, I suggest, generate a duty of mutual aid derived from the general notion of justice as reciprocity.

It is interesting to speculate how the practice of mutual aid might extend to those without a car at all. Suppose that, because of either loss of earnings or increasing infirmity, some of the old people in the community are no longer able to run a car. It might seem that, since they can no longer pay the 'premium'—the liability to give rides to others —the insurance model should entail that they are excluded from the benefits. Any help they receive would then have to be put down to charity rather than reciprocity. But those who have cause to fear that they may some day themselves be reduced to the same circumstances will favour extending the benefits of the practice as an insurance measure.

This is still reciprocity but in a more complex form. Those who contribute benefits in a given period do not necessarily have any expectation of being able to claim them in future from the present beneficiaries. But they expect to be able to make claims themselves in the future on others, as defined by the practice. At any given time, the young could get a short-run gain by reneging on the extension of mutual aid to the old. But a social practice, defined by informal norms and underwritten by informal sanctions (the exclusion from benefits of those who violate 'fair play' by failing to perform when required to) cannot simply be stopped and then started up again later. The age cohort that is thinking of reneging on its obligations to the old cannot, therefore, reasonably expect to be able to impose the same obligation later on their juniors.

The young have reason, derived from the insurance motive, for maintaining the extended practice in order to be in a position to bene- fit from it themselves later if they need to. This, of course, pre- supposes that those who make the sacrifices now will actually be around when they will stand to benefit from the operation of the same practice. We should therefore anticipate that reciprocity of this inter- temporal kind will be weakened by mobility, and this does indeed seem to accord with experience. If the community were known to be due to be dissolved in a few years' time (suppose, for example that its economy is entirely based on the exploitation of a non-renewable natural resource and that when that comes to an end its members will scatter), then we have to say that giving rides to those without cars would switch from reciprocity to charity.

It should be observed that waiving the 'premium' for some does not entail waiving it for all. Anyone who, relying on the practice to get him out of trouble, chose to save the expense of having a car or ran one that was notoriously unreliable would be condemned as a free (or cheap) rider. If he has no less reason for paying the premium than anyone else, it is unfair of him not to. He would therefore be excluded or—given that there is a humanitarian duty in life-and-death emergencies to help, which is not dependent on reciprocity—subject to condemnation. (We could, of course, extend the story to more generalized reciprocity, so that someone who relied on others for transport provided some other service to members of the community, but there is no need to get into such further extension here.)

I now have to say a little about the way in which justice as mutual aid underwrites compulsory redistribution. This theme has in recent years been taken up by economists under the label 'Pareto-optimal redistribution'.[18] Saying a redistribution is Pareto-optimal is to say that everybody prefers the distribution after redistribution has been carried out to the one before. The apparent paradox involved in saying that all might gain from redistribution is resolved by recalling that those who did not have a fire in a certain year have had their premiums redistributed to those that did; yet at the start of the year they thought they were better off with the insurance than without it, otherwise they presumably wouldn't have chosen to buy it. I shall not discuss other things that economists include under 'Pareto-optimal redistribution', such as redistribution required by altruism (feeling better if others are happy) or malice (feeling better if others are unhappy), since these do not have any relevance to justice. Some economists even include relief from individual or collective violence from the poor as a motive for 'Pareto-optimal redistribution', but this is only if we count handing over one's wallet to a mugger as a Pareto-optimal redistribution. I shall divide the case for redistribution deriving from considerations of reciprocity into three elements: first, insurance for categorical contingencies; second, insurance for non-categorical contingencies; and, third, redistribution through time.

First, then, by 'categorical contingencies' I mean specifiable misfortunes: being sick, going blind, being thrown out of work by a general recession or a sudden fall in the market for one's skills (for example, the redundancies of engineers and draughtsmen attendant upon the cut-back of the US aerospace industry). The state can accept risks (like that of compensation for long-term unemployment) that a private insurance company cannot. Suppose, for example, that a company were to offer a medical insurance policy to all in good health

---

[18] See Geoffrey Brennan, 'Pareto-Desirable Redistribution: the Non-Altruistic Dimension', *Public Choice* 14 (1973), pp. 43–67; and three essays in Harold H. Hochman and George E. Peterson (eds), *Redistribution through Public Choice* (New York, 1974): James D. Rodgers, 'Explaining Income Redistribution' (pp. 165–205); Richard Zeckhauser, 'Risk Spreading and Distribution' (pp. 206–28); and A. Mitchell Polinsky, 'Imperfect Capital Markets, Intertemporal Redistribution and Progressive Taxation' (pp. 229–58).

at age twenty-one, with a guarantee that it would never cancel it and that premiums would not reflect subsequent individual experience or health prospects. Rational risk-averse people would welcome such a policy; but, if they are free to opt out at any time, then those whose health is still good twenty or thirty years later would have an incentive to join a scheme that offered lower rates to those it accepted after a medical examination. The original scheme would thus be undermined, since only those in poor health would be left in it and would in effect form a pool of bad risks. This is a sort of prisoner's dilemma situation: at age twenty-one everyone would prefer the scheme with everyone staying in, but those who remain healthy have an incentive to defect. The solution is for the state to collect the premiums from everyone through ordinary taxes or a special social security levy.

Over and above this, it would be rational to insure against 'bad luck', and this is what I mean by the second head, insurance against non-categorical contingencies. Looking at his prospects at the age of twenty-one, say, a person with normal tastes would be willing to buy insurance, if it could be purchased, that would take some of his income if he is lucky enough to make a lot and give him some if he is unsuccessful. The state can achieve this by positive and negative taxation and, again, unless the state is going to enforce insurance agreements that do not allow for withdrawal on either side any time during the life of the insured person, only the state can bring about this kind of redistribution.

There are two obvious constraints on the amount of redistribution that would be generated by the state providing 'luck insurance' in the amount that would be purchased voluntarily. First, the redistribution package offered each person would have to be related to his expected income: redistribution from those with good prospects at age twenty-one to those with poor prospects at age twenty-one falls outside the present rationale.[19] And second, since the 'bad luck' to be insured against is simply imputed from an income that falls below the average for one with such prospects at age twenty-one, the problem of 'moral hazard'—the bane of all insurers—rears its ugly head. The perfect insurance (considered aside from moral hazard) makes the client indifferent between escaping the contingency insured against and suffering the contingency plus getting the compensation. But that means there is no incentive to avoid the contingency—lock doors, check wiring, avoid health risks, and so on. Where the probability of the contingency's occurring can be affected by choices, therefore,

[19] If we assume that the best the insurer could do in setting rates was to use educational level, achievement test scores, socio-economic background, race and so on as evidence, the risk to be insured against would be 'luck' as defined by Christopher Jencks in *Inequality: A Reassessment of the Effect of Family and Schooling in America* (London, 1973)—that variation in lifetime earnings not explained by such factors.

insurance must be less than perfect to avoid skyrocketing premiums or bankruptcy. If each person were offered a guaranteed income equal to the average for those with his prospects (that is, 100 per cent tax on income above and 100 per cent supplementation of income below), bad luck would be seriously contaminated by lack of exertion and the scheme would be in danger of going broke because of actual average incomes falling below those projected.

Finally, we should consider redistribution through time. If the normal human career is to have no earned income in the early years of one's life and again after retirement, then a lot of what looks like interpersonal redistribution, when viewed at a single point in time, may be thought of alternatively as intertemporal redistribution within each person's lifetime income. Economists have been particularly concerned with the state's role in distributing income backward. Babies and children cannot (legally) borrow to get themselves a good education, medical and dental care, a nutritious diet and so on; yet someone might see clearly, on reaching the age of majority, that it would have been worth paying money out in the future to have had those things earlier on. Even when the legal bar to borrowing falls at the age of majority, it is difficult to borrow much on future earnings. The problems set by making loans to be repaid out of future income over a long period are illustrated by the high rate of default in the USA on loans to college students. The state can overcome these problems by providing benefits, in the form of education, free milk, subsidized school meals, medical services, child allowances and so on, and then collecting the cost later in taxes.

Redistribution forward is easier to the extent that saving is easier than borrowing. But in an uncertain world, where in many countries no form of investment yields a positive (inflation-discounted) return, it is, I suggest, highly rational to want to have any private superannuation scheme or savings programme underpinned by a scheme of state pensions that is, when it comes down to it (whatever its insurance trimmings may be), a scheme for transferring from those who are earning to those who are retired. It may be noted that such a (non-actuarial) scheme corresponds to the extended practice of mutual aid in my example of the isolated community.

V Reciprocity and relations between countries

From the viewpoint of justice as reciprocity, we must say that even the meagre redistribution that takes place now, in the form of aid, soft loans and commodity contracts at above world prices, has to be counted as charity rather than justice. Justice as fidelity doesn't help: poor countries tend to break contracts (whether excusably or not need not be asked here) more often than rich countries. Justice as requital is a complicated matter. Obviously in the imperialist period raw materials were extracted and labour employed without adequate return, and there is now a case for reparations. The Banaban islanders, whose home was devastated by phosphate mining, are an example that has been in the news, but almost every colonial episode contained some element of coercive exploitation. It may be said that the descendants of the exploiters have no obligation to atone for the injustice of their ancestors; but surely they do if they are themselves richer as a result of that injustice and the descendants of the exploited are poorer.[20]

It is a good deal harder to show that current transactions fail to meet the standard of justice as requital. To my knowledge, the most elaborate and sustained attempt to argue that international trade between rich and poor countries is a process by which the rich exploit the poor is Arghiri Emmanuel's book *Unequal Exchange*.[21] According to Emmanuel, 'as far as the underdeveloped countries are concerned ... international aid has ceased to be regarded as a one-sided and gratuitous act on the part of the rich countries and is seen as an obligation that corresponds to a certain right of compensation.'

He goes on: 'Compensation for what? That is indeed the question, and this is what I have tried to answer' [p. 264]. As I understand it, the essence of his answer is that the large difference in wages paid in different countries for the same number of hours of qualitatively similar work (measured in terms of skill, physical exertion, and so on) shows that the system of international exchange is unequal. Thus, he says:

> While one may be able to find reasons, whether good or bad, to explain the difference between the wages of an American metal worker who controls a power press worth a million dollars and those of a worker on a Brazilian coffee plantation who uses only a simple machete, it is much harder to explain why a building worker who puts up a bungalow in the suburbs of New York has to be paid thirty times as much as his counterpart in the Lebanon, though both of them use the same tools and perform exactly the same movements as their Assyrian fellow worker of four thousand years ago. [pp. 263–4]

Surely it would be harder to explain how it would be possible to find building workers in New York at Lebanese (or Assyrian) rates of pay. Assuming the existence of some kind of labour market, work in rich countries will be better paid across the board than work in poor countries—hence the rule of thumb that the quickest way of judging

[20] For an analysis of some of the problems arising from the group reparations for misdeeds of earlier generations, see Boris I. Bittker, *The Case for Black Reparations* (New York, 1973).

[21] Arghiri Emmanuel, *Unequal Exchange: A Study of the Imperialism of Trade* (New York, 1972).

the standard of living of a country is to see what a haircut costs, because a haircut is a standardized service almost all of whose price is made up of labour costs. Even if two countries had no trading relations with each other (or with any other country) but one had a higher per capita income than another, we would expect identical work (for example, cutting hair) to be more highly paid in the richer country.

On Emmanuel's theory, the scale of unequal exchange in international trade today is enormous: it can be measured by asking what the terms of trade would be if wage rates were the same in all countries, and comparing that hypothetical state of affairs with the status quo.

> If we assume that wages account for fifty per cent of the cost of [third world] exports, and that the relevant rate of wages is one-twentieth of that prevailing in the advanced countries, a simple calculation will show us that the difference between the present value and the equivalence value is ... a difference ... in hundreds of thousands, of millions. If fifty sacks of coffee are at present exchanged for one automobile, whereas, in order to pay coffee plantation workers at the same rate as workers in the automobile industry, fifty sacks would have to be exchanged for ten automobiles, the loss suffered by the coffee producers and the gain made by the other party in this transaction are not *less than* the value of fifty sacks, but *nine times as much.*[22]

Now I think it is a perfectly intelligible view of the requirements of international justice that being born into one country rather than another should not determine one's fate to the extent that it does now, so that a person born into a poor society is condemned to almost certain disease, malnutrition and poverty while another, who has the good fortune to be born into a rich society, has an excellent chance of living a healthy and comfortable life. Later in the chapter (see below, section VI), I shall examine the conception of justice—justice as equal opportunity—from which such a view might be derived. But it seems to me simply perverse to try to derive any such notion from justice as requital, that is from the criterion of fair exchange.

To say, for example, that the poor countries actually lose from trading with the rich ones immediately raises the question why they should choose to trade at all in that case. Unless trade benefits both parties (compared with the absence of trade), the general presumption is that it does not take place. Doubtless, Brazilians would prefer obtaining ten automobiles in exchange for fifty sacks of coffee to obtaining one automobile; but, if we are asking whether or not Brazilians actually *lose* from exchange, the relevant question is whether or not they would be better off keeping the coffee themselves. Emmanuel

---

[22] Emmanuel, p. 368 (italics in original). Notice that this passage, which occurs in a reply to Charles Bettelheim, shows a shift in ground from the earlier one quoted, in that the standard is now taken to be one in which the pay of the machete-wielding coffee worker and the power press operative in the car plant is equalized.

nowhere suggests that they would be, and I see no reason to believe they would.

We must, of course, be careful not to abstract from the possibility of conflicts of interest within the poorer countries. 'Brazilians' do not, for example, collectively decide how much coffee to exchange for so many automobiles. One strand in the critique of the contemporary international economic order is that in many countries there is an alliance between foreign corporations and a small stratum of indigenous beneficiaries (importers, franchise-holders and so on) at the expense of the rest of the population. A poor country may therefore engage in uncoerced exchanges that are actually worse for the bulk of the population than no exchange at all. However, the fact that there are some countries that appear plausible candidates should not lead us to overlook the great range of ways in which poor countries handle their trading relations.[23] And we should not imagine that the elimination of trade that makes the trading country worse off as a whole than it would be without it could ever make very much difference to the contrast between rich and poor countries that now exists.

Justice as requital in exchanges is not, indeed, to be identified with a condition in which all that can be said is that both parties gain something from trade. As I suggested earlier (in section III), the criterion is that both sides gain equally from an exchange. Some economists would say that this is a hopelessly metaphysical notion but at any rate in simple cases its application seems fairly straightforward. Suppose someone is selling a house and there is one interested buyer. The seller would rather keep the house than accept less than £15,000, while the buyer would rather keep his money than pay more than £20,000 for the house. If the price is close to £15,000, the buyer realizes almost all the gain from the exchange, and if the price is close to £20,000, the seller realizes almost all the gain. Surely the gain is shared equally if the price is roughly half way between the two. Where variable amounts may be traded between the parties, the analysis is more complicated than where the only question is what price something like a house sells at. But the idea of an equal gain from the whole transaction (with the amount traded being whatever the parties agree on at the price set) still seems to me to make sense, at least in that gross departures may be detected.

We may now introduce another strand in the critique of contemporary international economics, which is popular in UNCTAD. This is that there is an asymmetry between the way in which goods typically exported by rich countries are priced and the way in which those typically exported by poor countries are priced. A car manufacturer sets his price and sells however many cars he can sell at that

[23] See Michael Moran, 'Review Article: The Politics of International Business', *British Journal of Political Science* 8 (1978), pp. 217–36.

price, whereas the raw materials and agricultural products that form the bulk of exports of most poor countries are much more likely to be sold on a competitive world market in which sellers will unload their goods at any price that leaves them better off selling than not selling. There is thus, it is argued, a built-in advantage for the industrial nations in international trade, because they can control production so as to obtain the profit margins they aim for.

As it stands, this claim is clearly overstated, since it is apparent that there is a good deal of competition in world markets between, say, the car manufacturers of different countries. A firm which arbitrarily decrees a certain profit margin and refuses to sell at any price that does not yield that margin is liable to find itself out of business. Suppose, however, that it were accepted that the industrial nations do gain differentially from the present set-up. How different would the distribution of income over the world look if the poor countries were to succeed in controlling the prices of their exports through some system of collective action? The answer is, as far as I can tell, that it would not look greatly different from the way it is now.

This may appear perverse when one considers the dramatic improvement in the economic circumstance of the oil-producing states that has been brought about by OPEC. But oil has two remarkable characteristics. First, the cost of extracting the oil from the largest deposits (in Saudi Arabia and the Persian Gulf) is a matter of a few cents per barrel: in Kuwait it doesn't even need to be pumped out, and all that has to be done is fill the tankers.[24] Second, for some uses there is no feasible substitute for oil, and these include the important ones of fuelling the internal combustion engine and providing raw materials for the petrochemical industry; and for the rest (especially heating and electricity generation) the substitutes available in most places are much more expensive, like coal or atomic power. Oil thus generates a lot of economic rent, and the appropriation of a much larger share of this economic rent by the countries with the oil naturally makes a noticeable difference.

At the opposite end of the spectrum from oil are commodities such as sisal and jute, whose maximum price is set by the point at which it is cheaper for users to switch to other fibres (including synthetics). Even ironclad controls over price could do little in these cases to redistribute income toward the producers. Justice as requital is satisfied even at a low price because, although the seller is not gaining much (compared with the next best use of the land or doing nothing at all with it) the buyer is also not gaining much (compared with the next most expensive alternative purchase). Equal exchange, it must be emphasized, has no inherent tendency to equalize the overall position

[24] Anthony Sampson, *The Seven Sisters* (New York, 1975), p. 94.

of the parties. It is concerned purely with the distribution of the gains from the transaction between them.

Obviously, the crucial question is whether most of the commodities exported by third world countries are more like oil or more like sisal and jute, and the answer is apparently that, although they form a spectrum, they lie mostly toward the sisal and jute end. It may be possible, for many products, to raise the price without too serious a drop in sales in the short run, but in the long run it will pay users to adapt to the higher prices by substituting other materials, using less, recycling and so on. It may be recalled, incidentally, that Emmanuel, in calculating the 'loss' from exchange to the poorer countries, took the amount they would get if they were able to sell the *present* amount of exports at a price *ten times higher*. But this figure has no significance because the sales at ten times the price would be far smaller. Perhaps in the long run tea will go the same way as handmade lace—too labour-intensive to be affordable. Perhaps it should. But it does not seem to me very sensible to say that tea is 'really' worth ten times what it costs now, and that tea pickers are being exploited by tea drinkers, if the effect of increasing the price of tea ten times would be simply to throw the tea pickers out of work.

Even leaving aside the tendency over a period of a few years for users to find substitutes, the introduction of an international cartel in commodities other than oil (the 'Integrated Programme') has only limited prospects. David McNicol has calculated, using short-run elasticities of demand, that a doubling of the prices of fourteen commodities would increase the incomes of the LDCs ('less developed countries') by $20.5 billion per year.[25] This is an amount less than twice the present sum of international economic assistance and is to be compared with the $80 billion by which the OPEC countries increased their oil revenues in *each* of 1974, 1975 and 1976 [McNicol, p. 133].

Even more serious than the relatively limited overall impact of these increases is their distribution among countries.

> The principal *gainers* would be the major producers of cocoa, coffee, cotton, copper and sugar.... The *losers* would be nations who export relatively low-value commodities and who import substantial quantities of other commodities—especially cotton, copper, sugar and wool.... India, the nations just below the Sahara, and many of the nations in northern Africa and southeast Asia export relatively low-value crops; and there is some indication that they tend to be importers of agricultural products. These nations, which are a majority of the poorest of the

[25] David L. McNicol, *Commodity Agreements and the New Economic Order*, California Institute of Technology Social Science Working Paper (1976). The fourteen commodities are cocoa, coffee, tea, wool, cotton, sugar, bananas, jute, sisal, beef, copper, tin and iron. Wheat and rice are imported heavily by LDCs and McNicol assumes that they would be excluded from price-raising efforts.

LDCs, would probably be net losers under a system of restrictive commodity agreements. [McNicol, pp. 132–3.]

Thus, the final result would actually be a widening of the existing gap between rich and poor countries.

I have been assuming that the Integrated Programme would operate on the basis of price-fixing and production quotas, with the redistribution from rich countries to poor countries proceeding from the higher revenues generated by the increased prices. It would, of course, be possible in principle (though hardly politically realistic in the forseeable future) for the rich countries to go further and offer to pay for more of the controlled commodities than could be cleared on the market. In the short run, the surplus could be stored but eventually only two solutions would be open. One is to subsidize sales so as to increase demand either on a regular basis (British agricultural policy until the 1970s) or in order to dump a particular 'mountain' that has accumulated (as the EEC has done). The other is to restrict supply by paying for non-production on the lines of the US 'acreage retirement' schemes. Subsidization would reduce the objectionable distributive effects of the straight production-quota scheme, whereas paying for non-production would do nothing about them. But both would be enormously expensive, and would constitute an irrational, inefficient and inequitable way of transferring income from rich countries to poor ones. The lessons of British and American policies toward farming would be equally applicable to global analogues: 'In the United States, as in Britain, farm subsidies have been both economically inefficient and socially indefensible, distributing benefits preponderantly to the wealthiest minority of farmers.'[26]

We still have to ask whether any case for international redistribution from rich countries to poor ones could be established under the third heading of justice as reciprocity—justice as mutual aid. The answer is, I think, negative. And it is negative precisely because the minimal similarity of circumstances required to underwrite obligations of mutual aid is lacking here. Justice as reciprocity, we must again emphasize, has no comfort to offer to those who are chronically bad risks. Just as banks prefer to lend to the rich rather than the poor, mutual aid extends only to those who are sufficiently well off to have a reasonable prospect of being able to reciprocate any aid they may receive when the occasion to do so arises.

> Such endeavours as the organized efforts in international development aid, or the objectives of the European Development Fund, and the proposed Southeast Asian Development Fund cannot be adequately understood in terms of reciprocity.... [The law governing diplomatic

[26] Graham K. Wilson, *Special Interests and Policymasking: Agricultural Policies and Politics in Britain and the United States of America, 1956–70* (London, 1977), p. 73.

immunity] is strictly conditioned upon reciprocal interest and reciprocal enforcement. . . . In any meaningful sense, however, there is no reciprocity between the interest of the United States or Britain or France in assisting, bilaterally and through multilateral institutions, the development of Tanzania or India or Colombia and the interest of these countries in receiving such assistance.[27]

To illustrate the point, even if the USA were hit in one year by a major earthquake, a serious drought and several disastrous cyclones, it could still pull through economically by borrowing or realizing foreign assets. The probability, in the lifetime of anyone now alive, that the USA will be asking Bangladesh for aid is so low as to mean that aid from the USA simply cannot be construed as mutual aid.

VI Reciprocity and relations between generations

On the face of it, there is no room for justice as reciprocity to operate between people who are not alive at the same time. ' "We are always doing", says he, "something for Posterity, but I would fain see Posterity do something for us." '[28] I think that is in fact roughly right. Since posterity cannot do anything for us, there can be no obligation arising from justice as reciprocity to do anything for posterity. However, there are two possible escape routes, and they are worth some examination.

The first line of escape has a powerful intuitive appeal to many people, for I have found that whenever I press the conclusion that justice as reciprocity does not have application to future generations somebody proposes it. I have not found it worked out in print, though Edmund Burke's *Reflections on the Revolution in France* contains some ideas in the general area. There is his famous vision of society as 'a partnership between those who are living, those who are dead, and those who are to be born'.[29] And there is the panegyric on the 'idea of inheritance': 'People will not look forward to their posterity, who never look backward to their ancestors. . . . The institutions of policy, the goods of fortune, the gifts of providence, are handed down to us, and from us, in the same course and order' [Burke, p. 53].

The line of argument is, I take it, as follows: since we have received benefits from our predecessors, some notion of equity requires us to provide benefits for our successors. The notion of equity involved

---

[27] Wolfgang Friedmann, 'The Relevance of International Law to the Processes of Economic and Social Development', in Richard A. Falk and Cyril E. Black (eds), *The Future of the International Legal Order* II: Wealth and Resources (Princeton, N.J., 1970), pp. 3–35, at pp. 12 and 13.

[28] Joseph Addison, *The Spectator*, no. 583.

[29] Edmund Burke, *Reflections on the Revolution in France* (Chicago, 1955 edn), p. 140.

is, it would appear, somehow related to reciprocity. In my discussion of justice as mutual aid (above, section IV), I considered a case in which the young provide transport for the old in the expectation that when they themselves are old the young will do the same for them. I emphasized there the advantage to all (taking a long time-span) of maintaining the practice, but clearly we can add that even if the young could somehow get away with neglecting the old now and yet still reintroducing the practice in time to benefit when they are old themselves, it would be unfair—a violation of justice as reciprocity—to do so. The extended reciprocity here runs in the opposite direction: having received benefits, we have an obligation of justice to pass on comparable benefits. The analogy lies in the fact that in both instances there is an ongoing practice from which we stand to benefit and which therefore creates a duty of 'fair play' to do our part in it.

I do not think that it is possible to sustain a completely general principle to the effect that the receipt of a benefit creates a *prima facie* obligation to pass on a similar benefit to others. R. M. Hare has recently put forward such a principle in a context somewhat analogous to the present one in that it involves the question of bringing people into existence as against providing for them. Hare argues that, if we are glad we were born, this entails that we ought (in the absence of countervailing reasons) to maximize the number of people born. And he derives this from what he calls a 'logical extension' of the Golden Rule, which he takes to mean that 'we should do to others as we wish them to do to us.' The extension is 'to say that we should do to others what *we are glad was* done to us'.[30]

There are two arguments against this extended Golden Rule. First, the result it reaches for issues of population is ridiculous. This, however, may be circumvented if it can be shown that the extended Golden Rule does not have these implications.[31] The more serious argument is simply that the extended Golden Rule is silly in quite straightforward cases not involving the difficulties imported by worrying about the claims of potential people. If someone offers me a toffee apple, out of the blue, and I accept it, does my enjoyment of the toffee apple create even the tiniest, most *prima facie*, obligation to distribute toffee apples to others? I do not see that it does. If it would spread happiness to give away toffee apples, *that* is no doubt a reason for doing so (though hardly one amounting to an obligation). But the reason thus generated does not seem to be in

[30] R. M. Hare 'Abortion and the Golden Rule', *Philosophy and Public Affairs* 4 (1975), pp. 201–22. The quotation is on p. 208, italics in original.

[31] For an argument, which seems to me plausible, to that effect, see George Sher, 'Hare, Abortion, and the Golden Rule', *Philosophy and Public Affairs* 6 (1977), pp. 185–90.

any way affected by whether or not I happen to have myself been the lucky recipient of a toffee apple. As a matter of moral psychology, it may be that receiving a toffee apple is what it takes to get my sluggish benevolent tendencies going, in bringing to my attention how much others might enjoy one. But that is, I suggest, another matter.

In my view, the so-called extended Golden Rule is plausible only in the context of a practice, when it becomes synonymous with justice as reciprocity (see above, section III). If there is a practice of handing round toffee apples and I have taken and enjoyed those given out by others it is unfair not to hand round some myself, just as someone who ducks out when it gets to his turn to buy a round of drinks is behaving unfairly.

If we could establish the existence of a practice of looking after the interests of later generations, there would seem to be some sort of case, based on justice as reciprocity, for saying we should play our part in the practice and take account of the interests of our successors. The obligation would not fit very well into the threefold classification I developed earlier, but I suppose it would best be regarded as a sort of extension of justice as requital.

The question then is, does such a practice exist, of which we are the beneficiaries? I am not sure exactly what kind of evidence is relevant to this question, but I would take it that the kind of thing we should look for is (a) evidence that our ancestors had a norm to the effect that the interests of future generations should be given serious weight in decision-making and (b) evidence that such a norm, if it was generally professed, was acted on. I cannot hope here to enter in any systematic way into such an enquiry. But it does not appear to me that the interests of later generations have ever played a very important role in public deliberations, still less in actual decisions. Let us take up the central issue—the degrading of the environment and the exhaustion of non-replaceable natural resources. My impression is that the only reason why our ancestors did not do more damage is that they lacked the technology to do so. I can see little evidence that they held back from anything that was technologically feasible and immediately profitable from any consideration about the costs they were imposing on their descendants. I do not therefore think that we would be under much of an obligation to our own descendants if we were constrained by nothing more stringent than the ecological morality of our ancestors. I am inclined, therefore, to suggest that the only implication of justice as reciprocity in this extended form is to give us an extra reason for adopting a more responsible attitude towards our successors. If we have some reason to do so anyway (which still, of course, remains to be shown), there is a bonus from justice as reciprocity in that we may be in on the foundation of a practice that will make it more likely that our successors will do likewise.

I now come to the second argument against the conclusion that we have no obligation to our successors derived from justice as reciprocity. This also appeals to the duty of fair play, but this time it is fair play among contemporaries rather than fair play over the generations. The argument is that, although we do not have obligations *to* future generations, we may have obligations *with respect to* future generations. The idea here is that, to the extent that the welfare of future generations is something nearly all of us as a matter of fact care about, it can be treated as a public good, and justice as requital (it will be recalled) requires us to play a fair part in contributing to a public good from which we benefit. That the 'benefit' is, as it were, a sentimental one directed at the future, rather than a personal one here and now, does not affect the logic.[32]

The obvious limitation to this argument is that the obligation with respect to future generations is entirely parasitic upon our actual sentiments about them. If we care about their welfare (or more specifically if enough of us care about their welfare to make it qualify as a public good), we can generate a derivative obligation among ourselves. But there is nothing in the argument that says we should care for their welfare. Since in practice it does not appear that many people have a time-horizon for public policy extending much beyond thirty years, this does not get us very far.

Discussions by experts of threatened crises in raw materials, energy, pollution, food shortages and so on generally appear to be founded on the belief that they have shown fears to be alarmist if they can produce evidence that we can probably get through the next thirty years without catastrophe. The notion that we should be thinking how to arrange things so that the human race has even a fighting chance of getting through the next ten thousand or hundred thousand years would, I am sure, be regarded by these experts as bizarre. The question of justice between generations is precisely the question whether we *should* care about the welfare of our successors, and what sacrifices we ought to be prepared to make now in their interests. I am not impressed by the bland assurance that all we have to do is feed in our own prejudices and they will come out as obligations of justice.[33]

---

[32] See D. Clayton Hubin, 'Justice and Future Generations', *Philosophy and Public Affairs* 6 (1976), pp. 70–83 and Thomas Schwartz, 'Obligations to Posterity', in R. I. Sikora and Brian Barry (eds), *Obligations to Future Generations* (Philadelphia, 1978).

[33] For a more extended discussion of this point see my paper 'The Circumstances of Justice and Future Generations', in Sikora and Barry.

VII Another principle of justice

My primary aim in this chapter has been to analyse the principle of justice as reciprocity and to show how limited it is in its application to problems of justice between nations and justice between generations. I have also tried to show that the attempt to derive more acceptable conclusions from justice as reciprocity than those that appear at first sight to follow (and I share the views of those who find those conclusions unacceptable) are pursuing an unprofitable enterprise. Their efforts are a tribute to the power and appeal of the paradigm of justice as reciprocity. But I am convinced that the way forward is not to devote further efforts to trying to square the circle, that is to say, trying to get non-outrageous conclusions from justice as reciprocity. The solution is rather, I suggest, to see if there is not some principle of justice complementary to justice as reciprocity that comes into its own when we move outside the special case of justice among contemporaries who are members of the same society.

I emphasize that it must be complementary because I believe that justice as reciprocity is here to stay. It is, as I suggested earlier (section I), a cultural universal and anyway it makes a lot of sense. Any theory of justice that tried to eliminate justice as reciprocity would be doomed from the start. We must therefore seek to show how justice as reciprocity needs to be supplemented, not displaced.

This can, I think, be easily done. The glaring limitation of justice as reciprocity is that it can say nothing about the initial control over natural resources. Once ownership rights are assigned, justice as reciprocity can tell us about fair trading. But it is silent on the crucial first stage. Theorists who wish to place fair exchange at the centre of their conceptions of justice, from John Locke to James Buchanan and Robert Nozick, have always recognized that some other kind of theory has to be brought in to get things started or that one must simply be agnostic about the initial distribution of resources.

We could, of course, take the heroic path of saying that justice as reciprocity is the only sort of justice and that however we may characterize the initial distribution of resources, 'just' and 'unjust' are not appropriate words. But that seems rather preposterous, since we surely want to have some distributive concept to evaluate distributions. If we can't have 'just' (or 'fair') we will have to invent some other; but we will surely want some distributive criterion.

Consider a 'state of nature' story. A number of people occupy a certain territory and live by hunting. It has been found by experience that bands of six are the most efficient for hunting, and on the principle of requital it is just for members of each band to be rewarded in accordance with their contribution to its success. Justice as mutual aid requires that a band experiencing a run of bad luck in hunting should be saved from starvation by others. But this does not entail systematic transfer from a more skilful band to a less skilful one.

So far so good. But now consider a development in this story. Suppose that, in one half of the territory, the terrain is more favourable, game is more easy to catch. Specifically, for any band (whatever its level of skill) exactly half as much effort is required in the more favoured half to catch the same amount of game. Now suppose that one half of the people in the area declare that access to the more favoured half of the territory is henceforth to be controlled by them. And suppose also that somehow they succeed in enforcing this against the others. (Call them the 'dominant group' and the others the 'subordinate group'.) The dominant group now has a choice. The members can hunt for themselves, catching an adequate supply of game with half the effort that the subordinate group has to exert to make the same catch. Or they can permit the members of the subordinate group to hunt in the favoured territory, on condition that they hand over a share of whatever they catch.

According to a common view, it makes a big difference to the analysis of the situation which of these paths is taken. If they offer a deal to the subordinate group and it is accepted, the members of the dominant group are living off the labour of the others; whereas if they simply exclude the others and hunt for themselves they are not. But this seems to me a misguided way of looking at the position. The advantage lies in controlling access to the favoured part of the territory, and the question of what use that advantage is put to is secondary. *Given* that the advantage is going to be maintained, the subordinate group would rationally prefer to have the option of hunting in the more favoured territory in return for giving up a share of the catch. So it would seem strange if the dominant group were to be judged more negatively for providing the option to the subordinate group than otherwise.

What has justice as reciprocity to say about all this? If the dominant group excludes the subordinate group, it has nothing to say. If the dominant group permits the subordinate group to hunt in return for a share of the proceeds, justice as requital says that there should be a fair exchange. But, since an hour spent hunting in the more favoured terrain is twice as productive as an hour spent outside it, it is obviously a fair exchange that the privilege should cost a share of the catch. On the question whether it is just for the dominant group to control access, justice as reciprocity is silent. If we want to make a judgement about the justice of that, it looks as if we must go to some sense of justice not derivable from justice as reciprocity. Tentatively, let me suggest that the principle is one of justice as equal access to natural resources.

To reinforce but at the same time refine this idea, let us turn to a society that is, by almost universal agreement, exceeding unjust—South Africa. I believe that, although some countries may be more violent and others more repressive, South Africa is *the* most unjust society in the world, but nothing I have to say turns on the acceptance of that view, which would require for its support much more about the distinction between injustice and other evils.

Let us now ask what it is that makes South Africa *economically* unjust. I suggest that there are at least these three features:

1. Non-whites are not allowed to unionize, and are paid less than the value they contribute to the economy.
2. Non-whites are provided with poor opportunities for acquiring education, and are prevented by the job reservation system from filling the better paid jobs, even if they are qualified.
3. Under apartheid, non-whites are prohibited from owning land in any of the more productive areas of the country. The so-called 'tribal homelands' are carefully chosen to be barren and devoid of mineral resources.[34]

The first of these points falls squarely within the scope of justice as reciprocity: non-whites are not allowed a fair bargaining position and are not receiving fair exchange for the value of their work. But the other two points cannot be related to justice as reciprocity. Suppose that non-whites *were* paid the full value of their product: the other two points would still be valid. Justice demands not only that people should be paid the value they contribute but that they should have a fair opportunity to increase the value they contribute. Justice as reciprocity has nothing to say about this.

It might perhaps be suggested that justice as requital can be employed to argue that non-whites are not getting their fair share of school expenditures, in that per capita educational costs of white children are many times those of non-white children. But it must be recalled that justice as requital demands only that benefits received should be matched to taxes paid. Apologists of the South African regime can say quite truthfully that since whites pay most of the taxes it is just, in this sense, that whites receive most of the benefits. This illustrates the way in which, given a fundamental pattern of injustice, justice as reciprocity operates merely so as to maintain it in equilibrium.

I think that this discussion of South Africa, sketchy as it is, can form the basis for a second shot at the principle we are looking for. It is, I suggest, none other than equality of opportunity, understood

[34] See Pierre van den Berghe, *South Africa: A Study in Conflict* (Berkeley and Los Angeles, 1967) pp. 196–8.

in a very broad sense that goes way beyond equal chances to get ahead in a meritocratic rat-race. The minimal claim of equal opportunity is an equal claim on the earth's natural resources. The maximum claim is that the same abilities and efforts should reap the same rewards. This, it may be noticed, is the driving force behind Emmanuel's criticism of the present international economic order. His error was, I believe, not in saying that there is something unjust about one person getting a huge multiple of the other's pay for performing the identical task, but rather in attempting to fit this idea in the framework of justice as reciprocity.

VIII Some implications of the principle

I realize that there are many difficulties in clarifying the conception of equal opportunity and also in thinking through its implications. In this closing section, I shall therefore tackle a more modest (but still formidable) task. I shall take up the narrow conception and ask what implications it has for international and intergenerational justice. This discussion is offered as a sketch of what might be said; I hope elsewhere to expand and refine it.

The main implication is that the claim of each country to control access to the natural resources of its territory cannot be accepted as absolute, nor can the claim of any given generation to use the earth's resources as it sees fit. It is wrong (to quote Burke again) for 'the temporary possessors and life-renters in [the commonwealth ... to] act as if they were the entire masters ... [to] cut off the entail, or commit waste on the inheritance' [Burke, p. 137]. The planet is the common heritage of all men at all times and any appropriation of its resources must be subject to appraisal from the point of view of justice.

It has to be said that recent moves in international forums do not suggest an easy road for the principle that the world's resources are a common possession of all men. The United Nations General Assembly has declared the 'permanent sovereignty over natural resources' of the country in which the natural resources occur.[35] The International Law of the Sea convention is apparently going to move away from the ocean as a 'common' by extending national territorial claims over the seabed and marine life rather than by internationalizing the sea's resources. And the emphasis that the third world countries are putting (through UNCTAD) on the raising of commodity prices as the favoured means of international redistribution is also inauspicious. As we have seen (section v), it has the same effect as the other two moves: it is good for those

[35] Charles R. Bertz, 'Justice and International Relations', *Philosophy and Public Affairs* 4 (1975), pp. 360–89 at p. 371, n. 9.

countries with resources but is if anything on balance disadvantageous for countries whose problem is that they are resource-poor. However, if it is assumed (not implausibly) that the only realistic alternative at present to national sovereignty is letting the rich countries have a free hand in using up the world's natural resources and that the citizens of rich countries will accept higher prices but not higher taxes, these moves can be understood as defining a politically feasible second best.[36]

It is important to see that, if it is a matter of justice to give countries more equal access to the world's resources, the duty to make transfers to a resource-poor country does not depend on the use made of the additional income by that country.[37] This is how justice differs from charity. If a man approaches me and asks for money to feed his wife and children, I can quite properly ask myself if there is reason to believe that he will spend anything I give him on buying alcohol. But an employer may not legitimately refuse to pay his employee what he owes him on the ground that he disapproves of the way it is going to get spent. This is not to say that there should not be some requirement that the employee support his wife and children; but there are two separate issues which should be kept distinct.

The application of this example in international affairs is as follows:

1.   Where aid is given as charity to relieve suffering, it is legitimate for the donor country to insist that the aid be disbursed to the needy within the recipient country.

2.   In as far as redistribution is required by the demands of justice, the criterion of justice is that countries, as collectivities, should have their fair share of the world's resources.

3.   Failure of a country to have a just internal distribution does not relieve donor countries of the obligations of international justice.

4.   International pressure, economic sanctions or even military intervention may sometimes be legitimate as a way of improving the internal justice of a society.

5.   The right of other countries to apply such pressure is not increased if the country in question is a beneficiary of international transfers based on justice. Nor is the right decreased if the country

---

[36] For a useful introduction to these questions see Oscar Schachter, *Sharing the World's Resources* (New York, 1977).

[37] Conservatives (or, if they are a distinguishable category, those who are reluctant to give up what they have got) naturally fasten on the argument that the obligation to redistribute is voided by the nature of the regime. See, for a string of similar arguments against redistribution, Robert W. Tucker, *The Inequality of Nations* (New York, 1977).

in question is a net contributor. (Of course, it is politically *easier* to bring pressure on poor countries, but that is a separate question.)

One final point. We might agree that the employer could, without committing injustice, withhold the pay he owes the employee if he knows that the employee is going to use it to buy an armoury and terrorize the neighbourhood or to destroy his family. But in an extreme case like that the employer (or anybody else) would also be justified in taking away money the employee already has. The international analogy is that a transfer to a country whose government plans to buy weapons for external aggression or internal repression may legitimately be cancelled; but in any situation where that would be legitimate it would also be legitimate to withhold any other payments that were due. (The UK government's freezing of all financial obligation to Rhodesia after the latter's Unilateral Declaration of Independence would be a case in point.)

What about intergenerational relations? I believe that the notion of fair access to resources can be deployed to deal with them. In my 'state of nature' example, it would surely be unfair (in a sense which has nothing to do with reciprocity) for one generation of hunters to hunt the game to extinction and leave their successors to starve. Access to the earth's resources can be unfairly distributed over time as well as over space.

What justice requires, I suggest, is that the range of opportunities open to successor generations should not be narrowed. If some openings are closed off by depletion or other irreversible damage to the environment, others should be created (if necessary at the cost of some sacrifice) to make up.

This conception of intergenerational justice has several attractive features. First, it is a global extension of a principle that families with possessions to pass on have traditionally espoused: 'Keep the capital intact!' Second, it underwrites the asymmetry that many people (including myself) feel between making successors better off, which is a nice thing to do but not required by justice, and not making them worse off, which *is* required by justice. And third, it does not make the demands of justice to our successors depend on our knowing their tastes—still less on our approving of them.[38]

[38] M. P. Golding, 'Obligations to Future Generations', *Monist* 56 (1972), pp. 85–99.

4

The sense of justice in the Common Law

Alice Erh-Soon Tay

I

Common lawyers, together with the country in which the Common Law was born and developed, have a certain reputation for matter-of-factness and practicality. They are, we are often told, the enemies of general speculation, of the bold proclamation of universal principles and, above all, of metaphysics. It is possible that Common lawyers do justice. If so, they believe that they do it best by talking about it rather little, and hardly ever in the abstract, by recognizing, as a fundament-tal truth, that justice is done concretely in balancing conflicting human interests, moral claims and even 'principles' of justice. For two centuries, since the decline of natural law thinking after Blackstone, the respected histories of English law and compendia of English law and legislation have contained little, if any, reference to the concept of justice in the abstract. English books on jurisprudence long either devoted virtually no attention to the topic or drew their views from a consideration of philosophers and others not learned in the Common Law. It was not, and probably still is not, the belief of Common lawyers that sound reasoning or moral sensitivity is best obtained by deduction from first or even broad principles. Civil and natural lawyers, many of whom have not been noted for their sympathy toward these attitudes, are liable to dismiss them as 'positivism' and to believe that they imply a vicious moral scepticism, a readiness to allow justice to be driven out by law. It is true that John Austin, in his lectures on jurisprudence in London more than one hundred and fifty years ago, was especially concerned to rid law and the philosophy of law of empty and portentous metaphysics and to separate law from morals. If justice was to have any precise and definite meaning for the lawyer, he argued, it meant conformity with the law, with the actual, existing law—the positive law. To call a law unjust, it followed, was to talk nonsense, to make noise instead of saying something or, in modern un-Benthamite parlance, to appeal to emotion and not to reason.

There are no doubt many who would like to believe that John Austin expresses correctly the spirit, traditions and procedures of the Common Law. They are wrong. The outstanding feature of the Common Law, and a principal distinction between it and so much of the civil law of the continent of Europe, is its flexibility, the deliberate open-endedness of its concepts, the extent to which it cannot be reduced to black-letter (so-called 'positive') law or divorced from the moral sentiments of the community in which it operates. Its language, its specific principles, its statutes and its authoritative decisions are infused with terms like 'fair', 'reasonable', 'proper', 'sound', 'commonsensical' and 'just'; judges are enjoined by the provisions of their oath and the law to 'do right', to 'deal justly'. They have agreed with Lord Denning that it is not a tautology to expect them to 'do right according to law' and though they no longer appeal to the timeless or God-given principles of natural law, they achieve much the same effect by reference to 'convenience', 'public policy', and their duty to do right. They have long held themselves to have a general duty and power to act as custodians of morals and guardians against wrong, to the extent, when there is no other way, of filling lacunae in the law or creating new law. It is true that there has been a great, and in my view, sound, suspicion in English law and among English lawyers of presumptuous readiness to innovate and of that vague jurisprudence which is sometimes attractively styled 'justice as between man and man', of palm-tree justice unfettered by rules, precedent or doctrine. The maxim, 'hard cases make bad law', expresses this concern with systematic justice and the belief that it is easily disrupted and ultimately made unjust, capricious, arbitrary, by a fireside equity that concentrates only on the single situation or the one urgent or obvious interest.

The term Common Law, which is derived, oddly, from the canon law concept *jus commune*, invites stress on the continuity between Common Law and custom, the legal traditions and ways of settling disputes of a community which existed before the Norman Conquest. William the Conqueror in fact undertook to respect such customs and laws. But the evolution of the Common Law as a system rested centrally on the specific justice that came to be offered by the king in competition with local and seigneurial justice. Unlike the latter, it was offered to all manner and estates of men, equally and impartially. It emphasized rationality and argument against trial by battle and ordeal. It combined the local juror with the external judge and gradually defined the functions of each. Thus justice for the English lawyer, by the beginning of the thirteenth century in the time of Bracton, came to be and has since been paradigmatically what is done in the royal courts. It is done there, self-consciously, in a certain manner, within a developing tradition and it is done in precisely that way, except by imitation or delegation, in no other courts or assemblies. For Royal justice is done as a public thing, by the crown through its judicial representatives as standing above and outside the private sectional interest, acting according to law and in a judicial manner. Such justice, as F. E. Dowrick has it in his very interesting study, *Justice According to the English Common Lawyers*, the English lawyer would maintain to be done adequately only 'when the trial of disputes or disorders is conducted within certain canons of fairness, and when the judge decides the case according to moral principles or takes into account the human interests at stake, or applies established laws'.[1] Dowrick has chosen his words carefully and well and they bring out the extent to which the Common lawyers' conception of justice goes well beyond the application of black-letter law or, as it is sometimes believed, of purely procedural principles.

Behind the beliefs of the Common lawyer there stands a more general set of conceptions, which he has in common with all those who belong to the Western legal tradition. These conceptions, and the tradition itself, are rooted in the remarkable impact on Western civilization generally of the ideas of law and legal technique introduced and developed by the Romans. They amount to the fundamental belief that law *counts*, that it is not only an outstanding feature of social organization, but that its rules, procedures and techniques are capable of dealing, justly and under the framework of general precepts and conceptions, with all important human activities. The Romans, indeed, whatever their other habits, were a 'law-inspired' people; they had created such a system of law, capable of counting in their own time and of again inspiring subsequent civilizations. The three great, original characteristics of Roman law as a living system up to the time of Justinian, as Professor Geoffrey Sawer has put it,[2] were first, a complexity which enabled it to cover the main social relationships of human life; secondly, a degree of abstraction enabling many of its principles to apply to a wide range of social relationships and over long periods of time without major change; thirdly, an autonomy of structure and development which gave law an independent role in the development of society as a whole. The subsequent history of Roman and Roman-inspired law, from the sixth century AD to the present, and of its relation to and interaction with Christianity, canon law, Germanic and other legal customs and

---

[1] F. E. Dowrick, *Justice According to the English Common Lawyers* (London, 1961), p. 29.

[2] G. Sawer, 'The Western Conception of Law', in Konrad Zweigert (ed.), *International Encyclopedia of Comparative Law* II (Tübingen, 1975), pp. 14–48 at p. 18. See also 'Editors' Introduction: Law, Lawyers and Law-Making in Australia', in A. E. S. Tay and Eugene Kamenka (eds), *Law-Making in Australia* (London and Melbourne, 1979), pp. 20–38 at p. 30.

procedures, is a complex story. But the ideal of a society based on law became stronger and stronger within that history, uniting the English Common lawyer and the continental civil lawyer and reaching its apogee in the great legal debates and reforms of the nineteenth century.

In the early history of England, these convictions were reinforced by the belief, found in other societies at particular stages of their history, that the king's justice was the foundation and *sine qua non* of the king's peace, that it replaced fighting by arbitration, violence by reason, arbitrariness and caprice by principled conduct. 'Justice', say the *Institutes* of Justinian in Book I, title I, 'is the set and constant purpose which renders to every man his due;' only a society based on law and with special custodians for legal work and traditions can guarantee such set and constant purpose and a consistent and devoted concern with the business of treating equals equally. Whatever the king's own motives may have been in offering his subjects justice, at a price and initially in competition with courts that historically did not derive their power from him directly, his success in the enterprise, for the Common lawyer, is testimony to its importance and credibility. That is why, as Dowrick argues [pp. 17–29], the conception of justice as adjudication, and above all as adjudication in the royal courts, is the foundation layer in the Common lawyer's and the Common Law's conception of justice. For the Common lawyer, justice in every aspect – in its source, its location and its procedures – is essentially public and not private, indissolubly linked with sovereignty, inalienable, incapable of becoming sectional, invisible or personal. The process by which these attitudes were formed and this conception of justice emerged may have been full of historical accident, of things done for other reasons. But for the Common lawyer, the process is profoundly historical, practical and yet complex. It is a learning by experience and not an application of concepts and a set of abstract principles that stand above and before experience, people and their problems in actual, historical situations. Law, he argues with Gierke, is the result of a common conviction, not that a thing shall be, but that it is. But what it is we can only see by having to work it out in practice. By itself, an act of parliament or a legal decision considered apart from the facts from which it arises cannot be pronounced just or unjust, good or bad law. It is in using them further that we learn their quality.

While the Common lawyer has seen the royal courts and what they do as standing at the centre of this conception of justice, it is well known that the Common Law developed many of its most important and attractive traditions in the struggle against royal authority. The king may be the source and fountainhead of all justice, though Blackstone thought that he was rather a reservoir. But since Chief Justice Coke's great confrontation with James I, Common lawyers have held that while the king may be the fountainhead of justice, he is not, as king, the best dispenser of it. The king's personal prerogative is mercy; justice is a matter of being learned in the law, not as an esoteric secret science, but as the record and distillation of experience. Coke, it is true, still put much emphasis on technique, on 'artificial' reasoning. In his time, and until the reforms of 1832–75 abolishing the forms of action, reorganizing the jurisdiction of the courts and merging the administration of Common Law and equity, Common Law, in its search for certainty and predictability, was dominated by comparatively rigid and formal questions of procedure, cause of action and type of remedy. This was so much so that Sir Henry Maine noted: 'So great is the ascendancy of the law of actions in the infancy of courts of justice, that substantive law has at first the look of being gradually secreted in the interstices of procedure.'[3]

But the tendency to burst out of procedural bounds in the interest of doing justice came from within. Thus during the period 1485–1832 a whole body of law, the law of equity, was developed to provide remedies and deal with wrongs that the Common Law courts could not consider. The lord chancellor, satisfied that there was no adequate remedy at Common Law, decided cases in the name of the king, 'to satisfy conscience and as the work of charity', drawing on the principles of natural justice current in the fifteenth and sixteenth centuries through the canon law and Roman tradition. Another, more restricted branch or body of law, the law of quasi-contract, was developed by judges quite specifically to deal with unjust enrichment in situations that the law of contract did not cover, but which seemed to them to cry out for justice. If I pay money to someone falsely thinking I owe it to him, there is no contract between us and I cannot in contract sue for its return. But that, said the judges, is patently unjust; it is unjust enrichment – a basis for recovery not known traditionally to Common Law – and gave a right to recovery as though there were a contract. In the eighteenth century a great and creative judge, Lord Mansfield, almost single-handed brought into being the formal law merchant based on Common Law principles and the customs, usages and moral and commercial expectations of merchants in the city. The nineteenth-century reforms merely made it possible to do justice more directly, more economically, without unnecessary constraints of procedure that reflected the reverence for form so often found in earlier law and complications and accretions that an antiquated formalism necessarily produces in its attempt, within the old system, to deal with new problems and demands. By the late nineteenth century, a series of great lawyers and legal thinkers had persuaded themselves and many others that this learning and artifice of reasoning of the Common Law (now including equity) in the end

[3] H. S. Maine, *Dissertations on Early Law and Custom* (London, 1883), p. 389.

came down to common sense, but common sense informed and made cautious and complex by a grasp of the subtle and often unobvious ramifications of human action and judicial decision. The Cartesian ideal is not the Common lawyer's: for him, plain speaking and plain dealing, sound judgement and common sense do not require the belief that everything is or should be clear and distinct, transparent to reason and capable of logical analysis into simples. On the contrary, they require the recognition of flux, complexity and historicity and of a certain intractability of human affairs.

II

Perhaps no modern English judge has been more willing to use the concept of justice *ex cathedra*, to give judgement according to the reason of the thing, with scant reliance on authority and much readiness to pronounce new principles, than Lord Denning. Yet for him, too, justice is not an abstract thing and in his lectures, *The Road to Justice*, he writes:

> When you set out on this road you must remember that there are two great objects to be achieved: one is to see that the laws are just; the other that they are justly administered. Both are important, but of the two, the more important is that the law should be justly administered. It is no use having just laws if they are administered unfairly by bad judges or corrupt lawyers.... [A] country cannot long tolerate a legal system which does not give a fair trial.[4]

This concept of justice as a 'fair trial', linked with and promoting the more general conception of justice as fairness, is indeed for the Common lawyer a *sine qua non*. It is not, of course, exclusive to or especially of the Common Law. As the rules of 'natural justice' – a technical term in the Common Law today – it has been summarized in the form that no man should be condemned unheard and that every judge must be free from bias. As such, they derive from the Latin tags *audi alteram partem* and *nemo judex in re sua* and have been held, in the Common Law itself, to be general principles of law common to civilized communities, belonging indeed to the common consciousness of mankind rather than to the science or specialized tradition of law. The rules of natural justice in the technical Common Law sense, however, are not an adequate statement of the canons of a fair trial at Common Law. They enunciate, rather, the minimum standard that the Common Law sets for all manner of hearings and tribunals, public or domestic, that have a duty to act judicially or quasi-judicially or that make determinations which affect the lives, significant interests and property rights of citizens and are not covered by specific exclusions. This supervisory role of the Common Law, long exercised through

4 Lord Denning, *The Road to Justice* (London, 1955). pp. 6–7.

the prerogative writs, is based historically on the prerogative power of
the crown to do justice throughout the realm; it has opened up a whole
field of administrative law in which the rules of natural justice are both
central and the subject of detailed consideration. Such consideration
in recent years has led to the gradual substitution for them of the
single, less formal concept of acting fairly, which in turn has made it
easier to import a wider body of Common Law attitudes and principles, if not formal canons, on the subject of acting fairly. Within the
work of the Common Law courts themselves, the notion of a fair trial
has had a more specific content. It is not easily derivable from the
Latin maxims alone (though incorporating them) or from the common
opinion of mankind, which has seemed to Common lawyers less than
satisfactory in its views on the conduct and administration of courts.
The canons of a fair trial at Common Law presuppose the forms and
procedures that have been evolved in England. They have been
summed up as involving the independence of judge and jury and the
absence of personal interest in both; the hearing of both parties and
consideration of all evidence, but evidence properly put before the
court and not hearsay; the presentation of strong cases on both sides;
the personal integrity – incorruptibility and impartiality – of the
judge; the carrying out of their proper roles by counsel with propriety
in the search for truth and the giving of reasons by the judge for his
decision,[5] reasons that show he is deciding on the evidence according
to rules and doctrine and not caprice. To this we may add, as Lord
Hewart did, for instance, in *The New Despotism* (1929), the fact that
the case must be heard in public, that the parties be treated as equals,
that the judge be identified and personally responsible in the moral
sense for his decision and that appeals to a higher judicial tribunal
from a court of first instance or judicial review be in principle possible.

These canons have not been empty phrases. They, like the rules of
natural justice, have been given flesh, applied in detail to a wide range
of circumstances, to new situations and new types of hearings and
determinations, by a vast body of case law and affected, for particular
purposes, by statute. In the United States, under the 'due process'
clause of the Federal Constitution, they have had even more technical
discussion and a more formal, though not necessarily greater, general
influence. In both countries, recent legislation has had the peculiar
and not wholly desirable effect of appearing to separate the canons of a
fair trial from the concept of just adjudication generally – something
that the Common lawyer has not traditionally done as sharply. New
circumstances, as we shall see, have not left these canons totally
unchallenged: governments seek, by statute, or by powerful pleading

[5] Denning, pp. 1–44; Dowrick, pp. 30–32. A number of the quotations that follow
have come to me conveniently through Mr Dowrick's excellent eye for the telling
phrase.

of affairs of state, public interest and policy, convenience and desirability, to exempt some of the activities of their servants and agencies from these canons. Both governments and citizens have urged, in the name of substantive equality, that parties should not always be treated as equals, that the full protection afforded by these canons should be set aside, in part, to minimize delay or cost that hits one party more than another and that there are types of enquiry and decision-making involving important interests of citizens that are not best conducted on a legal basis. There is force in all these points and judges and legislators have recognized and are continuing to recognize it. But the presumption of the Common Law is always in favour of natural justice and the canons that apply in the particular activity. That is the Common Law tradition and Lord Hewart was not wrong and not out of tune with public opinion in satirizing the alternative, attractive to the bureaucrat and the social engineer:

> The inhabitants of these islands are within measurable distance of an El Dorado where there will be no judges at all. In those isles of the blest . . . all controversial questions will be decided in the third floor back of some one or other government department; the decision so reached will not be open to appeal . . . by any means whatsoever; no party or other person interested will be permitted to appear or offer any evidence; the whole law will have been codified in a single interminable statute . . . no lawyers will be tolerated except a group of advisers, departmentally appointed; any questions likely to excite difference of opinion will be submitted to those advisers beforehand on hypothetical facts and behind the back of the parties; and the lord chancellor himself will have been exchanged for a minister of administration for whose office any knowledge of law, however slight, will be a statutory disqualification. Meanwhile, and until that happy day arrives, our fellow countrymen seem somehow to think not too unkindly of judicial decisions given in open court upon real cases by perfectly independent and impartial judges, who are individually responsible and who have heard both sides.[6]

The Common Law canons of a fair trial are now, in the Common Law world, to some degree and in some areas under attack as allowing formal justice to impede substantive justice, but the basic tradition remains and is strong. It is, in its details, neither a deduction from reason nor a conception of legal operation common to all civilized communites. Those raised in the civil law tradition and the more bureaucratic arrangements of continental Europe seem to have as much difficulty in grasping and sympathizing with the English law of evidence as they have in grasping the concept of a trust. The Common Law insistence that the role of the judge is not inquisitorial often strikes them as being commended neither by the interests of truth nor

[6] Lord Hewart, *Essays and Observations* (London, 1930), pp. 122–3, cited in Dowrick, pp. 38–9.

those of morality. Yet that law of evidence (discounting some inconveniences and irrationalities that should be and are being excised) forms in the main a most important and integral part of the Common Law's conception of a fair trial and its search for truth. (The simple story unchecked by rules designed to keep it testable, delivered straight from the heart and as the teller sees it, is almost always a pack of lies, unconscious self-deception and malicious innuendo.) But pride in these rules of evidence and insistence on the non-inquisitorial role of the court lie very deep and are no external, accidental, inessential thing. Thus, the Court of Appeal in *Jones* v. *National Coal Board* ([1957] 2 Q.B. 55) ordered a new trial when it found that the trial judge, with the best of motives and intentions, in order to clarify the issues before the court and expedite the conduct of the trial had interfered frequently in the course of argument by counsel on both sides and had taken upon himself the function of examining witnesses. Lord Denning, giving the judgement of the court on appeal ([1957] 2 Q.B. 55, 63), said this:

> In the system of trial which we have evolved in this country, the judge sits to hear and determine the issues raised by the parties, not to conduct an investigation or examination on behalf of society at large, as happens, we believe, in some foreign countries. Even in England, however, a judge is not a mere umpire to answer the question 'How's that?'. His object, above all, is to find out the truth, and to do justice according to law; and in the daily pursuit of it the advocate plays an honourable and necessary role. Was it not Lord Eldon, LC, who said in a notable passage that 'truth is best discovered by powerful statements on both sides of the question?' [*Ex parte Lloyd* (1822) Mont 70, 72n]. And Lord Greene, MR, who explained that justice is best done by a judge who holds the balance between the contending parties without himself taking part in their disputations? If a judge, said Lord Greene, should himself conduct the examination of witnesses, 'he, so to speak, descends into the arena and is liable to have his vision clouded by the dust of conflict' [*Yuill* v. *Yuill* (1945) P. 15, 20].

It is this non-Cartesian, indeed anti-Cartesian, conception of truth and justice as emerging from conflict rather than formal analysis, as requiring the balancing of claims and interests that are best urged in the first instance by those present and affected, that is distinctive of the Common Law. It constitutes, I believe, its great contribution to the theory of freedom and of justice. It is pluralist, empirical, conscious of human error and human limitation. It treats neither man nor the principles of law as abstractions under which real people and events, real claims and conflicts, are to be subsumed. It does not suffer from the illusion that enlightened self-interest, or the moral law, or the principle of utility establish directly and by themselves what either men or judges ought to do in the complex situations of the real world in which one decision constantly affects a myriad others. It does not formulate as a regular procedure hypothetical cases or play thought games with 'original positions' and unhistorical men. This is why, as Professor Bernard Rudden has also argued more fully and in somewhat different terms,[7] the Common Law hearing can be characterized as consisting of interwoven dialogues. There is the dialogue between the judge and his predecessors as he turns to and examines the precedents. There is the dialogue between the judge and counsel who set out the case before the court by presenting argument and the evidence of witnesses and also usually seek to guide the court in different directions—to hear differently, to appraise differently, to choose different principles or analogies, to decide differently. There is finally the dialogue between the judge and the jury in which he must sum up the evidence and explain the law in terms that bring it into relation with the understanding and the experience of the ordinary man. Professor R. Zippelius, surveying our law from another tradition, has correctly and sympathetically characterized this process as based on and embodying the empirical belief that truth is reached by a process of trial and error.[8]

Together with the process of trial and error that the dialogues embody and facilitate stands another process which to the Common lawyer is of the very essence of justice—the balancing of facts, interests and principles that cannot in practice be brought to a coherent unity or reduced to a common measure, that requires, in fact, the specific judgement of justice. A great American judge summed this up, characteristically, by way of specific example. In law, as he says, the measure of care imputed to that standardized being, the reasonable man, around whom so much of our legal measure of justice revolves, is dependent upon the value of the interests concerned:

> The law measures the risks that a man may legitimately take by measuring the value of the interests furthered by his conduct. I may accumulate explosives for the purpose of doing some work of construction that is important for mankind when I should be culpably reckless in accumulating them for pleasure or caprice. I may risk my life by plunging into a turbulent ocean to save a drowning man when I should be culpably reckless if I were to make the plunge for sport or mere bravado. Inquiries that seem at the first glance the most simple and unitary—was this or that conduct negligent or the opposite?—turn out in the end to be multiple and complex. Back of the answers is a measurement of interests, a balancing of values, an appeal to the experience and

---

[7] B. Rudden, 'Courts and Codes in England, France and Soviet Russia'. *Tulane Law Review* XLVIII (1974), pp. 1010–28.

[8] R. Zippelius, 'The Function of Consensus in Questions of Justice', in F. C. Hutley, E. Kamenka and A. E. S. Tay, eds, *Law and the Future of Society*, Beiheft N.F. Nr. XI, *Archiv für Rechts-s— und Sozialphilosophie* (Wiesbaden, 1979), pp. 117–24 at pp. 120–23.

sentiments and moral and economic judgements of the community, the group, the trade. Of course, some of these valuations become standardized with the lapse of years, and thus instantaneous or, as it were, intuitive. We know at once that it is negligence to drive at breakneck pace through a crowded street, with children playing in the centre, at least where the motive of the drive is the mere pleasure of the race. On the other hand, a judgement even so obvious as this yields quickly to the pressure of new facts with new social implications. We assign a different value to the movement of the fire engine or the ambulance. Constant and inevitable, even when half concealed, is the relation between the legality of the act and its value to society. We are balancing and compromising and adjusting every moment that we judge.[9]

Or consider this judgement by Lord Denning, sitting in appeal as Master of the Rolls, remembering that it is a reported judgement and thus part of those allegedly 'formal', 'conservative', 'abstract' precedents that make up the principal body of the Common Law and that do sound, in style and manner of argument, so different from the way in which civil law decisions have traditionally been reported:

This case is entirely novel. Never before has a claim been made against a council or its surveyor for negligence in passing a house. The case itself can be brought within the words of Lord Atkin in *Donoghue* v. *Stevenson*: but it is a question whether we should apply them here. In *Dorset Yacht Co. Ltd* v *Home Office* [1970] A.C. 1004, Lord Reid said, at p. 1023, that the words of Lord Atkin expressed a principle which ought to apply in general 'unless there is some justification or valid explanation for its exclusion'.

So did Lord Pearson at p. 1054. But Lord Diplock spoke differently. He said it was a guide but not a principle of universal application. It seems to me that it is a question of policy which we, as judges, have to decide. The time has come when, in cases of new import, we should decide them according to the reason of the thing.

In previous times, when faced with a new problem, the judges have not openly asked themselves the question: what is the best policy for the law to adopt? But the question has always been there in the background. It has been concealed behind such questions as: Was the defendant under any duty to the plaintiff? Was the relationship between them sufficiently proximate? Was the injury direct or indirect? Was it foreseeable, or not? Was it too remote? And so forth.

Nowadays we direct ourselves to considerations of policy. In *Rondel* v. *Worsley* [1969] A.C. 191, we thought that if advocates were liable to be sued for negligence they would be hampered in carrying out their duties. In *Dorset Yacht Co. Ltd* v *Home Office* [1970] A.C. 1004, we thought that the Home Office ought to pay for damage done by escaping Borstal boys, if the staff was negligent, but we confined it to damage done in the immediate vicinity. In *S.C.M. (United Kingdom) Ltd* v. *W. J. Whittall & Son Ltd.* [1971] 1 Q.B. 337, some of us thought that economic loss ought

[9] Benjamin N. Cardozo, *The Paradoxes of Legal Science* (New York, 1928), pp. 74–5.

not to be put on one pair of shoulders, but spread among all the sufferers. In *Lanchbury* v. *Morgans* [1971] 2 Q.B. 245, we thought that as the owner of the familiy car was insured she should bear the loss. In short, we look at the relationship of the parties: and then say, as matter of policy, on whom the loss should fall.

What are the considerations of policy here? I will take them in order. First, Mrs Dutton has suffered a grievous loss. The house fell down without any fault of hers. She is in no position herself to bear the loss. Who ought in justice to bear it? I should think those who were responsible. Who are they? In the first place, the builder was responsible. It was he who laid the foundations so badly that the house fell down. In the second place, the council's inspector was responsible. It was his job to examine the foundations to see if they would take the load of the house. He failed to do it properly. In the third place, the council should answer for his failure. They were entrusted by parliament with the task of seeing that houses were properly built. They received public funds for the purpose. The very object was to protect purchasers and occupiers of houses. Yet they failed to protect them. Their shoulders are broad enough to bear the loss.

Next I ask: is there any reason in point of law why the council should not be held liable? Hitherto many lawyers have thought that a builder (who was also the owner) was not liable.

If that were truly the law, I would not have thought it fair to make the council liable when the builder was not liable. But I hold that the builder who builds a house badly is liable, even though he is himself the owner. On this footing, there is nothing unfair in holding the council's surveyor also liable.

Then I ask: if liability were imposed on the council, would it have an adverse effect on the work? Would it mean that the council would not inspect at all, rather than risk liability for inspecting badly? Would it mean that inspectors would be harassed in their work or be subject to baseless charges? Would it mean that they would be extra cautious, and hold up work unnecessarily? Such considerations have influenced cases in the past, as in *Rondel* v. *Worsley* [1969] 1 A.C. 191. But here I see no danger. If liability is imposed on the council, it would tend, I think, to make them do their work better, rather than worse.

Next I ask: is there any economic reason why liability should not be imposed on the council? In some cases the law has drawn the line to prevent recovery of damages. It sets a limit to damages for economic loss, or for shock, or theft by escaping convicts. The reason is that if no limit were set there would be no end to the money payable. But I see no such reason here for limiting damages. In nearly every case the builder will be primarily liable. He will be insured and his insurance company will pay the damages. It will be very rarely that the council will be sued or found liable. If it is, much the greater responsibility will fall on the builder and little on the council.

Finally I ask myself: if we permit this new action, are we opening the door too much? Will it lead to a flood of cases which neither the council nor the courts will be able to handle? Such considerations have sometimes in the past led the courts to reject novel claims. But I see no need to reject this claim on this ground. The injured person will always have his claim against the builder. He will rarely allege—and still less be able to prove—a case against the council.

All these considerations lead me to the conclusion that the policy of the law should be, and is, that the council should be liable for the negligence of their surveyor in passing work as good when in truth it is bad.

I would therefore dismiss this appeal.[10]

III

'Justice must not only be done but be seen to be done.' The canons for a fair trial or hearing enumerate certain forms for achieving justice, forms that must be observed publicly, visibly, that stand as signs of a society's and a profession's devotion to justice. But they are not, to the Common lawyer, sufficient or in fact capable of being abstracted from the content of the hearing and the decision, from the considerations that weigh, properly or improperly, with those taking part. It is here that the conception of the judgement of justice as a balancing of matters and principles properly taken into account is crucial. There is no question, in the Common Law, with all its emphasis on defining issues and restricting the matters before the court, of failing constantly to bring in, and to require to be brought in, what is *relevant* to just determination. This will include, of course, the law and principles of the law, past discussions and decisions that are to be held pertinent or 'distinguished'. It will include moral sentiments and standards of behaviour, expectations and aversions that may reasonably be expected to govern the behaviour of men at particular times and in particular circumstances. It will include, as Mr Dowrick has reminded us, considerations of welfare and utility, of public interest, of morality where it is appropriate for the law to uphold it, and of social justice. Constantly, because the judgement of justice, as Professor Julius Stone has argued,[11] includes a creative leap and not a direct deduction from simple universal principles, the lawyer makes use of open-ended terms that invite judgement to enter at every step, in selecting what is relevant, reasonable, fair. He does so within a system which, for the able and imaginative, does not inhibit and has not inhibited creativity, the capacity to meet new situations and demands, often with decisions that prove to be the revolutionary start of far-reaching developments. But the function of the system is to inhibit (for nothing can stamp out) arbitrariness and prejudice, impetuousness and a disregard for consequences or for the rights of those who are not there to claim loudly and without concern for others. Empty

[10] *Dutton* v. *Bognor Regis Urban District Council* [1972] 1 Q.B. 373, *per* Lord Denning, MR, at pp. 397–8.

[11] See especially his *Law and the Social Sciences in the Second Half Century* (Minneapolis, 1966).

talk of 'morality' and 'justice' without consideration of how its claims would affect a total system of just rules and just determinations is no substitute for law or justice in the concrete sense. The possible conflict there is the reason that law has often been presented, so Cardozo reminds us,[12] 'as something to which morality and justice are not merely alien but hostile'. Cardozo sees the judicial process as involving the operation of four forces: the force of logic or analogy; the force of history; the force of custom; and the force of justice, morals and social welfare, of the *mores* of the day.[13] The Common lawyer puts special weight on justice as judicature, on the concept of the fair trial and on doing justice according to law. But he has never believed and could not read two cases without ceasing to believe that justice in the law can be done or is ever done without constant recourse to conceptions that transcend anything that might be called formal or strictly black-letter or procedural justice, to conceptions of 'natural', 'moral' and 'social' justice. That there should be continuous dispute among judges about the extent to which these conceptions should be invoked and allowed to disturb old law and create new is only natural; it is part of the dialogue and of the ebb and flow that is essential to justice and to the spirit of the Common Law. It is in fact striking how many of the allegedly radical new departures in creating 'a law for the second half of the twentieth century', from products liability to greatly increased duties of employers to employees, from the setting aside of unequal contracts to giving the citizen greater protection against governmental arbitrariness, have come out of the Common Law courts, sometimes in bold and imaginative decisions, sometimes in small and at first scarcely noticeable steps, before engaging the attention of legislators and becoming embodied in statute. The Common Law has had many great and creative periods when judges reworked and extended its principles to meet major social change. The twentieth century has been as creative as any and the suggestion that the Common Law's concern also with precedent, system, doctrine and formalism has resulted in stultification is made possible only by ignorance. It is true, of course, that there are areas of law—such as contract—in which radical departures are both possible and necessary today; there are other areas—such as the law of trusts, concerned with interests and arrangements that are intended to last for generations, where the recognition of new problems and new conditions has to proceed cautiously. Above all, the creativity of the Common Law has lain, generation after generation, not in elaborating scholastically concepts of formal justice but, on the contrary in seeking to do right

---

[12] Benjamin N. Cardozo, *The Nature of the Judicial Process* (New Haven, 1924), p. 134.

[13] Benjamin N. Cardozo, *The Growth of the Law* (New Haven and London, 1924), pp. 61–2.

substantively and responsibly, recognizing new wrongs and harms, new dangers and problems, but also recognizing that there were almost always competing interests and considerations involved. 'I do not think so ill of our jurisprudence', said Lord Atkin in the classic case *Donoghue* v. *Stevenson* in 1932, 'as to suppose that its principles are so remote from the ordinary needs of civilized society and the ordinary claims it makes upon its members as to deny a legal remedy where there is so obviously a social wrong.' He proceeded to find, for the first time in English Common Law, a manufacturer liable for harm caused by a defective product to a consumer with whom he had no contract and of whom he had no specific knowledge, on the basis that he could reasonably have foreseen that harm would ensue to one such as the consumer for whose use the product is intended. Why? Because we have a duty to our neighbour and while the law must define who is our neighbour, for what purposes, in ways that will probably restrict our liabilities to make human intercourse and commerical life possible, it is not its job simply to ignore the most patent demands of morality and the moral sentiments of mankind because no action has existed before.

Legal justice, as it is often called, is far more in the actual practice of the Common Law than the application of abstract, procedural canons of fairness and impartiality. Without these, it is true, there is nothing, but by themselves they could hardly ever lead to a decision. As Professor Chapman notes,[14] in drawing a distinction between 'fairness' and 'justice' we speak of a fair trial but of its just outcome (though we also speak of 'fair shares'). Fairness as in 'fair trial' deals with usages governed by rules, while justice is also concerned with considerations, such as needs, essentially extraneous to the result and involves connotations of balancing, weighing, recognizing complexity and rendering a final decision which are not involved in judgements of fairness. It is also untrue, as Professor Stone goes on to argue in the present volume, that legal justice is confined to treating equals equally. Logically, that may be the simpler task, but the whole point of a system of rules, as Professor Stone says, is to discriminate, to make distinctions, to treat some in one way and others in another. The judgement of justice, in Common Law, does not shirk the harder task of treating unequals unequally. Hans Kelsen, among others, has argued[15] that the making of such discrimination is necessarily time-bound, that it varies with shifting, moral sentiments and beliefs and that 'justice' is therefore not a satisfactory instrument of reason and does not provide a firm logical foundation for, or criticism of, legal

[14] John Chapman, 'Justice and Fairness', in C. J. Friedrich and J. W. Chapman (eds), *Justice: Nomos VI* (New York, 1963), pp. 147–69 at pp. 147–8.
[15] Hans Kelsen, 'The Pure Theory of Law', *Law Quarterly Review* L (1934), pp. 474–98 at pp. 474–82, and *What is Justice?* (Berkeley, 1957), p. 21.

norms. The Common lawyer is content with that. He has long not thought that justice is timeless, independent of the sentiments of actual people in actual communities, immune from fashion, ideology or interest. But he has not shirked the task of reaching decisions in the knowledge that not all interests can be reconciled, that not every one can be made happy and that not all decisions would be good ones. He has believed that he is better fitted to make them when it comes to questions of justice because of his independence, because of the system and tradition, the body of rules and doctrine in which he works and because he has made the pursuit of justice his life's work. It is not difficult to draw attention to the limitations of such professionalism, its involvement with caste, its predisposition toward caution and conservatism, its lack of immunity from the consistent production of grey and black sheep. But if we study with the same jaundiced attention politicians and administrators from the point of view of their concern with justice as the set and constant purpose to give every man his due, with full consideration for consequences, we are far less impressed. Immediate demands are usually made in the name of justice and it is not surprising, therefore, that the politician, whose stock-in-trade is giving the appearance of immediate and sympathetic response, should be looked to by those who have new demands as the fountainhead of 'justice'. But he relies, in the end, on the Common Law to clear up the mess. Its record for doing that, over many centuries, is by and large impressive. There is much in our society, perhaps almost everything in it, that is workable because in the end the citizen can rely on determination by the courts. The effects of that spread far beyond the circle of those who have the wit or money to go to law themselves and they infect, through the strength of the legal tradition in Common Law countries, the legislative acts and adminis- trative arrangements and habits of the society as a whole.

The most common informed and literate attack on the Common Law today is an internal one consisting of complaints, like those voiced by Professor P. S. Atiyah in the field of contract and tort, that the whole conceptual structure of particular areas of law has rested on and been the carrier of nineteenth-century liberal philosophies and is therefore in need of urgent revision. On the amount of revision required, the extent to which nineteenth-century liberalism is an unsatisfactory philosophy for our day, there is dissension among lawyers as there is dissension in the community. But revisions are certainly taking place under the leadership of reforming judges, lord chancellors and attorneys-general and not only as the result of statutory innovations which often merely follow and push further recent developments in the Common Law. They are in fact frequently not mere revisions but fundamental reappraisals of whole areas of Common Law which for the most part nevertheless maintain and build up its systematic concern for justice. A less literate and informed attack on the Common Law as dispensing 'legal' or 'formal' justice and not doing 'real' justice seems to me fundamentally misplaced. The justice of the Common Law, I have argued, is not 'formal' or 'legal' as opposed to substantive; the belief that it is so is characteristic of the disappointed litigant, of the man, group or class with unrecognized or unsatisfied demands which to the litigant for a time seem more important than anything else in the world. Of course, stridency gets a better hearing in the political arena than in the legal case and new demands are more easily given initial satisfaction by political proclamation or simple statute than worked into a complex system that has regard for consequences before they happen and for the rights of others before they protest.

Elsewhere,[16] Professor Kamenka and I have discussed the various ways in which the traditional procedures of the Common Law are not suited to a whole range of modern conditions and require amendment and supplementation through the development of new procedures, new types of courts and tribunals, new rules of evidence, and so on. The weak and deprived, in particular those not able to confront others with the confidence and self-assurance of factual equality, are now more than ever in our minds and it is the fashion to solve their problems more quickly and directly by bureaucratic-administrative rather than legal means, by treating them as recipients of services or special consideration assured for them by government. There is much in this that calls for procedures and ways of working that are not those of the Common Law, though such procedures and ways of working consistently run the risk of turning human subjects into objects, of keeping the deprived spiritless and dependent. The proper attempt to avoid this by procedures for administrative and judicial reconsideration and review, for giving peoples 'rights' to benefits, 'rights' to be heard and to participate, are all parasitic on the strength of the Common Law and its traditions and will survive only as long as it survives. There is no question of treating the Common Law at any stage of its development as final, or as capable of dealing with all social problems. But the peculiar and enviable reputation throughout the world that the countries of the Common Law system have acquired for their capacity for a meticulous and sustained concern with justice and the gradual correction of their own abuses is rooted in the sense of justice of the Common Law. It is a sense that is neither purely formal nor incapable of accommodating social and moral justice and

[16] Eugene Kamenka and A. E. S. Tay, 'Beyond Bourgeois Individualism: The Contemporary Crisis in Law and Legal Ideology', in Eugene Kamenka and R. S. Neale (eds), *Feudalism. Capitalism and Beyond* (London and Canberra, 1975), pp. 126–44 and the same authors' contributions to A. E. S. Tay and Eugene Kamenka (eds), *Law-Making in Australia* (London and Melbourne, 1979), pp. 20–38 and pp. 247–62.

unlike many versions of the latter, it constantly remains human.

I have written of a *sense* of justice, which involves but is not exhausted by principles of fairness, equality, respect for persons, a concern with social adjustment and well-being, a capacity to recognize wrongs and make room for rights. The account of justice I have given is an ostensive one: justice is what is done in Common Law, as a result of its traditions, doctrines and procedures. Any abstract, 'philosophical' definition of justice, I believe, like Aristotle's or Justinian's, will be so open in character as to postpone everything that is of interest, everything that makes justice real. Making it real, I have sought to show, is not a matter of deduction from or mechanical application of general principles. It is a pursuit, requiring judgement and a sense of justice at every step. It is thus itself a specific, historical and practical activity, carrying with it an ideology, requiring specific custodians, assuming a division of labour and the integrity of particular concerns in society. To say that justice is the balancing of concerns and interests is not to deny that it is itself a concern and interest of a specific sort, that has its own requirements, that it shapes people and societies as well as 'serving' them. The sense of justice, certainly, was not invented by the Common Law and is not exclusive to it; it is part of the Western legal tradition, rooted in and from time to time again drawing upon procedures, principles, concepts and maxims associated with Roman law. It is also known to other traditions. But I do not believe, myself, that we will get a better appreciation of the 'idea' of justice, or a better technique for actualizing it, by seeking some fundamental kernel or set of principles common to all Western legal systems, let alone to all legal systems wherever they be. There are different conceptions of justice between which we must choose and some legal systems, I believe, safeguard justice better than others. How long, in the face of many pressures, they will continue to do so is another matter.

5

Justice not equality[1]

Julius Stone

I Introduction

Even those for whom the making of a demand in title of justice is but a thump on the table have to concern themselves with the question why certain demands inspire such gestures and with the effects of this kind of invocation in human confrontations and adjustments. It is ground common to both sceptics and devotees of justice that the history of mankind records the successive failures of various criteria of justice to sustain themselves. Sceptics and devotees differ in what they infer from this sad history.

When we reduce justice-demands to thumps on the table, the resolution of conflicts is abandoned to the play of other forces. When we persist in asserting certain demands in title of justice, we acknowledge at any rate the need to continue the search for criteria of justice which can maintain themselves. In that case, we are also likely to think that the endlessness of the search is to be explained, not by any lack of significance, but rather by the endlessness of changing problems. We may also offer other reasons, but this one surely carries special weight amid the formidable tempo of change now found in all existential spheres of human life and culture.

One related tendency of social, political and jurisprudential theorists in the present century has been to seek criteria of justice of vastly simplified indeterminacy or ambiguity, such as 'fairness' and 'equality', in the hope of escaping the admitted perplexities involved in grappling directly with questions of justice. Generally, such attempts reduce themselves to the argument that all issues of human justice are to be resolved by reference to the criterion of equality or to some modality of it. Two features of this century, particularly since the rise

---

[1] This chapter is a revised version of remarks at the opening symposium of the World Congress on Philosophy of Law and Social Philosophy. A fuller exposition, 'Justice in the Slough of Equality' appears in the centennial issue of the *Hastings Law Journal* (1978), vol. 29, no. 5, pp. 995–1024.

of cultural and ethical relativism, have contributed to the remarkable upsurge of faith in the principle of equality. One is the phenomenal expansion of the role of logic, mathematics, physics and the natural sciences generally, in determining the material and spiritual nature of our culture. The notion of equality, carrying as it does a certain *soupçon* of logically or mathematically demonstrable certainty and objectivity, has an apparent appropriateness in such a culture. Another is that the notion of equality, used as a weapon in social, political and international struggles, has had a most remarkable record of success in the story of modern Western societies. It has had such success from the French and American Revolutions onward and still surges forward in 'liberation movements' of all kinds. In historical perspective also, therefore, equality has come to seem like an idea whose time has finally arrived.

It is part of my present purpose to show that this tendency to reinterpret justice as equality is not justified theoretically or by the results that have been or might be achieved through such reinterpretation.

II Pilgrimages to the mecca of equality

Twentieth-century pilgrimages to the mecca of equality often emerge from older and more familiar landscapes. Kant's attempted demonstration of the innate right of equal freedom of the will of each member of society, as springing *a priori* from the nature of ethical enquiry, still dominates (though usually cryptically) many current attempts to reduce justice to terms of mere equality.[2] Some have used Kantian themes to champion entrepreneurial initiative and related concepts of political liberty, as in F. A. Hayek's *Road to Serfdom*.[3] Some, like Rawls, have rather thinly covered over Kant's *a priori* 'truth' with a no less indecisive and much more mysterious postulate of 'the veil of ignorance', from behind which we are to make judgements of 'fairness' and 'equality'.[4]   Most thinkers, however, are deterred from overtly passionate crusades for equality by Perelman's incisive point that only issues of 'formal justice' can be intellectually ('philosophically') controlled by the notion of equality. Issues of what he terms 'material justice' (which are of course the issues about which men murmur, cry out, struggle and even die) escape such control.[5]

[2] See Julius Stone, *Human Law and Human Justice* (Sydney, 1965) pp. 82–104.

[3] F. A. Hayek, *The Road to Serfdom* (Chicago, London and Sydney, 1944); see also Stone, *Human Law*, at pp. 99–104.

[4] See J. Rawls, *A Theory of Justice* (Cambridge, Mass., 1971), especially pp. 136–42, 333–50.

[5] See Ch. Perelman, *De la justice* (Brussels, 1945); Stone, *Human Law*, pp. 325–30; J. Stone, *Legal System and Lawyers' Reasonings* (Sydney, 1964), pp. 325–37.

Even Rawls, when he approached the problems we associate with the welfare state, unabashedly sidestepped or penetrated the 'veil of ignorance' which (in his view) guards our access to the virtues of 'fairness' and 'equality', and replaced them with compassion toward the least fortunate. This, of course, assures some legitimate breathing-space for the welfare state. But by thus accommodating the discriminations unavoidable in welfare programmes, Rawls is at odds with the *main* stream of egalitarian individualism proceeding from Kant. For he would thereby be subjecting the presumption of equality to vastly indefinite qualifications, even if he were also to specify more clearly than he has how the inequalities, which his theory could legitimate, lead with certainty to benefit the least fortunate. This, still, does not lead Rawls to question the general hegemony of the equality notion, or to give adequate attention to its often-exposed deficiencies.[6]

Continued acceptance of this hegemony of the notion of equality, and blindness to its inadequacies as the pretended core of justice, characterize many powerful thinkers, even when they seem to accept Perelman's cardinal point about the difference between formal justice and material justice.

The distinguished array of talents that has converged toward the banner of equality from many areas of social science and philosophy obviously is not to be dismissed as naively ignorant of the actual differences between human endowments, whether among individuals or groups. Nor surely are they insensitive to the possibility that differences in endowment may require differential treatment in terms of justice. It is precisely because there is no such naivete that the protagonists of equality tend to state their positions in terms of a *presumption* of equality, rather than equality *simpliciter* While equality of treatment (they admit) is not necessarily justice in every case, they would still insist that justice requires equality of treatment until and unless good reasons for departing from equality have been shown.

III Empirical presuppositions of equality criteria

D. E. Browne[7] has drawn our attention to the many thinkers who now seem to be committed in various ways to the view that 'the presumption of equality' stands at the centre of justice, albeit subject to rebuttal. He defines them (and I adopt his criterion) as those thinkers

---

[6] Rawls, pp. 60–67, 302–3, 311–15, and *passim*. 'Equality' figures in some form in seven main rubrics of the index to *A Theory of Justice*. It requires much imagination and indeed guesswork to find from the index the relevance of the welfare state to his Second Principle (p. 60); or indeed the relevance of his Second Principle to the justification of 'inequalities'. This last (and the welfare state) earn no index rubric at all!

[7] D. E. Browne, 'The Presumption of Equality', *Australasian Journal of Philosophy* LIII (1975), pp. 46–53. See, for example, R. S. Peters, *Ethics and Education* (London,

who, without preliminary regard to empirically found similarities in the relevant badges of entitlement of individuals, assert that all individuals have a right, until the contrary is shown, to an equal distribution or to equal treatment. And he correctly distinguishes such precepts from Aristotle's classical position that equals are to be treated equally and unequals unequally. Aristotle's formula leaves it to the proponents both of equality and inequality to prove empirically whether the persons, among whom justice is to be done, have characteristics entitling them to similar (equal) or different (unequal) treatment.

None of the grounds which can be offered for such a metaempirical 'presumption of equality' seems sustainable.

A first such ground, based on the Kantian *a priori* proof of the equal innate freedom of all individuals, proves far too much (or far too little) to be accepted as helpful at the present juncture of social and political interventionism in Western societies. This kind of ground would proceed through the *a priori* proof of individual free will from the nature of ethical enquiry, to a proof of the free will of all individuals, and thus to a proof of the equal free will of all, and finally to a proof of equality as such, all without reference to empirical findings. The difficulty with this is that it also tends to establish the individualistic doctrine of illimitable free will, and most thinkers really desire to escape, by the presumption of equality, from the consequences of this very doctrine.

Second is the argument from the essential nature of rules by which justice (it is said) must be dispensed. The very nature of rules, the argument runs, means that they apply equally to all who fall within their terms. But, of course, any legal or ethical order consists of a multitude of rules, and most of this multitude are concerned, by the very differences of fact on which they are predicated, to dispense *un*equal shares or treatment among individuals, according to differences in their relevant badges of entitlement. In its neglect of this discriminating function of *rules*, as distinct from the equality innate *in a single rule*, this second argument, like the third, which draws the presumption of equality from the common humanness shared by individuals, begs the question it is used to prove.

1966), pp. 117–43; S. I. Benn, 'Egalitarianism and the Equal Consideration of Interests', in J. Pennock and J. W. Chapman (eds), *Equality: Nomos IX* (New York, 1967), pp. 61–78. See generally, S. I. Benn and R. S. Peters, *Social Principles and the Democratic State* (London, 1959); Hugo Bedau, 'Egalitarianism and the Idea of Equality', in Pennock and Chapman, pp. 3–27; I. Berlin, 'Equality' in *Proceedings of the Aristotelian Society* LVI (1956), pp. 301–26; A. C. Graham, 'Liberty and Equality', *Mind* LXXIV (1965), pp. 59–65; J. R. Lucas, 'Against Equality', *Philosophy* XL (1965), pp. 296–307.

Certainly, the third argument from common humanness assumes without empirical enquiry not only that humanness is a relevant badge of entitlement, but that *it is the one dominantly relevant* in issues of just distribution or treatment. J. R. Lucas has observed that, to derive an equality norm from the humanist observation that 'a man is a man for a' that', we would have to frame an argument somewhat in the form:

> All men are men
> All men are equally men
> Therefore all men are equal.

And he observes wittily that, if we substituted 'numbers' for 'men' in this syllogism, we would have the obviously fallacious argument:

> All numbers are numbers
> All numbers are equally numbers
> Therefore all numbers are equal. [Lucas, p. 297.]

The initial argument has a certain adventitious strength, because the positive affect surrounding the symbol of 'common humanity' exposes those who deny the adequacy of this argument to charges of *inhumanity*. (This exposure might be reduced but is not wholly removed by substituting the word 'humanness' for 'humanity'.) Yet it is critical to make this denial and to show that it is not a sign of inhumanity, but rather an attempt to remove a thought-block which hampers performance of the tasks of justice, and perhaps even of those of humane compassion.

A concession should here be made to those indulging in the presumption of equality, the need for which D. E. Browne has perhaps overlooked. This is that the three arguments above, inconclusive as they are when used to prove what share or treatment individuals are in justice entitled to, are still ways of stating *an important presupposition* of all enquiries into justice. For such enquiries cannot begin until the constituency of individuals among whom justice is to be done has been delimited, until, in short, 'the justice-constituency' has been identified. And the arguments from *a priori* free will and common humanness do, at this level, afford the directive that all human beings physically in or within the sway of a given justice-constituency *ought to be counted within it also for the purpose of doing justice*.[8] This, of course, was a great question in many ancient societies, including Aristotle's Greece. It remains so in some contemporary societies. All of the arguments discussed, then, are a

---

[8] Intensified, of course, by religious ideals of 'the brotherhood of man' and 'the fatherhood of God'. This chapter does not aim to explore questions of justice between humans and other species or between humans and their environment.

necessary step toward raising questions of justice, but cannot resolve these questions, including the question whether persons shall be treated equally or unequally.

The triumphant landmarks of the notion of equality in history, referred to above (p. 98), were in times and societies in the West where significant classes of human beings were excluded from the justice-constituency within which they found themselves. The directive power of the equality notion did extend to the removal of those gross exclusions, and the power of equality as an emotive symbol contributed to success in this. Once all human beings came to be included within the justice-constituency, the tasks of determining what was just between them and their fellows could begin. Recognition of common humanness, of human equality in that sense, is thus, as we have observed, a necessary step toward raising the questions of justice, toward asking when persons shall be treated unequally or equally according to their badges of entitlement. But it cannot answer these questions.

The justice-relevant similarities or differences which determine entitlements of individuals thereafter cannot be derived from the equality notion. They escape its ambit in two vital respects. The notion of equality itself cannot determine for us what features are to be seen as similarities or differences relevant to justice (that is, as constituting badges of entitlement) in particular kinds of issue between particular classes of individuals. Further, it cannot determine for us the incidence in empirical fact of relevant similarities or differences among the individuals concerned. Yet this incidence must surely affect the question whether it is sensible to begin in an actual society with the presumption, here under question, that equality prevails, that is, that relevant similarities overwhelmingly predominate.

To admit the role of the equality-in-humanness principle as critical to the threshold problem of delimiting the justice-constituency, then, still leaves it essential to say that equality and its modalities do not provide an adequate core criterion of justice, at any rate *for problems of our Western democracies.* For, however it be elsewhere, the justice problems of countries like, for example, Australia, the United States and the United Kingdom, are not mainly problems of gross exclusion of human beings from the justice-constituency in which they find themselves. The problems in such societies at this stage are rather those of determining what shares and treatment are to be accorded to individual members in conformity with justice-relevant similarities and differences. And the decisions generally turn on those very questions mentioned above (p. 102) which escape control by the presumption of equality.

These limits to the usefulness of the notion of equality for problems of justice are apparent even when, as under the equal protection clause of the US Constitution, the question is not whether justice can be resolved into equality, but rather one of applying an express constitutional directive that equality shall govern state action.

The limits have become very apparent to all who work with or study that clause, especially since we have entered the era of 'affirmative action' and 'reverse discrimination'. Whatever biases there may be in relation to the merits of cases like *DeFunis* and *Bakke*,[9] there is a widening consensus that judicial efforts to set even minimal standards of tolerable justice by manipulating the equality notion have produced an uneasy morass of unprincipled decision-making.

IV Equivocations of equality

This poor performance with the notion of equality even for the purpose of implementing the equal protection clause is due in major part, as is its inadequacy as a core criterion of justice, to the treacherous ambiguities and self-contradictions which it conceals.[10] The notion may be taken to refer, first (and as seen above, p. 101, very usefully), to the threshold question of delimitation of the membership of the justice-constituency. It is other concealed multiple references which cause the trouble. For it may refer, second, to the demand that all members of a justice-constituency come under the same uniform rules. And in that second reference it ignores the plain injustice to any human beings who might still be excluded from the constituency. It also ignores the fact that the uniform rules to which all are submitted may merely be *equally unjust* to all. And it further ignores the fact that a uniform rule superimposed on pre-existing relevant differences between the factual situations of members may also be grossly unjust. Third, equality may refer to a requirement, quite at loggerheads with the second reference above (to uniformity of rule), that the rule differentiate among individuals according to the diversity of their situations *so as to produce a greater degree of equality among them after the rule has been applied*. The feature designated as equality under this third reference is not application of a uniform rule, but involves the

---

[9] *DeFunis* v. *Odegaard*, 416 US 312 (1974); *Regents of the University of California* v. *Bakke*, 46 L.W. 4896–936 (1978), affirming in part *Bakke* v. *U.C.* 18 Cal. 3d 34, 553 p. 2d 1152 (1977). Archibald Cox's *Role of the Supreme Court* ... (1975) 56–118, well stresses the need 'to articulate principles', without specifying the tensions involved between justice and equality (in its diverse versions) here examined. Yet his references to 'legitimation' and to 'natural law' indicate some sensitivity to them.

[10] Cf. in relation to this notion in international justice, Julius Stone, 'Approaches to the Notion of International Justice', in R. Falk and C. E. Black (eds), *The Future of the International Legal Order* I, *Theories and Practice* (Princeton, New Jersey, 1969), pp. 372–460.

very opposite of that. Equality in this third sense of greater *resultant* equality is achievable only insofar as the applicable rules of law do discriminate in favour of those actually initially disadvantaged.

V Reverse discrimination problems

The contemporary use of the Equal Protection Clause of the Fourteenth Amendment to the United States Constitution provides a fascinating practical illustration of the problems discussed above.

Although the Equal Protection Clause was first interpreted as prescribing that the same rule must be applied to all, this meaning had not been left unqualified. The clause has also come to be interpreted to mean that members of the society can (and indeed should) in appropriate cases be protected by laws which differentiate among them according to pre-existing factual inequalities, in order to bring about a resultant (or residual) greater equality.

These conflicting meanings are but one set of the equivocations which beset the notion of equality; but they underlie some of the massive controversies of the last two decades since *Brown* v. *Board of Education* [347 US 483 (1954)].

In fact, it has not been possible to apply even the Equal Protection of the Laws Clause merely in terms of the ideal of equality. As Dworkin has well observed,[11] that clause makes the concept of equality a test of state action, but it does not stipulate *any particular conception of that concept*. In this light it ceases to be surprising that Dworkin's own valiant effort to explain how DeFunis's exclusion in favour of a less intellectually qualified black ends in the conclusion that unequal treatment will be justified as long as the victim still is 'treated as an equal'. He is concerned here to assert (on grounds far from self-evident) that the 'right to treatment as an equal' is fundamental, and 'the right to equal treatment' merely 'derivative' from it.

This distinction begs the question which of the possible references of 'equal' protection is the predominant one though (as just seen) he himself recognizes the choice to be open under the Equal Protection Clause. Moreover, the very right to 'equal treatment', which he is at pains to derive from his Kant-like axiom about 'treatment as an

---

[11] R. Dworkin, 'The DeFunis Case: the Right to Go to Law School', in *Taking Rights Seriously* (London, 1977), p. 226. See also R. Dworkin, 'Why Bakke has No Case', *New York Review of Books*, 10 November 1977, p. 11. The use of Mr Dworkin's justification of reverse discrimination to illustrate what I have ventured to call the slough of equality is not invidiously intended. His efforts to marshal learning to contemporary issues and the coverage and imagination which have often accompanied this have drawn general admiration. His work has been chosen precisely because of this admiration and because he has offered a rationale of this very area.

equal', has itself at least two potentially conflicting meanings. The meaning Dworkin here assumes is that 'equal treatment' means equal distribution under a uniform rule.[12] But 'equal treatment' can also mean, as seen above (pp. 103), treatment by a differentiating rule which results in a greater residual equality between the persons concerned. And resort to this latter meaning would succour the minority claims in DeFunis and Bakke situations, without resort to Dworkin's vague notion 'treatment as an equal', which is here in question. In the welfare state, indeed, which seems to be a main context of Dworkin's own thinking, this second kind of residual greater equality produced by deliberately discriminatory rules is an everyday phenomenon. But, of course, for Dworkin to have relied on *this* meaning of 'equal treatment' (rather than on the overriding primacy of 'treatment as an equal') would still require him to give good reasons for choosing it. And those reasons could *not* be *in terms of equality*.

Dworkin's efforts to explain the notion of 'treatment as an equal' are on two levels. On the one hand, he says, 'treatment as an equal' requires only that we accord equality of respect or consideration or concern, and the like. On the other hand, as if in response to objections to the vagueness of this, he seems finally to explicate 'treatment as an equal' as meaning that discrimination may be resorted to, at the cost of *unequal* treatment, for the advancement of the conditions of an 'ideal society', or in furtherance of an 'ideal' which will in turn foster a 'better society'.

The essential question here is, does either of these levels of explanation depend decisively on the centrally quantitative notion of equality-as-justice? As to the latter level, subordinating 'equal treatment' to the task of securing the conditions of an 'ideal' or 'better' society, it must be obvious that what is decisive is the notion of 'ideal' or 'better'. But even the former level, explaining 'treatment as an equal' as 'equality' of respect or concern, and the like, turns out on close scrutiny not to be controlled by equality-as-justice. Dworkin's assertion is that the displacement of DeFunis by the minority applicant, despite its departure from 'equal treatment', still 'treated' DeFunis 'as an equal' because it accorded 'equal respect' to him. His purported demonstration of this 'equal respect' is by an argument that other admission tests might be as just as that of intellectual merit, provided they are supported by the prospects of plausible social benefits, such as providing better legal services to the minority communtiy. So that it is clear that what are here being compared are not *quantities* of respect as between the claimants, but rather in-

---

[12] See the much clearer statements of J. R. Lucas (p. 298), who exposes in general the unavoidable built-in contradictions, as well as overlappings, between these two modalities of 'equality'.

tellectual merit as a test with any other plausible social benefits. One value is being compared with an indeterminate range of other imaginable values.

VI The US Supreme Court's opinions in Bakke

With all the controversies surrounding the United States Supreme Court's decision in *Regents of the University of California* v *Bakke* of 26 June 1978, its outcome rings clear in support of the present point. Even when the court is applying the constitutional precept of the Equal Protection Clause, we find, at the critical watersheds of judgement, that it is not equality but some wider notion such as 'justice', or a society that is 'not race conscious', or 'not oppressive', which is decisive. The five judges who constituted the majority which held that the Supreme Court of California[13] erred in prohibiting the university 'from establishing race-conscious programs in the future', consisted of Mr Justice Powell (who announced the judgement of the court), and the Justices, Brennan, White, Marshall and Blackmun, who concurred on this issue in a single joint opinion. (We may refer to these latter four judges as 'the Brennan Four'.) The remaining four justices, Stevens, Burger, Stewart and Rehnquist, disposed of the case on the basis of provisions of Section 601 of the Civil Rights Act 1964 other than its non-discrimination provision—namely its categorical prohibition of 'exclusion' [46 L.W. 4934–6]. This removes any bearing of their opinion on the above issue. The five majority judges were agreed that Section 601 'goes no further in prohibiting the use of race than the Equal Protection Clause' [46 L.W. p. 4911].

How did the five majority judges draw from the Equal Protection Clause their view that the use of race as a criterion is not prohibited in 'benign' discrimination remedying disadvantages of members of a group resulting from past unlawful discrimination? Since their respective tolerance of race-conscious criteria has very different ambits, I take Mr Justice Powell's views and those of the Brennan Four separately.

For Mr Justice Powell the decisive point was that the benign discriminatory provision must be shown to be necessary for protecting a substantial *and* constitutionally permissible purpose or interest of the state.[14] Since what was to be justified in the *Bakke* case was the departure from equality involved in benign discrimination, it is obvious that the justifying 'purpose' or 'interest' invoked by Mr Justice Powell cannot be the attainment of equality in that same sense;

---

[13] *Bakke*, 18 Cal. 3d 34, 553 p. 2d 1152.

[14] 46 L. W. p. 4906, citing *In re Griffiths*, 413 US 717, 722–3 (1973). For a fuller analysis of the U.S. S.Ct.'s decisions see Julius Stone, 'Equal Protection ... Forward from Bakke' *Hastings Constitutional Law Quarterly*, Fall, 1979.

for then no question of its 'constitutional permissibility' would arise. At nearest, it might be the approximation to that condition—that is, in this case, to a percentage of minority entrants proportionate to that of the minorities in the general population. But this is precisely the purpose that Powell denies [at p. 4906] can ever be permissible under Title VI of the Civil Rights Act of 1964. There were other purposes of the University of California in the *Bakke case*, apart from the above rejected purpose of securing a percentage racial representation based on racial quotas, which (other requirements being met) Mr Justice Powell would regard as permissible. These were: (1) to ameliorate 'the disabling effects of identified discrimination' (p. 4906); (2) to improve delivery of minority health services (p. 4907); (3) to diversify the student body so as to produce a robust exchange of ideas, speculation, experiment, creation and so on [p. 4908]. Though some indirect relation to equality may possibly be found in the first of these other purposes, the values they represent can clearly not be expressed or contained in any norm of equality. So that for Mr Justice Powell some value other than equality was finally decisive.

At first sight, the same may be said in respect of the assertion by the Brennan Four that 'our cases have always implied that an 'overriding statutory purpose' could be found that would justify racial classification.'[15] This 'overriding purpose' seems to refer to values other than equality; otherwise how could it be said to 'override' the equality prescribed by the Equal Protection Clause?

Yet, on further analysis, the matter is more obscure. For the Brennan Four (disagreeing in this respect with Mr Justice Powell) held that even the fixing of numerical quotas proportionate to population was a permissible remedial measure against the effect of past discrimination[16] On this basis the 'overriding purpose' could be said to be the achievement of 'equality', albeit in a sense of equality different from that in title of which Bakke claimed that the remedial measures violated his claim to it, or which Mr Justice Blackmun called 'idealistic equality' [p. 4932]. Even this in-some-sense-equality-seeking purpose cannot, however, rehabilitate equality as the decisive value in play. For, by hypothesis, race-conscious criteria in remedial discriminatory preferences impair the equality of the non-preferred. So that the confrontation is between two vindications of 'equality'. Equality, being on both sides of the argument, cannot decide it as long as its meaning does not shift—as indeed it here does—from equality in the sense of application of a uniform rule, to equality in the sense of application of discriminating rules which, precisely by their discrimi-

---

[15] 46 L.W. 4896 at p. 4919, citing a string of cases, ending with *McDaniel* v. *Barresi*, 402 US 39 (1971) and *North Carolina State Board of Ed.* v. *Swann*, 402 US 43 (1971), supporting race-conscious desegregation plans in schools.

[16] L.W. 4896 at pp. 4921, 4924 and n. 58, Blackmun J. at p. 4932.

nation, increase the resultant factual equality (see above, section IV). Even if the only critical point is whether one meaning of equality still overrides the other, careful analysis must conclude that this point itself cannot be decided without reference to a value other than equality.

The majority positions, therefore, on the main issue in *Bakke* still support the present thesis as to the non-decisiveness of the equality notion in current rulings under the Equal Protection Clause, even when the remedy approved is by allocation of discriminating numerical quotas to redress under-representation of a particular race. But, of course, the Brennan Four would admit, under the tests they adopt, other 'important government objectives' (including presumably those mentioned above approved by Mr Justice Powell) as legitimating the discriminations involved in benign discrimination or affirmative action [p. 4920].

For the Brennan Four, as for Mr Justice Powell, therefore, it remains true that beyond the simplest cases of gross and grossly arbitrary exclusion of individuals from the justice-constituency, the values preferred by the judges, even in applying the constitutional norm of equal protection, are not contained within the notion of equality. Beyond those simplest cases, decisions require, if they are to be intellectually comprehended, to be referred to some wider value norm or norms of what is due between members of society. If we are unhappy with the term 'justice', which is a millennial symbol for such a wider norm, can we be much happier with the judicial reliance on 'important governmental objectives'?[17]

Mr Justice Blackmun's sensitively eloquent separate opinion almost expresses the present thesis, and certainly well illustrates it. He pointed out that 'governmental preference has not been a stranger to our legal life', instancing veterans, handicapped persons and Indians, even aside from the *ad hoc* constitutionally protected progressive income tax. Further, 'in order to treat some persons equally, we have to treat them unequally. We cannot—we dare not—let the Equal Protection Clause perpetrate racial supremacy' [p. 4933]. The inference is permissible that in his view equality is no more the final value-criterion which legitimates preference for those suffering from the effects of past racial discrimination than it is what legitimates preference for veterans, or handicapped persons, or Indians. With great respect, I would agree with this.

---

[17] Brennan Four opinion, 46 L.W. 4896 at p. 4920, citing *Califano* v. *Webster*, 430 US 313, at p. 316 (1977).

VII Equal protection under the US Constitution in general

The preceding section shows the spurious role that the presumption of equality plays in support of reverse discrimination. The same point can be ventured more generally about most other decision-making under the Equal Protection Clause.

In a notable analysis of this body of decisions, John Bishop[18] has observed that, in the face of the wide prevalence of severe inequalities among members of society, the choices which have to be made under the Equal Protection Clause are not between treating people equally and unequally but between justified unequal treatment and unjustified unequal treatment. He does not confront (naturally enough, in the context of the Equal Protection Clause) the important consequential question discussed in section III above, whether the incidence of justice-relevant inequalities—where equality must yield to other values—is so predominant that 'the presumption of equality' should be abandoned or even reversed. But at the least, whenever unequal treatment is held justified, the constitutional protection of 'equality' receives (as it were) new modalities.

The focus of the Equal Protection Clause is limited to infringements arising from state action, but the underlying theory of equality-as-justice is relevant to the ethical evaluation of all action. The more complex, wide-ranging and refined a legal order, the more will it proliferate masses of rules distributing benefits and burdens among social members. The rules will distribute scarce resources among members of society based on the facts stated in each rule. The set of facts on which each rule is predicated may be different from the facts of all different rules,[19] precisely because they are different rules. All these different sets of predicated facts involve differences of legal distributions corresponding to differences in persons, or differences in issues, or both. State action involving such differentiations is subject to judicial evaluation under the Equal Protection Clause. The corresponding evaluation in terms of justice is not so limited. In both spheres, the narrower and the wider, it is clear that the prescribed equality does not necessarily mean governance of all by the same rule. For such a meaning would strike down a great mass of rules of every legal system of any complexity.

To detect objectionable departures from uniform rules, American courts (as already mentioned) resort to various devices. One of these is

---

[18] J. Bishop, 'Justice as Equality in the New Equal Protection', mimeo paper, A.S. L.P./60a, Australian Society of Legal Philosophy (1974).

[19] Of course, there may be overlapping between rules, some times so great as to create a distinction without any difference, or meaningless category or convergence of rules. But this pertains to the imperfections of the particular rules.

the category of 'suspect classification', of which some of the earliest were classifications by skin colour or ancestry.[20] Even these classifications were not mechanically stricken down under the clause if it could be shown that under 'strict scrutiny' the classification was necessary to serve some 'compelling state interest'.[21] The Warren Court added to this category of requiring strict scrutiny those discriminating rules which, although not containing suspect classifications, have the effect of impairing the 'fundamental' rights or interests of the person to whom they applied.

These judicial inventions transcend the notion of equating justice with equality. The characterization of a classification as 'suspect' must spring from some value other than equality. That another value is the source is even clearer when rights or interests are characterized as 'fundamental'. Thus, the problems now debated in relation to the so-called 'new equal protection',[22] into which the *Bakke* rulings have to be fitted, may not be so new.

It was Justice Harlan who, in *Plessy* v. *Ferguson* [163 US 537, 559 (1896)], rejected the principle of separate but equal as satisfying equal protection and who formulated the oft-quoted aphorism that 'our constitution is colour blind.' It was another Justice Harlan, of a much later generation, who protested in his dissent in *Griffin* v. *Illinois* [351 US 12, 34 (1956)] that the majority holding under the Equal Protection Clause produced the anomalous result that a constitutional admonition to treat all persons 'equally' meant in that case that the state must provide free of cost to one class of persons that for which all others were required to pay. This result might still be explained in terms of equality if the interpretation of equality chosen is that one which yields a greater ('residual') equality between subjects after application of the rule, rather than that which requires only equality by uniform application of the same rule. But the criterion which

[20] The specific prohibition of bills of pains and penalties figures explicitly and separately in the constitutional amendments from the beginning.

[21] Though originating in decisions in the 1940s based on the equality implied from the Fifth Amendment due process clause, requiring strict scrutiny of *racial* classification (*Hirabashi* 320 US 81, esp. 100–102 (Stone, C.J.), 111–112 (Murphy J.) (1943) and *Korematsu* 323 US 214 (1945)), the so-called new equal protection was mainly elaborated to cover other than racial 'suspect categories', and the invasion of 'fundamental rights', by the Warren Court in the 1960s. See the discussion in Harlan J.'s dissent in *Shapiro* v. *Thompson* 394 US 618 (1969) endorsed by the majority in *San Antonio Independent School District* v. *Rodriguez* 411 US 1, at 31–34 (1973). On the 'newer' equal protection, see G. Gunther, '. . . A Model of a Newer Equal Protection' (1972) 86 *Harv.L.Rev.* 1–48.

[22] See *United Jewish Organizations* v. *Carey*, 430 US 144 (1977); *Shapiro* v. *Thompson*, 394 US 618 (1969); *Harper* v. *Virginia Board of Elections*, 383 US 663 (1966); *Reynolds* v. *Sims*, 377 US 533 (1964); *Douglas* v. *California*, 372 US 353 (1963); *Griffin* v. *Illinois*, 351 US 12 (1956).

would be decisive would be the one which leads to the choice of this version of equality, rather than the one requiring uniform application of the same rule. And *that* criterion is obviously some value *other than equality*.

Later cases confirm that more than a choice between two conflicting versions of equality is involved in the affirmative action requirement. The decisive final issue is not really apt for disposition in terms of equal protection of the laws; its meaning is more properly sought in terms of minimal acceptable standards of justice, or the avoidance of unacceptable arbitrariness and unreasonableness. In short, it points to the need for some kind of revived doctrine of substantive due process. The problem with this is, of course, that substantive due process is thought to be dead in American constitutional law, if not also buried.[23] When the majority in *Harper* v. *Virginia* [383 US 663 (1966)] suggested that a poll tax of $1.50 would violate equal protection not only of those unable to pay it but also of those unwilling to pay it, the decision cannot be explained under even the modality of 'residual' equality.

In any case, when affirmative action decisions are ostensibly drawn from the concept of equality, it is other policies or values on which the judgement is actually based. In *Shapiro* v. *Thompson* [394 US 618 (1969)] the majority held that a one year residence requirement in a state for entitlement to public assistance there violated equal protection; in reality, as Harlan's dissent points out, they were choosing between the value of fulfilling subsistence needs for all persons and the value of rewarding persons settling in the state on the basis of the merit (in the eyes of the State concerned) of continuous residence in that state.

This shift from decision-making based on justice identified with equality, to decision-making according to justice *tout court*, is also very manifest in the court's fixing upon impairment of fundamental rights or interests as grounds for requiring strict scrutiny. The constitutional precept of equality, after all, is in no way limited to fundamental rights and interests, so that classification of rights and interests as fundamental or not is no more than a peg on which the court hangs its straight judgement of justice, whether legal support of

---

[23] The US Supreme Court has not struck down a single economic regulation as violative of substantive due process since *Thompson* v. *Consolidated Gas Utilities Corp*, 300 US 55 (1937), in contrast with its decisions in the three decades preceding the landmark case of *Nebbia* v. *New York*, 291 US 502 (1934), during which numerous such regulations succumbed. Substantive due process has been decried by members of the present court, although the due process clause of the Fifth Amendment has been a tool used in expanding personal rights in the last decade. See, for example, *Shapiro* v. *Thompson*, 394 US 618 (1969), majority opinion by Brennan, J.

a particular kind or claim violates in some respect the tolerable minima of justice. Behind the equal protection complexities of *Serrano* v. *Priest*[24] is a judgement of justice about the place of quality of education among these tolerable minima. Moreover, the range of rights and interests labelled fundamental is more varied, and certainly more capricious, than the range of suspect classifications. And the puzzles of equal protection become even more perplexing when the judgement depends on the interaction between *degree* of 'suspectness' and *degree* of 'fundamentalness'.

VIII What must then be salvaged of the equality criterion?

At this point we may perhaps take stock of the rule that the equality notion can play in the drama of justice, and the roles that it cannot play. The only indubitable role (as seen above, pp. 101–3) seems to be at what has been here called the preliminary threshold level, at which the assertion of the equality of human beings requires that all human beings physically within, or within the sway of, the community be taken into account as members of the justice-constituency.

Equality in humanness as a basis for including all humans among the members of the justice-constituency in which they are found, however, tells us nothing (as seen above, p. 101) about their equality or inequality in other respects. It may be argued, contrary to this, that equality in humanness carries at least one other clear precept of justice—namely that all members of the justice-constituency are entitled to the minimum material resources of food, shelter and medical care necessary for maintaining biological existence. The entitlement of all human beings to such minimal material subsistence is undoubtedly a requirement of justice. But it is quite superfluous to introduce equality as an explanation of this. The subsistence entitlement, as sanctified for example in the considerable achievements of this kind in Western welfare states, is adequately explained by the very fact of common humanness. It adds nothing to the claims of all members of society to humanness to say that they are *equally* human. The justice-duty arises from the biological needs of human beings not from any philosophical superstructure of equality we mount upon these.

A similar answer has to be made to the somewhat more ambitious argument that equality also prescribes minimal educational, intellectual and political endowments, converging into a right of each freely to form and express his demands and opinions and have them responded to along with those of others by those in authority. It has indeed, been my view, *in no way dependent on the equality notion*, that

---

[24] 5 Cal. 3d 584, p. 2d 1241, 96 Cal. Rptr. 601 (1971); *contra, San Antonio Independent School District* v. *Rodriguez*, 411 US 1 (1973).

the very nature of Western democratic societies, as dedicated to the maximum possible satisfaction of human demands, requires that such a minimal endowment of mind and spirit be regarded as a virtual absolute of justice in such societies. In such societies (I wrote in 1946):

> The irreducible minimum requirement of legal justice is in a broad sense procedural. It is that society shall be so organized that men's felt wants can be freely expressed; and that the law shall protect that expression, and provide it with the channels through which it can compete effectively for (though not necessarily attain) the support of politically organized society. The special importance of the claim to free expression and its implications have been repeatedly stressed in this work; it carries with it vital corollaries notably as to the responsibility of those who exercise power.[25]

This precept rests on the mere fact of membership in a justice-constituency dedicated by hypothesis to the maximum satisfaction of human demands. Here again it seems not necessary to resort to the notion of equality as its basis. Participation of all members of a community in its affairs is better seen as an immediate presupposition of justice in a society so dedicated.

Nor is the equality notion any more necessary or adequate, even if we were to suppose that the material resources of a community were inadequate to meet the biological subsistence-needs of all the members. If, for example, we supposed that only 10 per cent of the subsistence-needs of all members of a society can be met, there is no persuasive reason why we should decide to condemn all the community to death by sharing those inadequate resources *equally* among them, rather than draw lots for the 10 per cent of the community who should use the available resources in order to survive; or rather than allow the 10 per cent of youngest adults to survive; or rather than allow the 10 per cent who are most talented to survive; or (even) rather than allow to survive the 10 per cent comprising the youngest persons and sufficient number of related adults required to look after them. Any of these, perhaps even others, could be argued for; and the choice of one or other (or some combination of them) is a matter too complex, wide and momentous to be dictated by equality. What are involved are wider values for which we use the symbol 'justice' or some similar symbol. And, of course, even for justice the question would be clearer than the answer.

IX Perils of pretending that equality is justice

I have argued that there is no pot of justice at the end of the rainbow of equality. Even when the equality notion is explicitly sanctified as a constitutional precept, as in the Equal Protection Clause, wider

[25] Julius Stone, *The Province and Function of Law* (Sydney, 1946, reprinted 1961, 1968), at p. 785.

concepts of justice have to be invoked to give it meaning. This should the less surprise us in view of the treacherous nests of ambiguities, antinomies and even contradictions concealed within the equality notion.

Finally, I wish now to identify some dangers and distortions to justice which may result when, despite all this, equality is treated, without adequate empirical basis, even if only presumptively, as the equivalent of justice.

First, when we indulge the presumption of equality, and this presumption is unrebutted, justice may be going the way of equality on a mere mechanical test of burden of proof. Yet lawyers, at least, do not need to be reminded that the mere test of the burden of proof does not warrant a conclusion *as true*. Similarly, this mechanical test of burden of proof about justice does not warrant a conclusion *as just*.

Second, conversely, when the opponent in the contest for justice does succeed in rebutting the presumption of equality by showing justice-relevant differences, equality still does not, even then, guide us to justice. For it is admitted on all sides that when relevant differences are shown, justice requires not equality but rather differentiation in distribution or treatment. We then still have to look for criteria other than equality corresponding to the justice-relevant differences.

The evils of the presumption of equality, however, are not merely these negative ones that it may direct us to an 'equality' which is unjust, or leave us stranded on shores of justice for which equality has no maps. A More positive evil is that, in so far as we thus reduce justice to equality, we may fall into habits of thought which obfuscate the real tasks basic to the doing of justice in contemporary Western democracies. These are, first and above all, the identification and explication of differences between human beings which are relevant to making justifiable discriminations between them; and, second, the structuring of justice-rules corresponding to these differences.

This point should, perhaps, be restated more directly. The appeal to justice, which is so persistent and endless in human society, prods us to provide reasons why some solutions proposed as 'just' deserve more approval than others or than the *status quo*, or why situations condemned as 'unjust' deserve corresponding disapproval. It drives toward recognition and articulation about the values which men are pressing for sanctification as worthy of general approval and (in this sense) just. More important still, it challenges us to select among these values those supported by the reasons we find strongest, or to make adjustments between them and other values by compromise and sacrifice of more or less of each. These processes of recognition, articulation, persuasion by reasons, selection and adjustment are all critical parts of the maturation and refinement of human society.

Yet the effect of simplifying justice into equality is to conceal, truncate, foreclose or disguise by fictional or ambiguous formulae the range of values involved in justice-controversies. By the same token it tends to impede or block or confuse the above essential processes. And I agree, not least in this, with Roberto Unger[26] that the predicament of liberal society will repeat itself unless we recognize the need for (and, I would add, manage to find) 'criteria by which to choose between different ways of ranking, among legitimate and illegitimate uses of power and among permissible and prohibited inequalities'.

No Western people has shown the sweep of concern with justice, or probed more deeply into its relevance to all aspects of a complex economically organized democratic society, than the people of the United States. No people has struggled more earnestly to hold on to the enclaves of justice which it has won against the surrounding wilderness and against the divisions within itself.

Precisely because of this appreciation and admiration for American achievements, I find myself dismayed by the rather demonic efforts to find simple answers to the grave questions of justice of this last quarter-century by expeditions into the slough of equality. Distinguished students of the Equal Protection Clause have lamented (as already observed) the inadequacy of judicial reasonings which now weaken the application of that clause to the values of human personality. This paper signals a wider fear for the whole arena of human justice, if we continue to seek shortcuts to justice through mirages hovering over the slough of equality.

---

[26] Roberto Mangabeira Unger, *Law in Modern Society* (New York, 1976), pp. 239–40.

6

Marxism, liberalism and justice

Wiesław Lang

In this chapter I shall counterpose the Marxist idea of justice with contemporary bourgeois theories of justice. The first part is devoted to a reconstruction of Karl Marx's basic outlook upon the problem of justice and to characterizing the main tendencies in the progress of ideas and practices relating to justice in socialist countries today. The second part deals critically with what I take to be the most representative bourgeois theories of justice. Here, I am mainly concerned with normative theories of justice in their material aspect, especially with theories of social justice. Meta-ethical aspects of the theory of justice and problems of legal justice, especially the theory of retributive justice, are dealt with only marginally.

I The Marxist concept of justice

Reconstructing Marx's concept of justice has been the subject of numerous philosophical works of a Marxological nature. The general outline presented here therefore does not claim to be especially original.[1]

The main difficulty in reconstructing Marx's views on justice lies in the fact that Marx in his works did not treat the concept of justice as an autonomous subject. The term 'justice' appears in Marx's writing mainly in connection with his critique of bourgeois ideals and

---

1 See. R. Dahrendorf, *Marx in Perspektive: Die Idee des Gerechten im Denken von Karl Marx* (Hanover, 1953); R. C. Tucker, *Philosophy and Myth in Karl Marx* (Cambridge, 1961); G. Vlastos, 'Justice and Equality', in Richard B. Brandt (ed.), *Social Justice* (New Jersey, 1962), pp. 31–72; R. Hancock, 'Marx's Theory of Justice', *Social Theory and Practice* 1, pt. 3 (1971), pp. 65–71; G. Temkin, *Karola Marksa obraz gosodarki komunistycznej* (Karl Marx's Vision of the Communist Economy, Warsaw, 1962). For my presentation of the Marxian idea of justice, I am most indebted to E. Żyro, 'Aksjologiczna treść pojęcia sprawiedliwości w pogladach Karola Marksa' (The Axiological Content of the Notion of Justice in the Thought of Karl Marx), *Etyka* no. 1 (1966), pp. 191–219.

concepts of justice and with the critique of social relations based on private ownership of the means of production. The idea of justice is included within the critique of those social relations which Marx calls unjust and in the Marxian vision of the communist society. Therefore, a purely semantic analysis of the meaning of the term 'justice' in Marx's works is not the right method of reconstructing the Marxian idea of justice.

It is by no means unintentional that Marx eschews abstract analysis of the concept of 'justice in general'. This is in conformity with Marx's motto, 'philosophers have so far only interpreted the world; the point is to change it.' Marx's philosophy is first of all a practical one, a philosophy of action. In Marxist philosophy justice is not a ready abstract formula invented by philosophers by means of purely intellectual operations of learning, part of 'the world of values'. It is rather an ideal of relations among people created in practical activity, especially in the historical process of the struggle of progressive social classes for abolishing inhuman conditions of existence. Radical humanism, according to which 'man is the highest being for a man', is the philosophical premise of the Marxist critique of capitalistic social relations. This fundamental consequence of the critique of religion, the axiological assumption of Marxism, is for Marx equivalent to the categorical demand for abolishing all those relations in which man is a humiliated, enslaved, forsaken and contemptible being. For Marx that kind of relation is unjust. Social relations based on the exploitation of man by another man, those in which the producers of goods, constituting the majority of people, have no control over the means of production and the fruits of their work, are then clearly unjust. 'Though the world of civilization and culture is the work of all people,' Marx writes in the *German Ideology*, 'yet first [it is the work of] all of the working people.' But only the privileged part of the society takes advantage of goods of this world and provides for its own needs at the expense of the working classes. Since Marx denoted all forms of harm done to men as unjust, he undoubtedly saw as just the absence of exploitation of man by man and the elimination of plunder, subjugation, discrimination, and privilege at the expense of others. The social relations that consist in living off one's own work, using the fruits of one's labour and disposing over it oneself—that is just for Marx.

The principles defining such a state of relations he labels the 'ordinary principles of justice' [Żyro, p. 199]. It is the practical and theoretical negation of inhuman social relations, that is, of relations destroying fundamental generic features of man, which leads to the formation of a positive purview of the concept of justice in Marxian philosophy. The idea of justice is defined by the leading axiological assumptions constituting the ethical basis of the critique of the existing social relations. Justice means granting each individual what he deserves in virtue of his humanity. In its broad meaning, it is understood by Marx as a principle of granting each human individual suitable rights irrespectively of any social contribution whatsoever. People are to be treated equally not because of their actual equality in some respect, but just because they are people.[2] This is expressed in the Marxian formula, 'from each according to his capacities, to each according to his needs.' It is a principle that leads to much controversy because it may be interpreted variously according to the axiological assumptions on which the interpretation is based. In the light of Marxian philosophy, it is a radically egalitarian concept of justice, although it does not imply a naive belief that there is a natural equality of people or that all people have identical needs.

Only elementary needs indispensable to the maintenance of the physical existence of man, such as the needs of food, sleep, satisfying the sexual urge, clothing, shelter and so on, are common to all people. Meeting those needs is necessary to develop and meet higher needs which are different for different people. According to Marx, people are equal only in the sphere of elementary needs. Granting all persons an equal right to satisfy and develop various needs and secure optimal conditions for their realization in a style of life worthy of man is the consequence of the principle 'to everyone according to one's needs'. Of course, the way in which people take advantage of the equal, objective conditions which give them equal opportunities of shaping their own personalities and their own concepts of life may be significantly different, just as individual styles of life may differ, although all these are realized according to the principle 'to each according to his needs'. The realization of this principle, however, does not mean the unlimited satisfaction of all possible, individual needs. There are many factors limiting the range of individual needs which can be satisfied. Among these factors the following seem to be most important:

1.   the objective, potential opportunities of individuals as limited by their genetic endowment (the limitation is due to the first part of the formula 'from each according to his capacities');
2.   the objective technological, cultural and economic possibilities a society has of satisfying different needs of the people;
3.   the system of values and rules dominant in the society. The principle 'to each according to his needs' should be interpreted as follows: to each according to his needs within the bounds of the physical and mental abilities of the given human individual, within the bounds of the objective possibilities of the society for realizing a state of things that would satisfy definite needs and within the limits set by

[2] See Vlastos, p. 48; Żyro, p. 201.

basic norms and values dominating in the society. Only the needs conformable with all these limitations are to be considered as reasonable and morally acceptable needs which ought to be satisfied.

The role played by desert, based on an individual's contribution to the production of socially useful goods, in the Marxist concept of justice as expressed in the principle 'to each according to his needs' remains an open problem. In spite of some appearances it seems to me that this idea is intrinsic to the genuine Marxian concept of justice. Within the principle, 'to each according to his needs', for individuals capable of doing socially useful work contribution to such work (desert) is the only moral basis for benefiting from the limited quantity of goods and for participation in their distribution. The requirement of contributing socially useful work for individuals capable of such work, however, is not a criterion or measure for distributing goods among people. According to Marx, the ideal of social justice based on the principle of 'to each according to his needs' can be fully achieved only in the classless communist society, his general vision of which he sketched in his *Critique of the Gotha Programme*. Full collectivization of the means and tools of production and the achievement of a high standard of development of productive forces, enabling an abundance of goods to be produced, are the objective preconditions for realizing the postulate, 'to each according to his needs'. Nevertheless, in his *Critique* Marx criticized the concept of the equal distribution of income because he considered human individuals unequal as far as their capacities and needs are concerned.

Apart from the fundamental, broad concept of justice as an ideal whose realization is to take place in communist society, Marx formulates a narrower concept of justice expressed in the following formula: 'from each according to his capacity, to each according to his work.' Justice is understood here as granting a man what he deserves in accordance with his contribution to work.

According to this principle, not only socially useful work itself but the worker's effort and the social value of the work and especially its results are the moral foundation for measures and criteria for the qualitative and quantitative apportioning of goods. This principle of justice in the narrow meaning is to be realized in the socialist system, which is the first progressive phase of communism as a social formation. Realization of the ideal of social justice in the broad meaning is limited in the socialist system because elements of marketing still play a significant role and the quantity of produced goods is limited and therefore has to be distributed according to desert. Socialism abolishes economic grounds for the exploitation of man by man, but as Lenin emphasizes, unjust social differences connected with the realization of the principle, 'to each according to his work', will remain in socialism.

The two principles of social justice—'to each according to his work' and 'to each according to his needs'—are formulated by Marx as principles governing the two successive phases of development of the socialist-communist formation (socialism and communism). They seem to have no intrinsic meaning and can only be properly comprehended on the basis of the whole outlook constituting the theory of scientific socialism.

Within the structure of that theory, both principles are subordinated to a superior one, to the principle of the actual equality of opportunities. This is the radical principle of social equality, the main core of the Marxian concept of justice in the broad meaning. It is the superior principle of justice in the phase of socialism and of communism, although its realization takes a different course in each of these phases. When detached from the principle of equality of opportunity, the two remaining principles lose the sense they are given in Marxist philosophy and acquire a thoroughly different meaning. The principle, 'to each according to his work', detached from the principle of equal opportunities becomes the principle of competitive meritocracy, while the principle, 'to each according to his needs', justifies all kinds of social inequalities in the sphere of distribution of goods; it can be interpreted as a principle justifying an aristocratic or caste social order.[3]

The principles of social justice in its broad and narrow meaning as formulated by Marx are undoubtedly principles of distributive justice, because they concern distribution of goods in society. However, it seems wrong to interpret the Marxist theory of society as involving a concept of distributive justice exclusively. According to Marx the distribution of consumption goods in a society is determined by the system or distribution of ownership of the means of production. This latter distribution is a feature of the mode of production itself. A just distribution of material goods was not the final moral good for Marx. He explicitly warned against understanding scientific socialism as a theory of distribution of goods. In *The Critique of the Gotha Programme* he criticized primitive communism, which reduces justice in human interrelations to a just distribution of goods; for him to do this was to remain under the influence of private property, to universalize it instead of abolishing it. The intrinsic sense of the Marxian ideal of justice achievable in communist society is the liberation of the individual from the negative consequences of private ownership of the means of production and from slavish subordination to the division of labour. There is thus a marked connection between the Marxian theory of justice and the theory of alienation and

[3] See J. Danecki, 'Marksowska koncepcja równości spolecznej: Próba rekonstruckcji i interpretacji' (The Marxian Concept of Social Equality: an Attempt at Reconstruction and Interpretation), *Studia Nauk Politycznych* 1 (1972), pp. 9–32.

emancipation. The essential injustice of a social system based on the private ownership of means of production consists in divorcing the producers from control over the means of production and the products of their work, as well as turning work, a generic feature of man, into an activity which serves only to satisfy individual needs. Communism as a system making real the Marxian ideal of social justice is aimed at creating social conditions in which work will become man's most important need and the intrinsic moral value that makes sense of human existence. This does not mean any work whatever, but meaningful work. Work can be meaningful when producers of goods have full control over the means and conditions of work and over the social utilization of its results. Work becomes meaningful only when the division between the productive function of work and its political and social aspects is abolished.[4] The right to meaningful work is through the Marxian ideal of justice as a funda-mental human right, a basic social value. No consumption good is equivalent to the value of meaningful work. Lack of opportunity of doing meaningful work can not be compensated for by any welfare services. The right to meaningful work differs remarkably from the right to employment guaranteed in constitutions of some capitalist countries to today. Participation in the control of conditions of work, and of the distribution and social utilization of produced goods, gives human work moral sense, makes it meaningful.

The economic effectiveness of a social system is also a relevant value from the point of view of the Marxist concept of justice. The contradiction between productive forces and social relations finds its expression in the consciousness of the working classes as a negative moral evaluation of outdated relations of production, which have become fetters on productive forces and make impossible the full utilization of the manufacturing potential of production or its further development for the good of the society. Such relations are considered unjust. But social relations stimulating the development of productive forces usually receive a positive moral appreciation.

In Marxist philosophy, the concept of justice remains in close connection with the Marxian concept of morality, although the classics of Marxism were not explicit about the mutual inter-relationship of the two notions. The concept of a morality based on Marxism seems broader than that of justice. Differences in the objective sphere seem to be the following:

1.   Moral norms mainly regulate relations among human individuals. Principles of justice concern primarily all relations between the

---

[4] A. Eshete, 'Contractarianism and the Scope of Justice', *Ethics* LXXXV (1974), pp. 38–49.

individual and the society and between social groups and classes [Żyro, p. 217].

2. Justice is claim-oriented. Principles of justice, among other things, define claims of individuals in relation to the society and morally justifiable rights of the society concerning individuals (laying on them duties concerning the society).

Morality, however, is conceived by Marx not only as a system of commands, prohibitions and mutual claims, but also as a set of principles regarding mutual goodwill among people. This is a super-rogatory concept of morality which does not restrict man to granting another what he deserves but tells him to give much more.

The Marxian idea of justice is a dynamic, open concept shaped in the process of historical development of societies. Therefore Marx opposed the ideals of a just social system as formulated by utopian socialists. The realization of justice in the narrow meaning ('to each according to his work') proved to be much more complicated in the practice of the socialist countries which came into existence in the twentieth century than Marx had anticipated in *The Critique of the Gotha Programme*. Difficulties and limitations in the realization of the Marxian concept of social justice appeared in socialist countries mainly in connection with their historical genesis and the historical conditions of their development. In spite of Marx's and Engels's former expectations, but in accordance with the prognosis formulated by Lenin, underdeveloped countries and those exhausted by the two last world wars were the first countries to enter along the path of socialism. 'Catching up' and fast industrialization were the basic duties to be realized in those countries in the period of the construction of the foundations of socialism. In the first phase of the construction of socialism, postulates of justice had to be partly subordinated to the requirements of the political stabilization of the socialist system, the consolidation of its defence forces and accelerated economic development. The objective difficulties consequent on these unfavourable starting conditions, and especially those arising from the requirements of economic development, have resulted in substantial limitations in realizing the principle, 'to each according to his work.' The inequalities in distribution of national product among different social and professional groups play, to some extent, the role of a stimulator in the development of important branches of the national economy or of different regions of the country. The criteria of social distribution of primary goods are based not only on the principle, 'to each according to his work', but also on reasons of a purely economic character. Apart from the economic factor, the sources of some economic inequalities in a developed socialist country include the different genetic endowment of individuals, the institution of the family as a fundamental social unit of the socialist community and the law of inheritance in the sphere of personal property, still in force in socialist countries. On the other hand, the realization of the principle, 'to each according to his work', is limited in practice by the social policy of socialist countries, which tends to maintain the egalitarian structure of socialist societies and guarantees the realization of the principle of equal opportunities as the basic principle of social justice. The following social ventures are aimed at the realization of a certain minimum of basic services, accessible for all people on equal terms:

1. Providing a certain minimal equal standard of living for all citizens regardless of their individual desert. This especially concerns such basic goods as natural environment, health services, housing and primary education.

2. Limitation of the gap between individual incomes. Income still remains a measure of desert, but within the bounds and proportions limited by law.

3. Providing for disabled people suitable living conditions corresponding with the general standard of living of the society.

The postulates of social justice in the broad meaning which find expression in the principle, 'to each according to his needs', might have seemed utopian in the nineteenth century, yet they have become fully realizable in the second half of the twentieth century as a result of the prospects and changes created by the scientific and technological revolution. In particular, the prospect of a technological overcoming of the basic limitations and negative features of industrial civilization, connected with the division of labour and with the stultifying discipline of industrial production, has essential significance for the realization of justice in the future communist society.

II Bourgeois theories of justice

In contemporary Marxist-Leninist theory we can distinguish three types of evaluations, with regard to philosophical doctrines constituting the subject of critical analysis—substantive, methodological and functional. These types correspond with three aspects on the basis of which Marxist theory considers social and philosophical doctrines. Substantive evaluation is an evaluation of the statements contained in a doctrine from the point of view of the values of truth or falsehood. Methodological evaluation is based on the instrumental evaluation of the value of the methods applied in the criticized theory for formulating and solving problems which are the subject of the said theory. Functional evaluation is an evaluation of the ideological role which the criticized theory plays in given historical conditions. According to the hypothetical presupposition of Marxist theory, every social or philosophical theory plays a 'eufunctional' or dysfunctional role in relation to a specified social arrangement and to basic social groups (social classes) singled out by the structure of the said arrangement. A functional analysis of a theory strives to explain both the historical genesis of the theory and its function in the social arrangement under study.

Various kinds of relations of a rather complicated character take place between the types of evaluation distinguished. These are not linear deterministic relations. The ideological function of a theory has an essential influence upon its cognitive and methodological value. But the evaluation of the ideological function does not univocally prejudge the evaluation of the theory's cognitive and methodological value. The truth or falsehood of the theory's propositions is independent of the evaluation of its ideological function as reactionary, conservative or progressive.[5]

The ideological character of bourgeois theories does not in the least negatively prejudge their cognitive value. The opinion that the ideological character of a theory strips it of scientific value requires the acceptance of two assumptions which I regard as completely false.

1. That a scientific theory is by definition free from valuation.
2. That any ideology constitutes a distortion of the reflection of reality.

The first assumption implies that there is possible a 'pure' non-ideological and non-evaluating social theory or social philosophy. Assumptions of this kind constitute a particular type of neo-positivist fallacy. The second assumption has its original source in the early Marxian concept of ideology as set out in the *German Ideology*, and also as developed in Karl Mannheim's sociology of knowledge. I do not accept this point of view. I follow rather the concept of ideology elaborated on the ground of the modern Marxist–Leninist philosophy, which defines ideology in purely functional terms, regardless of the cognitive value of the propositions qualified as ideological. I also do not accept a primitive, now discarded, interpretation of Marxism, according to which the truth of a theory is equivalent to its social progressiveness while every contemporary bourgeois theory is by definition reactionary and false.

Almost all bourgeois theories of justice are linked with liberal ideology, with liberal economic, political and philosophical doctrine. The concept of justice implied by classical liberal doctrine constitutes

[5] Jerzy Kmita, 'Norma metodologicznego neutralizmu aksjologicznego' (A Norm of Methodological Axiological Neutralism), in Ilja Lazari Pawłowska (ed.), *Metaletyka* (Warsaw, 1975), pp. 463–85.

the moral justification of the mechanisms of the capitalist free market economy. According to this theory, the justice of the apportioning of goods is assured automatically by the mechanisms of the capitalist market, supplemented by judicial law enforcement which sanctions the individual outcomes of the market game. The moral source of the justice of the market system is the principle *'laisser faire—laisser passer.'* The legal equality of the persons competing on the market is the safeguard of the fairness of the market game, considered to be fair competition. There are no extra-market standards for evaluating the distribution of goods. The just distribution is the distribution which is the result of the proper functioning of the market. The assumptions of the classical liberal doctrine make impossible the formulation of any specific problems of social justice considered as distributive justice.

The philosophical underpinning of the liberal theory is utilitarian ethical philosophy. Already in the nineteenth century two trends were to be distinguished in the development of the liberal theory—a humanitarian, progressive and reformist trend represented mostly by John Stuart Mill and a conservative anti-egalitarian trend advanced by Herbert Spencer. Spencer's concept of justice was based on a specific interpretation of Darwin's theory of evolution. The representatives of both trends were committed to the problem of improving the social conditions of the market economy (Mill) or morally justifying the social outcomes of this economy (Spencer).

The crisis of classical liberal economic and political theory in the twentieth century is linked with the historical shift of the capitalist formation from the free market economy phase to the phase of corporate monopolistic capitalism and with the sweeping structural crisis of the capitalist system. The inefficiency of the market mechanisms in the sphere of the regulation of fundamental socio-economic processes has become evident. The bourgeois liberal state is breaking down and the capitalist welfare state is emerging. The historical landmarks of our century are the successful proletarian revolutions, the coming into being of the socialist states, the breakdown of the old colonialism, and the successful struggle for the liberation of the people living in the areas of former colonies. The egalitarian idea of social justice formulated by the Marxist philosophy and advanced in the programmes of the communist and socialist movement becomes the watchword of the struggle of the working classes in the whole world. 'It seems very likely that at some later date our own age may be described as the age of egalitarian movements,' Thomas Platt writes.[6] Social justice has become the central issue for contemporary bourgeois political and legal thought. As A. M. Honoré has written:

[6] Thomas Platt, 'Equality Actual and Legal', *Journal of Social Philosophy* VI (1975), at p. 14.

During the last century the emphasis has shifted from analysis of justice *tourt court* to that of social justice. Indeed justice by itself no longer arouses the responses it once did. Perhaps this is because modern social and economic developments have made it clear that individual justice, justice between wrongdoer and victim, is only a partial and incomplete form of justice. We find that in this century the notion of social justice has everywhere received attention.[7]

In the first half of this century the answer of bourgeois ethical philosophy to the increasing demand for a philosophical under-pinning of the idea of social justice was mainly negative. It consisted in the tendency to avoid or eliminate the problem of social justice in the field of scientific investigation. In ethical philosophy the discussion was reduced to the controversy between traditional natural law concepts of justice and modern relativistic meta-ethical theories, strictly linked with the neo-positivist model of science. The limitation of the philosophical discussion to these two conceptions, considered as contradicting and excluding each other, made impossible the formulation of the problem of social justice on the plane of ethical discourse. The conceptual framework of traditional natural law theories was not appropriate for dealing with the specific problems of social justice in the twentieth century, while the meta-ethical theories of justice exclude *a priori* the formulation or consideration of any concept of social justice. The methodological assumption of these theories was a strict distinction between the ethical and meta-ethical point of view. They explicitly limited the scope of scientific discussion on ethical and moral matters exclusively to the meta-ethical plane. Ethics is conceived as the logical study of language and becomes irrelevant to the real moral issues. All ethical questions in the proper sense of the word (normative questions) are characterized as unem-pirical, unscientific. Consequently all problems of justice in the material sense, particularly all concepts of social justice, are also characterized as unscientific. Material concepts of justice become merely the rationalizations of emotional or non-rational individual attitudes. The discussion of the concept of justice has been limited mostly to the meta-ethical analysis of justice in the formal sense identified with legal justice and with the principle of impartiality. The contribution of twentieth-century moral philosophy to the solution of pressing social problems has been minimal.

A remarkable shift in bourgeois social and ethical philosophy is to be observed since the 1960s. The neo-positivist model of science and the heuristic value of the conceptual distinction of ethics and meta-ethics has been challenged. This change of approach to ethical problems on the plane of methodology and the theory of science has resulted in the

---

[7] A. M. Honoré, 'Social Justice', in R. S. Summers (ed.), *Essays in Legal Philosophy* (Oxford, 1968), p. 61.

scientific rehabilitation of the problems of normative ethics. Justice in a material sense, including the concepts of social justice, has become the object of ethical theories developing rational underpinnings for the concept of justice.

The ideological function of contemporary theories of justice is defined by their relation toward the basic structure of society, that is, the system of ownership of the means of production. This relation also constitutes a basic criterion of the functional classification of contemporary theories of justice. On the basis of this criterion, contemporary Western theories of justice may be divided into two fundamental groups—conformist and nonconformist. Conformist theories directly or indirectly accept the capitalist economic structure based on private ownership of the means of production, whereas nonconformist theories challenge the capitalist economic and social system of private ownership of the means of production from the point of view of principles of justice. Most Western theories of justice have a conformist character. Clearly nonconformist theories of justice are the theories based on Marxist–Leninist philosophy. The acceptance of the capitalist socio-economic structure appears in conformist theories in various forms: (a) direct acceptance (apologetics); (b) acceptance hidden by reticence through by-passing the question of economic structure; (c) indirect acceptance consisting in the acceptance of the opinion that the society's economic structure (the system of ownership of the basic means of production) is completely irrelevant to the problem of social justice; (d) indirect acceptance consisting in the philosophical negation of the objective standards of a justice-oriented evaluation of the economic structure of the society (emphasizing the subjective character of values and of any moral evaluation of the economic structure).

Conformist theories justify both the fundamental social inequalities of contemporary highly developed capitalist states and the fundamental social and economic mechanisms—the source of existing inequalities.

These theories differ from each other in the following points:

1. the evaluation of the present state of social inequalities (proper, too great, too small);
2 the views concerning the need for certain changes in the existing division of the national income, and consequently, the answers to questions whether and to what degree the disproportions existing in the social division of basic necessities should be reduced or evened out by way of a limited redistribution of the national income carried out through extra-market mechanisms, in particular through the social policy of the state;
3. the evaluation of the functioning of social and political mech-

anisms performing an equalizing redistribution of the national income;

4. theoretical concepts justfying, in the ethical sphere, the present state of social inequalities or the efforts to correct the state's social policy.

Differing opinions on the last question play the most essential role. In the sphere of conformist theories, controversies concern the method of moral justification of the existing state of things and problems of ethical standards relevant to the underpinning of current justice-oriented attitudes, more than a substantive evaluation of the actual state of social inequalities and postulates concerning its change. Most conformist theories are compatible in the basic scope of their ideas relating to the moral evaluation of basic social inequalities and methods of limiting them. They differ, however, from each other in their theoretical justifications.

I suggest the following classification of the main types of conformist theories: (1) liberal conservative theories, appearing both in their extreme (Hayek) as well as in their more moderate versions (Nozick, Bell); (2) progressive-reformist theories, among which we may distinguish (a) liberal theories, (b) egalitarian theories, (c) post-industrial theories (connected with the myth of post-industrial society; (3) reactionary theories, among which biological-genetic and cultural theories (Blanfield, Jensen, Shockley) play a fundamental role.

All conformist theories, except those of a clearly reactionary character, are liberal theories. But they are liberal in different senses because they value differently liberty and equality. The conservative and reactionary theories have their original source in the anti-egalitarian interpretation of liberal doctrine advanced by Herbert Spencer. They take a clearly anti-socialist and anti-communist ideological stand. They also criticize and totally reject the theoretical concepts and the practices of the capitalist welfare state. The reformist theories of justice are historically linked with the progressive and humanitarian trend of liberalism developed by John Stuart Mill. These theories develop the theoretical and axiological underpinning of the theory and practice of the welfare state. They can be properly considered welfare state theories, although they give clear preference to the capitalist and economic system and reject communist ideas of social justice.

Liberal conservative theories of justice

The most representative liberal conservative theories of justice are those of F. Hayek and R. Nozick.[8] F. A. Hayek's concept of justice is

[8] F. A. Hayek, *The Road to Serfdom* (Chicago, London and Sydney, 1944); *The*

an integral part of his general idea of society and social development, particularly of his theory of economy, state, law, politics and morality. Hayek totally rejects the idea of purposeful and conscious human activity aimed at the formation of a social system. He particularly rejects the possibility of the purposeful formation of a social or economic system based on a preconceived model of social justice (distributive justice) or on ethical standards accepted consciously in advance. Hayek puts forward underpinning arguments based on a theory of knowledge, a theory of the development of institutions and a theory of human nature. Any purposeful pattern-oriented social policy is impossible, he argues, because human knowledge is too limited, because the most rational social economic and political institutions emerge spontaneously in the course of historical evolution and because human nature is anti-social and egoistic.

There are no scientific laws of social development, and knowledge of social facts gives no premises for the far-reaching prediction of social developments. The conscious and deliberate construction of a social system therefore cannot be based on scientific grounds. Economic and political settings which emerge in the long run of history as by-products of spontaneous, even of irrational, human practices have proved to be superior in rationality and efficiency to institutions created consciously according to rational preconceived patterns, far-reaching plans and projects. While Hayek's approach to social change and social engineering is, in many respects, very close to Karl Popper's philosophy of science, it is even more radical and less consistent. He rejects so-called piecemeal engineering, which Popper considers an appropriate means of purposeful, conscious social change in an open society, but on the other hand calls for great social change in contemporary capitalist states. He demands restoration of the free market economy by the abolition of the institutions of the welfare system and by the limitation of the role and activities of monopolistic corporations which disturb the functioning of the free market and challenge the principle of fair competition. He considers the carrying out of these reforms a necessary condition for the full implementation of commutative justice.

Constitution of Liberty (Chicago and London, 1960); *Individualism and Economic Order* (Chicago and London, 1948); *The Confusion of Language in Political Thought, with some Suggestions for Remedying It*, Institute of Economic Affairs, Occasional Paper no. 20 (London, 1968); *Law, Legislation and Liberty* 1, *Rules and Order* (Chicago and London, 1973); R. Nozick, *Anarchy, State and Utopia* (New York and Oxford, 1974).
In my presentation and critical analysis of Hayek and Nozick's views, I have profited from an unpublished doctoral thesis by Wojciech Sadurski, assistant professor in the Faculty of Law of Warsaw University, 'Polityczna aksjologia neoliberalizmu' (Political Axiology of Neoliberalism Exemplified in F. A. Hayek's Theory, 1977). This dissertation also contains an excellent Marxist analysis of the concept of commutative justice.

Hayek also develops an axiological argument against the ideas of social planning or engineering. The implementation of an ideal of social justice considered as distributive justice is not only theoretically and practically impossible for him, but it is also inadmissible from the standpoint of the supreme moral values accepted by Hayek, especially from the standpoint of the value of personal individual liberty. The moral justification of the collective promotion of social justice can be based only on the idea of the objectivity of values or on general agreement concerning the fundamental values which are supposed to be promoted. But values are individual and subjective and no general agreement on fundamental values, especially on principles of justice, can be reached.

Every model of the distribution of goods is an arbitrary idea. The compulsory enforcement of any ideal of social justice Hayek regards as a violation of personal liberty and an act of despotism. The implementation of any model of distribution carried out by the state is, according to Hayek, a real threat to the free and open society. It challenges the very foundations of this society and is a direct road to serfdom.

Principles of justice, for Hayek, are ethical standards which can be applied only to the behaviour of individuals. It makes no sense to apply ethical standards to the evaluation of a social system or economic structure. Especially, it makes no sense to speak about a just or unjust distribution of income in a free market economy. In a market system there is no ethical question of the distribution of goods at all, because in that system there is no distributor of goods.[9] The income of different persons is the outcome of the work of spontaneous forces, not of any conscious activities. The problem of the distribution of goods and of distributive justice, thus, is inherent only to the socialist system. In a capitalist economy, social justice is only a dangerous mirage, really a socialist idea. The relations between the persons participating in the market game for Hayek, however, can be subjected to a specific kind of ethical evaluation, based on the principles of commutative justice. The concept of commutative justice is developed by Hayek as a counterposition to distributive justice [Hayek, *Constitution*, pp. 440–41, nn. 10–11].

Commutative justice—Hayek draws on Aristotelian terminology here—means the principle according to which services rendered should be rewarded according to the value they have for the recipients.

---

[9] F. A. Hayek, 'The Principles of a Liberal Social Order', *Il Politico* XXXI (1966), pp. 601–17, at p. 611. The same point of view is advanced by Ludwig von Mises in *Le socialisme* (Paris, 1952), originally published in German as *Die Gemeinwirtschaft; Untersuchungen über den Sozialismus* (Jena, 1932), English translation by J. Kahane, *Socialism: an Economic and Sociological Analysis*, new enlarged edn with epilogue (London, 1951).

This value is articulated in the price which people are ready to pay for service, regardless of the moral deserts of the people rendering the services. There is no link between commutative justice and the personal circumstances, virtues, needs or desires of the parties. All these factors are completely irrelevant to the market value of services and products of human work.

Commutative justice ensures freedom of choice of the persons who are the parties to transactions. The contrary principle of distributive justice—that results of the work should be valued and paid according to the deserts of the people performing the work—is in Hayek's opinion a socialist principle, incompatible with the freedom of the choice of persons engaged in interactions. The principle of distributive justice challenges the freedom of choice of possible courses of action as well as the freedom of choice of occupation and profession.

Inequalities in the distribution of goods resulting from the functioning of the (genuinely) free market, for Hayek, cannot be considered unjust. They are the results of free and fair competition. All kinds of social policies and ventures correcting the results of the market game, especially all redistributive measures tending to reduce the inequalities brought about by market economy, are morally inadmissable. Hayek's theoretical and axiological arguments are thus used to challenge progressive taxation, the welfare system and social security arrangements. Individual charity is the only proper way to help those who cannot compete [Hayek, *Constitution*, pp. 299–300].

Hayek develops similar views on the questions of education and medical care. In a capitalist free market society there are neither theoretical nor moral reasons to justify state-subsidized free education or free medicare for poor people. The social worth of people who have been successful on the economic plane is greater than the worth of the poor and disabled. Higher and university education and medicare should be treated as commodities sold on the free market. Their price should be established by the economic rules of supply and demand. Every form of organized public help for the poor disturbs the process of natural selection.

The principles and postulates presented above are in Hayek's theory the logical consequences of the limitation of the notion of justice to the concept of commutative justice. The concept of commutative justice has its philosophical underpinning in Hayek's idea of human nature and moral responsibility.

Hayek accepts the traditional ethical assumption of liberal and neoliberal economic theory that human nature is egoistic and that therefore people should be egoist and care only for their own interest.[10]

[10] Hayek, *Constitution*, p. 84; *Individualism*, pp. 14–15. Cf. Ludwig von Mises, *Le gouvernment omnipotent* (Paris, 1947), p. 341, published in English as *Omnipotent Government* (New Haven, 1944).

Egoistic concern with one's own business is an ethical attitude most advantageous for the society as a whole. The egoistic motivation of individual behaviour is the only basis for the general well-being of society. People are morally responsible only for their own individual behaviour and its immediate consequences. The far-reaching effects of human conduct are unpredictable and unknown and cannot be the subject of responsibility. Only immediate face-to-face relations between people can be the subject of moral evaluation and ethical responsibility. Abstract knowledge of the misery and sufferings of the millions of people on earth whom we do not know personally can evoke our compassion but cannot really motivate our everyday behaviour and decisions. Our moral responsibility is limited to the people we meet and the relations with those we are in touch with [Hayek, *Constitution*, p. 84; *Individualism*, p. 14].

A concept of justice very close to Hayek's idea of commutative justice has been developed by Robert Nozick in his *Anarchy, State and Utopia* [Nozick, pp. 150–160]. Nozick's ethical and social theory is undoubtedly more subtle and sophisticated than Hayek's. Nozick calls his commutative theory of justice an entitlement theory. According to him, the possession of things considered to be goods is just if the title of possession is just. The requirements of justice are met when people own or hold the things which they have acquired legitimately. The just or legitimate title to acquisition and possession of things is legal title. Injustice takes place when people have things without legal title, that is, when they have acquired the things they have by theft, blackmail, violence, unfair competition, and so on.

This theory, according to Nozick, is historical, because the history of the existing distribution of goods and not the structure of the distribution is the proper criterion of justice. Nozick criticizes and rejects the concepts of 'patterned distribution' based on 'end state' principles. Consequently he rejects also the criteria of 'patterned distribution', intrinsic to the idea of distributive justice, being natural dimensions, such as needs, merits and so on.[11] Justice based on the concept of historical entitlement is a non-patterned justice. The system of entitlement is well founded when it is based on individual goals of individual transactions. No broader concept of a goal is needed for the justification of the entitlements. According to the entitlement theory everyone is expected to do what he decided to do and everybody ought to receive what he has done for himself and what other people have done for him.

Nozick rejects the egalitarian idea of the axiological priority of the principle of human equality and develops a sharp critique of the redistribution of income achieved by the system of progressive

[11] In particular, Nozick advances a sharp criticism of Marx's concepts of meaningful work, exploitation and workers' control and of John Rawls's theory of justice as fairness, pp. 246–61 and 183–228.

taxation. He argues not only that progressive taxation as a re-distributive measure challenges the principle of historical entitle-ments, but also that progressive taxation is unfair, because it ignores different and incomparable needs of individuals.[12] People with higher incomes simply work more in order to satisfy their more sophisticated and expensive needs. People with lower incomes do not have such needs, but having more free time they achieve some pleasures easily without extra labour.

To make his theory more feasible and objective, Nozick introduces the concept of the competent and objective observer. Here his theory differs clearly from the theory of Hayek, in which there is no room for such a concept. Nozick's theory of justice is extremely formalistic. He conceives justice merely as a legal procedure for the acquisition of possession and the circulation of goods. In both Nozick's and in Hayek's theory the concept of justice is divorced from the idea of desert or merit.

There are some more moderate versions of liberal conservative theories of justice, which admit the possibility of the redistribution of income through welfare policy but only so far as concerns the social minimum. But the provision of a social minimum is considered not an implementation of social justice but rather a humanitarian means of maintaining social peace.

The common feature of liberal conservative theories of justice is that these theories accept clearly the priority of liberty in relation to the principle of equality and the priority of the economic efficiency of the social system in relation to the requirements of justice. They challenge on moral grounds the compulsory enforcement of the redistribution of incomes. Charity as a voluntary enterprise is advanced as the most proper or only admissible way of helping the poor and disabled.

They take for granted the thesis of neoliberal economic theory that the total growth of national income settles automatically all social problems and conflicts, because it improves the situation of the disadvantaged groups of society. The growth of economic potential makes irrelevant the problem of the distribution of goods. Distributive justice (social justice) makes no sense in a society of abundance of consumer goods. In such a society the inequalities in the distribution of goods cease to be a serious and significant problem for the people. The best way of settling the social problems which are the objects of the egalitarian theories of justice is not to change the pattern of distribution but to stimulate maximal growth of the economic potential of the society.

The critique of the conservative liberal theories of justice is an

[12] Similar criticisms of progressive taxation are developed by Bertrand de Jouvenel in *The Ethics of Redistribution* (Cambridge, 1951).

embarrassing task, and especially from a Marxist standpoint. They have been criticized from different points of view and it is difficult to add something genuinely new. The ideological character of the conservative theories of justice is so clear that it does not need to be proved. I will focus my critical analysis on the most striking fallacies, inconsistencies and failures of these theories.

The fully conformist attitude of liberal conservative theories of justice toward the capitalist economic and social system is beyond doubt. Hayek's theory is an open apology of an outmoded and obsolete nineteenth-century liberal model of capitalism. Other conservative theories are not so clearly apologetic and their acceptance and philosophic affirmation of capitalism is presented in more general and neutral terms. The implicit assumption of all conservative liberal theories is that the capitalist system needs no moral justification.

These assumptions lead to substantial inconsistencies in the theories of justice developed by Nozick and Hayek. Nozick says that his entitlement theory is a 'non-patterned' theory of justice and does not imply any 'end-state concepts'. But that is simply not true. The parajuridical concept of historical entitlement makes sense only within a legal system which is structured according to a definite substantive pattern. That must be a legal system safeguarding private property in the means of production and consumption. Only if the legal system patterned by the requirements of capitalist market economy can be recognized as a just system, can the transaction performed within the system be also considered as morally just. The concealed assumption of the entitlement theory of justice is that the bourgeois legal system is just. The non-patterned theory of justice (entitlement theory) underpins the moral justification of the distribution of goods within the capitalist system, but is of course not applicable to the justification of the system itself. The same difficulty applies to Hayek's concept of commutative justice. If the notion of commutative justice is to have any moral content, the justice of the capitalist system must be assumed *a priori*; Hayek's contention that the social system or economic structure cannot be the object of moral evaluation (cannot be considered as just or unjust) is incompatible with the concept of commutative justice.[13]

The theories of justice developed by Hayek and Nozick are

---

[13] The theory developed by Ludwig von Mises is much more precise and consistent. According to Mises, the choice of one of the two possible forms of social organization—that based on private ownership and that based on collective ownership of the means of production—is the moral issue. The only moral criterion relevant to the choice of a social system is the economic efficiency of the system. But the logical consequences of a chosen social system cannot be the object of moral evaluation. Everything that is intrinsically unavoidable or necessary for the proper functioning of the chosen system is *ex definitione* morally just. Mises, pp. 357, 504, 591.

intrinsically linked with the concept of perfect procedural justice. These extremely formalistic and legalistic theories are close to some recent concepts of legal justice advanced in contemporary bourgeois legal philosophy. Justice is identified with legal equality, which is conceived as the pure formal principle of legal impartiality. On this interpretation the concept of legal equality does not presuppose any sort of actual equality and is not challenged by any lack of it. The requirement of legal equality is met when existing actual inequalities are either legally justified (just inequalities) or when they do not need any moral or legal justification because they do not fall within the scope of legal and moral evaluation (natural inequalities). They are legally and morally irrelevant inequalities.

All that legal impartiality requires is that we 'treat all men alike, except where there are relevant differences between them.'[14] The crucial issue, of course, is what is meant by 'relevant differences' and how these differences are to be defined. On Hayek's theory, the only relevant differences between persons are the differences required or produced by the competitive market economy system. Within the framework of Nozick's concept, the relevant differences are determined by the legal procedures of the acquisition of goods.

The formalistic legal approach to the problems of justice is a very peculiar feature of the liberal conservative theories of justice. This way of considering justice is in clear contrast with recent trends prevailing in jurisprudence and with recent developments of law in the contemporary world. 'There is in advanced industrial or post-industrial societies today a widespread crisis in law and legal ideology which goes to the very core of social conceptions and hence of 'philosophical' discussion of the nature and function of law', Eugene Kamenka and Alice Erh-Soon Tay write in their penetrating study of the contemporary crisis in law,[15] and that crisis is in particular the crisis of the traditional formalistic concept of law.

The meta-ethical grounds of liberal conservative theories of justice are also marked by some substantial inconsistencies resulting from the compromise between the assumptions of traditional liberal theory and the concepts advanced in recent bourgeois ethical theories.

Hayek accepts the philosophical assumption according to which there is a logical link between facts and values, value judgements and theoretical judgements, and rejects the radical epistomoligical dualism of 'is' and 'ought'. But while this could open the way to the concept of the objectivity of values, Hayek's reasoning is not in that

[14] S. I. Benn and R. S. Peters, *Social Principles and the Democratic State* (London, 1959), p. 128. Cf. S. Hook, *Political Power and Personal Freedom* (New York, 1959).
[15] Eugene Kamenka and Alice Erh-Soon Tay, 'Beyond Bourgeois Individualism: the Contemporary Crisis in Law and Legal Ideology', in E. Kamenka and R. S. Neale (eds), *Feudalism, Capitalism and Beyond* (London, 1975), pp. 127–44, at p. 127.

direction. He accepts the claim regarding the subjectivity of values, the claim of traditional liberal theory. The inconsistency characteristic of traditional liberal theory—between its claim regarding subjectivity of values and the need for social consensus to produce or justify the fundamental moral values of the capitalist market economy system and the objective standards of evaluation of the outcomes of the market game—thus remain unsettled in neoliberal conservative theory, especially in Hayek's theory. [16] Nozick tries to overcome the inconsistency by introducing the concept of an objective and competent observer, but this concept does not help him much. The idea of an objective observer seems incompatible with the concept of non-patterned justice.

On the axiological plane the real hierarchy of values implied by neoliberal doctrine is revealed in Hayek's theory. Hayek has formulated his axiological standpoint clearly; it is unjust and unfair to enforce any compulsory redistribution of income because this violates the personal freedom of choice. It is completely fair and just to let some people die of starvation or because of insufficient medicare, if the miserable situation of these people is the outcome of the fair competition on the free market. Their death will even improve the general well-being of society. Hayek conceives freedom in a purely negative way—only as freedom from interference by the state or other people. Freedom of choice, for him, can be challenged only by immediate and purposeful actions of other people. Therefore the compulsory redistribution of income is a serious violation of human freedom of choice, but the conditions of living in which people are deprived of food, shelter, medicare are completely irrelevant. The merit of Hayek is that he has formulated his standpoint so clearly. The supreme value of Hayek's axiological system is not the freedom of choice of a real human being but the freedom of choice of *homo economicus* as a participant in the market game. The protection of the liberty of the successful gambler is the most important function of Hayek's concept of justice.

The empirical foundations of neoliberal conservative theories of justice undoubtedly contain many sound and interesting observations of social reality. But the selection of the empirical data is clearly determined by conservative ideology. Therefore the generalizations that underpin the conservative concept of justice are substantially wrong or misleading, and the sophisticated theoretical models used in these theories are deprived of explanatory power.

Hayek's theory of knowledge, for example, completely ignores the dynamic acceleration of the social sciences in this century. Hayek gives a clear preference to prejudices and traditional irrational

---

[16] Hayek has been criticized on this point by some conservative liberal authors. See e.g. Irving Kristol, *On the Democratic Idea in America* (New York, 1972), p. 98.

knowledge of social phenomena because this kind of knowledge is much more suitable for the empirical underpinning of his concept of justice than modern theories of social structure, social change and social development. This attitude is characteristic of all conservative theories. The same objections apply to Hayek's theory of social institutions. It is true that the institutions which came into being spontaneously in the course of historical development may be very often more efficient than consciously created institutions. But there is no such general regularity and there are strong historical and sociological arguments challenging this hypothesis. Hayek ignores the fact that, without new economic theories such as Keynes's, without the implementation of far-reaching plans and projects of social change and without consciously created institutions, the capitalist system would not have survived until now.

The psychological assumptions concerning human nature accepted by Hayek and other representatives of neoliberal doctrine are the traditional utilitarian concepts of human nature intrinsic to liberal economic and political theory. These assumptions are vague and deprived of any empirical evidence on the ground of modern psychology. It is true that egoistic motivation plays an important role in the stimulation of human behaviour. But the claim that man is by his nature an egoistic and anti-social being has the same cognitive power as the opposite contention, according to which human nature is social and altruistic.

The argument based on the concept of human needs is also a vague speculation, ignoring important elements of empirical knowledge of the dynamics of human needs. It is perfectly true that people with different incomes have usually different needs, particularly as concerns cultural needs. The structure and hierarchy of needs of people with high incomes does differ from that of people with low income. But it is also empirically true that the people with high income have quite different chances and possibilities of developing their needs from those of the people with low income, for the distribution of income is also the distribution of conditions shaping human needs. This empirical fact is completely ignored by the neoliberal theory of justice and the whole argument against the distribution of incomes is based on a simplified and distorted concept of human needs.

Some important assumptions of Hayek's and Nozick's theory of justice clearly contradict empirical knowledge. The fundamental theoretical assumption of these theories is the contention that the parties of the transactions compete on the free market on equal terms and have the same opportunities to win. This contention is not true even in reference to the capitalist free market economy in the nineteenth century, not to mention that it is obviously false in reference to present day monopolistic capitalism.

The neoliberal hypothesis that economic growth automatically solves social conflicts has no empirical basis in the contemporary world. The most developed capitalist countries with the highest rate of economic growth are torn by social conflicts. The growth of the economic potential of capitalist societies seems to intensify social tensions and stimulate the consciousness of deprivation of the disadvantaged and exploited social classes.

It can be argued that these objections are not well founded from the methodological standpoint because the assumptions of neoliberal theories of justice are not empirical propositions about social or psychological actuality but merely postulates for a theoretical model. Assumptions of such a model can be of a counter-empirical character. If this interpretation is right, then we may ask about the cognitive value and explanatory power of this model.

There is no social reality in reference to which the theoretical model of society implied by neoliberal conservative theories can prove its explanatory and predictive power. This kind of modelling is a tool of ideological distortion of the real image of the structure of capitalist society. The empirical ground of liberal conservative theories of justice seems to be very poor.

Reformist theories of justice: John Rawl's *A Theory of Justice*[17]
In contemporary Western ethical philosophy, John Rawls's theory is undoubtedly the first attempt to create a comprehensive normative theory of justice in the material sense, constituting a basic element of the general theory of morality and ethics. Rawls's theory has had great publicity; for some years it has been the central topic of discussion in Western ethical and political thought. Rawls's concept of justice has been subject to a thorough and penetrating criticism from various philosophical and ideological positions. Radically contradictory evaluations and interpretations of his theory have been formulated.[18] I shall try to present a brief reconstruction of the essential points of Rawls's theory and to advance a critical analysis of this theory from a Marxist point of view.

Rawls rejects the methodological distinction between ethical and meta-ethical discourse. His theory is to provide not only an explication of the principles of justice as fairness, but also their scientific justification, consisting in a systematic presentation of good reasons for accepting the proposed concept of justice. These reasons are very

---

[17] Cambridge, Mass., 1971; Oxford, 1972.
[18] As John Chapman points out: 'It has been called Christian (Stuart Hampshire), Hobbist (Anthony Flew), individualistic with a vengeance (Robert Nozick), Gladstonian and Spencerian (Brian Barry), illiberal and socialist (Daniel Bell) . . . and liberal revisionist (C.B. Macpherson).' J. W. Chapman, 'Rawls's *Theory of Justice*', *American Political Science review* LXIX (1975), pp. 588–93, at p. 588.

sophisticated, involving the construction of an abstract and complicated theory of the process of choosing the principles of social system. Rawls develops a social contract type theory as an ideational reconstruction of the decision-making process. The model of this process is the bargaining game among self-interested parties designed to solve Kant's problem of deriving substantive moral and political principles from the purely formal criteria of rationality. The linking of Kant's theory of social contract with the contemporary theory of decision-making is an original idea. Making use of the ideational model of social contract, Rawls describes the process of choosing principles of a social system by free and equal subjects in conditions of uncertainty (limited knowledge), assuming finiteness of goods and a generally advantageous socio-economic situation. Presupposing a whole series of ideational assumptions, the author characterizes in detail the so-called 'original positions' of hypothetical choosers concluding a hypothetical social contract [pp. 122–6, 136–50, 530–41]. This contract is to define the fundamental principles of the organization of society and the rules of participation in this organization.

The construction of the original position of the choosers is to constitute a fundamental argument justifying the equity of the suggested concept of justice. In the hypothetical situation of choice postulated in Rawls's 'original position', the allegedly rational rule of choice is the 'maximin rule', according to which one should choose the best alternative from among a set of the worst—least advantageous—alternatives. The two principles of justice suggested by Rawls constitute a solution of the problem of justice in accordance with the maximin rule [pp. 152–7]. The choice of principles of justice in accordance with the above-mentioned rule minimizes the risk of a choice made in conditions of uncertainty by hypothetical representative persons concluding a hypothetical social contract under the veil of ignorance.

The version of social contract suggested by Rawls, then, is an ideational solving-model for hypothetical choices of principles of justice, not a historical assertion. His theory is not subject to evaluation from the point of view of truth or falsehood, but only from the point of view of its usefulness in solving the problems the author is attempting to deal with. The model assumes that the fulfilment of the conditions postulated by the original position guarantees the hypothetical choosers making a completely rational decision concerning the choice of original principles of justice (principles of a just organization of society). But the requirement of the postulate of the veil of ignorance excludes the possibility of making a rational decision in this matter.[19] Choosers not informed about the current state of develop-

[19] See Hans Oberdiek's review of J. Rawls, *A Theory of Justice* in *New York University Law Review* XLVII (1972), pp. 1012–28, at pp. 1012–26.

ment of the productive forces of the society for which they are to choose principles of justice and about its level of civilization cannot make a rational choice of principles of social justice.

A rational choice of principles of justice is also impossible without a knowledge of alternative economic structures defined by the technical and civilizational level of the society. The present planet-wide technical and civilizational level of humanity creates the possibility of a choice between two opposing socio-economic systems: the capitalist system based on the private ownership of production and the socialist system based on the social ownership of the fundamental means and tools of work. The choice of one of these prejudges and limits the rationality of choosing a concept of justice as a principle of the organization of society and the distribution of fundamental goods. The rationality of the maximin rule depends (among other things) upon the degree of probability that the chooser of the principles of justice will live in a non-egalitarian society, in which there will exist significant differences in the distribution of primary goods. Only when this probability is high may the maximin rule be considered a rational directive for the choice of principles of justice.[20] The maximin rule may, as a principle of minimization of risk, be a rational rule of choice of principles of justice in the conditions of a capitalist state. The mechanism of a capitalist economy functions on the basis of a zero-sum game. Each participant in this market game must bear an enormous risk of failure, multiplied by the threat of wavering markets, the probability of a recession and crises. In the capitalist system the life success of an individual is to a large extent determined by his initial position in regard to primary goods (prestige, income, education). However, his position is to an equally large extent determined by his class situation. Utilization of the maximin rule as a guideline in choosing principles of justice in the socialist system would be a completely irrational thing, since the risk of failure of an individual caused by his innate characteristics and initial social position is minimized by the socialist socio-economic system (the socio-economic rights of citizens).

The maximin rule, therefore, is a rational principle of justice only in highly non-egalitarian systems. It is completely irrelevant in choosing between the two opposing competitive socio-economic systems, capitalism and socialism, and irrational in a socially egalitarian society.

The assumption made by Rawls, according to which the economic structure of the society is irrelevant so far as the choice of original principles of justice is concerned, is evidently false. It constitutes a kind of ideological bias, stemming from the conformist character of Rawls's theory. To be sure, Rawls states that both the capitalist and

[20] Compare Brian Barry, *The Liberal Theory of Justice* (Oxford, 1973), pp. 87–107.

the socialist society may or may not fulfil the requirements of justice, but in Rawls's deliberations there appears an undeniable preference for the capitalist economic system connected with the private owner-ship of means of production, the market economy and a liberal democratic political system [Esheté, p. 46]. The original positions, however, do not unequivocally prejudge a rational choice of principles of justice even in the capitalist system. The rationality of the maximin rule depends on accepting certain additional empirical premises concerning the variant of the capitalist system and the position which in the accepted system of values is attributed to the principle of the maximization of chances and the minimization of risk.

The scope of application of the maximin rule as a directive of rational choice in conditions of uncertainty is therefore rather limited, and some authors totally question the rationality of this directive in a decisional situation fulfilling the postulates of the original positions.[21]

The ideological character of this directive is beyond doubt. Only within a system of values characteristic of the capitalist socio-economic order may the maximin rule be presented as a rational directive for choosing principles of justice, though even within these ideological assumptions the scope of its application is limited. Rawls attempts to assign universal value to this directive with the aid of the accepted concept of rationality and the postulates of the original position, but the choice of the two principles of justice (justice as fairness) can be justified as rational only on the basis of value-oriented assumptions corresponding with the bourgeois-liberal value system.

The two principles of justice, the choice of which is determined on the ground of Rawls's concept by the original positions of hypotheti-cal choosers, are the central points of the entire theory. The first principle is that each person is to have an equal right to the most extensive basic liberty compatible with a similar liberty of others. The second principle is that social and economic inequalities are to be arranged so that they are both (a) to the greatest benefit of the least advantaged, and (b) attached to the offices and positions open to all under conditions of fair equality of opportunity [Rawls, pp. 60–65, 250, 302].

The first principle of justice is a formulation of the basic ethical postulate of the classical liberal doctrine and since the second principle is subordinated in a lexical order to the first, Rawls's theory of justice is a liberal theory of social justice. In relation to the classical liberal doctrine it is a revisionist theory. The innovatory character of Rawls's theory in relation to this doctrine lies in point (a) of the second

[21] See David Lyons, 'Rawls versus Utilitarianism' *Journal of Philosophy* LXIX (1972), pp. 535–45; Stanley Bates, 'The Motivation to Be Just', *Ethics* LXXXV (1974–5), pp. 1–17. Rawls admits, p. 153, that 'clearly the maximin rule is not, in general, a suitable guide for choices under certainty'.

principle, called the difference principle. It is presented as a direct result of the maximin rule as a directive for choosing principles of justice in original positions.

The difference principle is the principle of social justice. But it is a concept of purely distributive justice relevant for non-egalitarian class-structured societies. It is mainly redistributive, in fact implying an implicit acceptance of the existing patterns of the original distribution of primary goods, with all its creation of 'naturally' privileged or underprivileged groups.[22]

The lexical priority of the first principle of justice over the second (especially over the difference principle) implies two assumptions which are intrinsic to traditional bourgeois liberal doctrine: (1) that liberty is a more important and higher value than actual equality; (2) that political liberty is quite independent of the distribution of primary goods. But in contrast with the representatives of conservative liberal theory, Rawls is aware of the impact of economic conditions on the realization of liberty. Consequently he introduces the concept of the value of liberty, but limits its scope of reference to the perspective of the historical developments of the social systems. He ignores the relation between the value of liberty and the ordering of the two principles of justice, though the value of liberty may be different for different groups and classes of society. Including the value of liberty in the main structure of Rawls's theory of justice challenges the ordering of the two principles of justice and consequently the very foundations of the whole concept of justice as fairness.[23]

The theoretical underpinning of the difference principle is based on an assumption which is empirically not true: the assumption that inequalities in the distribution of primary goods and constitute an indispensable condition for technical progress and the system's economic productivity and are an indispensable and irremovable structural characteristic of every society, irrespective of the state of development of its productive forces and economic base. This assumption is empirically false (or at least irrelevant) in relation to the economics of a relative abundance of primary goods conditioned by the attainment of a very high level of development by the productive forces. Here the differentiation in the distribution of primary goods

---

[22] See Ota Weinberger, 'Begründung oder Illusion. Erkenntniskritishe Gedanken zu John Rawls Theorie der Gerechtigkeit', in *Zeitschrift für Philosophische Forschung*, Band 31. Heft 2 (1977). Wolff also writes: 'By focusing exclusively on distribution rather than on production, Rawls obscures the real roots of that distribution.' R. P. Wolff, *Understanding Rawls* (Princeton, New Jersey, 1977), p. 210. See also the papers by Milton Fisk and Richard W. Miller, in Norman Daniels (ed.), *Reading Rawls* (Oxford, 1975), pp. 53–80, 206–30.

[23] See Norman Daniels, 'Equal Liberty and Unequal Worth of Liberty', in *Reading Rawls*, pp. 253–82.

ceases to play any role whatsoever in stimulating the productivity of work and maximizing social inputs. Even in the economics of a relative scarcity of goods, this assumption does not define sufficient conditions (but only the necessary condition) of the maximization of social inputs and work productivity. Neither can the inequalities in the distribution of primary goods be considered guarantors of the economic efficiency of a social system. Particularly they are no guarantors of such efficiency from the point of view of the least advantaged social groups. From the point of view of objective rules of social development, the struggle of the exploited classes for reducing or completely abolishing such inequalities is a struggle for an arrangement of socio-economic relations whereby existing social inequalities cease to be economically justified. The historical result of this struggle is the economic and cultural advancement of classes occupying the least advantageous social positions from the point of view of the distribution of primary goods. This advancement of their real perspective is the basic stimulus of the growth of productivity of work or of technical progress.

The empirical criteria needed for practical interpretation and application of the difference principle are completely vague. The principle justifies inequalities in the distribution of social goods only so far as the existence of these inequalities is advantageous for the least advantaged social groups. The minimization of inequalities in the social distribution of goods is inadmissible if it causes a deterioration of the situation of these social groups. But Rawls does not formulate any criteria on the basis of which one could empirically determine whether the existence, or enlargement, of the inequality of distribution of primary goods in a given social arrangement is justified, that is, whether it fulfills the requirements of the difference principle [Chapman, pp. 589–90]. According to Hayek, capitalism has always satisfied the difference principle. To Marxists, Hayek's contention is evidently false, but in my opinion Rawls on this question would also share the Marxist view. His theory, however, does not supply any operative arguments on the basis of which one could repudiate Hayek's statement. Such arguments are supplied by the Marxist analysis of capitalism and in particular the Marxist theory of exploitation. This historical conservatism of Rawls's theory consists in the fact that the difference principle provides a moral justification for social inequalities considered necessary at a given historical stage of the development of productive forces. The contention that social inequalities are necessary in given historical conditions, so far as the interests of the most underprivileged social classes are concerned, is a self-confirming statement, which plays an 'eufunctional' role in relation to a social arrangement based on social inequalities. It reflects the interests of the classes dominating in the given arrangement, and plays the role of an ideological stabilizer in a class-structured society, slowing down the further development of productive forces. Any similarity to the historical approach of the Marxist theory of social development is only apparent. Marxist theory does not identify the historical necessity of social inequalities in certain socio-economic formations with the moral justification of these inequalities which facilitate the exploitation of one person by another. Marxist theory postulates a moral critique of these social inequalities, regardless of the economic function they may play in specific historical conditions. The struggle for social equality stimulates the development of productive forces in all historical conditions, with the result that existing antagonistic class divisions and the ensuing differences in the distribution of primary goods cease to be historically necessary divisions and differences.

On a global scale Rawls's theory is a non-egalitarian and conservative theory in a double sense:

1. It assumes a non-egalitarian structure of society with regard to the distribution of primary goods as an indispensable condition of the economic productivity of the social system (an unequal distribution as an incentive to productive work).
2. It assumes that a large society consists of 'non-comparing groups' and that this helps to keep down envy, 'for people will not resent inequalities they do not notice' [Chapman, p. 590].

Rawls clearly underlines the non-egalitarian character of his theory of justice and both criticizes and repudiates radical egalitarian theories. H. A. Bedau puts it thus: the Rawlsian idea of the 'system of fair inequalities provides the nearest thing we have to a rational assessment of why the poor should allow the wealthy to keep most of that wealth and not, as in Marxist ideology, seek to expropriate it without so much as a thank you.'[24]

It seems to me, however, that one must evaluate differently the meaning and function of Rawls's theory within the capitalist system. In relation to the classical liberal theory it is a clearly revisionist theory. The revisionist character of this theory finds expression in two fundamental questions: (1) Rawls formulates the substantive ethical standards for evaluating the distribution of goods as standards completely independent of the mechanisms of the capitalist market economy (Rawls thus disregards the concept of an allegedly perfect procedural justice based exclusively on market mechanisms); (2) Rawls also repudiates the concept according to which the mechanisms of the capitalist market automatically ensure a just division of goods

[24] H. A. Bedau, 'Inequality, How Much and Why?', *Journal of Social Philosophy* VI (1975), p. 25.

compatible with the extra-market standards of justice, that is, an imperfect procedural justice [Rawls, pp. 85–86].

Though Rawls basically accepts the non-egalitarian economic structure of capitalist society, his difference principle heads toward a reduction of the range of differences in the distribution of social income within this structure to the advantage of the least advantaged social groups. It justifies the transfer of social income from the top to the bottom of society as a principle of social justice and not as based on a principle of charity to the poor, or of bribing the poor in order to maintain social peace. The difference principle justifies the moral right of the least advantaged social groups to a growing participation in the distribution of social income and not merely to securing a social minimum.

This participation is justified exclusively by the growth of social differentiation in the distribution of goods and the global growth of social income. It is not dependent on the size and character of the contribution of these groups to the creation of social income. However, this concept is characterized by complete elasticity and the degree of egalitarianism is more or less undefined. Rawls does not say how large these transfers are to be. In practice how egalitarian the principle is depends on the relationship between total income and its distribution. Neither does Rawls propose any upper limits of the range of social difference in the distribution of primary goods.

But it should be noticed that his theory is not a specific political programme. It is rather a philosophical concept, the task of which is the creation or justification of moral standards of evaluation and criticism of the functioning of socio-political systems and social policy programmes of a contemporary highly developed industrial state. It is not the volume of the suggested redistribution in the social distribution of goods that is essential, but rather the ethical justification of that redistribution contained in Rawls's theory of justice. His theory is thus undoubtedly a moderately egalitarian brand of liberal theory, progressive and reformist in comparison with other versions of the liberal theories (Hayek, Bell, Nozick) and in comparison with reactionary theories of a cultural or biological and genetic character (Jensen, Shockley). Thus Rawls's theory is the object of sharp criticism by representatives of the conservative versions of the liberal theory.[25]

In specific American conditions, Rawls's theory may constitute the optimal philosophical and ethical justification of social reform programmes connected with the 'Great Society' idea and in particular the 'War on Poverty' programme of the mid-1960s. It also seems that in the United States, John Rawls's theory of justice constitutes a

[25] See Nozick, pp. 150–60; and D. Bell, *The Coming of Post-industrial Society: a Venture in Social Forecasting* (New York, 1973), pp. 440–46.

philosophical substitute for the European social democratic concepts of justice and the welfare state theory. The fact that these ideas are alien to traditional American philosophy, partly explains the enormous sympathy Rawls's theory has aroused in the USA as well as the sharp criticism it ran into from representatives of the liberal theory.

An essential characteristic of Rawls's theory is the striking disproportion between the wealth of assumptions in the ideational model and the wealth of empirical material constituting a potential scope of application of the model, on the one hand, and the scarcity of empirically solvable problems to which this model finds an operative application, on the other. The statements which the author derives, by way of a quasi-deductive process, from the assumptions of the ideational theory of social contract turn out to be true in relation to such a numerous (practically unlimited) class of the most diversified social situations that the cognitive value, and the predictive force, of these statements become negligible.[26]

The explanatory power of the social contract theory and bargaining game model has proved to be very limited in relation to the consideration of the problems of social justice in contemporary societies. The impossibility of deriving substantive principles of justice from the purely formal criteria of rationality is also evident in Rawls's theory. The theory reveals the conservative ideological function of the contractual model in relation to fundamental social and political issues of contemporary world.

Rawls accepts assumptions which make possible the belief that the problem of ownership of the basic means of production is irrelevant to the philosophical problems of social justice. These are assumptions which at the same time make Rawls's entire concept empirically irrelevant. Considering the economic structure of a society to be a problem irrelevant to the question of social justice is a hidden form of ideological acceptance of the economic structure existing in a given society. Thus it is not the ideological character of Rawls's theory in general, but its ideological conformism in relation to the capitalist economic structure that has substantially limited its cognitive value.[27]

According to R. P. Wolff [p. 210] the main source of the failure of Rawls's theory is that 'the economic models employed by Rawls exhibit the same concern with a distribution to the exclusion of production'. This approach is characteristic of all liberal theories of

---

[26] See Z. Ziembiński, Rawlsa ogólna teoria sprawiedliwości (John Rawls's General Theory of Justice: a Critique of the Book *A Theory of Justice*), *Etyka* no. 13 (1974).

[27] 'Rawls's failure grows naturally and inevitably out of his uncritical acceptance of the socio-political presuppositions and associated modes of analysis of classical and neoclassical liberal political economy,' Wolff writes, p. 210.

justice. The failure of Rawls's concept of justice confirms Hayek's contention that the idea of social justice is incompatible with the fundamental assumption of liberal theory. As Wolff puts it, 'Rawls's enormous sophistication and imaginativeness show us that the failure is due not to any inadequacies in the execution, but rather to the inherent weakness of that entire tradition of political philosophy of which *A Theory of Justice* is perhaps the most distinguished product.'

Egalitarian theories of justice

There are some liberal progressive and reformist theories of justice that are more egalitarian than Rawls's. Although they are liberal in their foundations, they do not stress the priority of liberty over the principle of equality. Some even clearly emphasize the priority of equality, an actual equality, as challenging the value of the concepts of formal justice and of impartiality.

A moderately egalitarian concept of justice is the compensatory theory of justice, linked with the concept of so-called preferential treatment in American legal doctrine.[28] The idea of compensatory justice, conceived as a principle of preferential treatment for disadvantaged groups, has been clearly formulated in American legal philosophy by Thomas Platt. Platt develops an anti-formalistic interpretation of Sydney Hook's definition of justice as the principle of equal concern [Hook, p. 36]. On this interpretation the principle of equality is not a prescription to treat in identical ways people who are unequal in their physical or intellectual nature, but a policy of equality of concern or consideration for human beings whose different needs may require different treatment. For Platt, certain forms of actual equality are necessary conditions of the realization of legal equality. If some important conditions of living are unequal, legal equality, implying a principle of impartiality, becomes a form of maintaining and preserving actual inequalities.

One of the most egalitarian bourgeois theories of justice seems to be the concept of justice advanced by A. M. Honoré. According to Honoré, 'the principle of social justice resides in the idea that all men have equal claims to all advantages which are generally desired and which are in fact conducive to human perfection and human happiness' [Honoré, p. 91]. For Honoré, actual equality of opportunity is the main core of the notion of social justice. He thus formulates two fundamental principles of social justice. The first principle requires

---

[28] See R. A. Wasserstrom, 'Racism, Sexism and Preferential Treatment: an Approach to the Topics', *University of California Law Review* 24 (1977), pp. 580–619. These concepts and programmes of 'preferential treatment', 'affirmative action' or 'reverse discriminations' are sharply criticized by liberal conservative lawyers, sociologists and political theorists, as the programmes which clearly challenge the traditional egalitarian idea of equality; see Bell, pp. 413–39.

that all men be considered merely as men and apart from their conduct and choice have a claim to an equal share in all those things which are generally desired and are in fact conducive to their well-being. According to the second principle there is a limited set of factors which can justify departure from the principle embodied in the first proposition. These are the choice of the claimant or the citizen on the one hand and his conduct on the other; there are also certain principles of individual justice dealt with under the rubrics of 'the justice of transactions' and of 'special relations'. Honoré emphasizes that there is no single formulation by which the content of social justice can be adequately expressed. Honoré does not define clearly the relation between liberty and equality, but he identifies social justice with a set of principles of equality and conceives justice and liberty as equally important moral values. The demands of liberty, he claims, 'frequently conflict with those of justice' [Honoré, pp. 63, 92].

In contrast with Rawls's theory, the concept of social justice developed by Honoré is also concerned with relations between nations: 'thus the demand for aid for underdeveloped countries is part of the demand of social justice on a worldwide scale', he writes [p. 92] and he stresses the radical practical consequences of his concept of social justice.

Egalitarian concepts of justice have been also advanced in some recent philosophical critiques of John Rawls's theory of justice as fairness. Brian Barry develops, as an alternative to Rawls's theory, an egalitarian concept of justice based on the idea of 'altruistic cooperation', which ought to be realized at the expense of the efficiency of the social system [Barry, pp. 166–8]. The axiological assumptions and underpinnings of such bourgeois egalitarian theories of justice are very close to the assumptions of the Marxist ideal of justice expressed in the formula, 'to each according to his needs.' This is particularly true of the concept of justice developed by A. M. Honoré, which seems to be inspired by Marxist ideas.[29]

But these radical egalitarian theories also differ substantially from the Marxist theory of justice. They rest on purely distributive concepts of justice. They do not consider the fundamental problem of social justice, which is the problem of the control of the means of production by the working classes of society. Therefore these theories remain within the ideological and conceptual framework of bourgeois liberal doctrine.

---

[29] See also G. Vlastos, 'Human Worth, Merit and Equality', in Joel Feinberg (ed.), *Moral Concepts* (Oxford, 1969), pp. 141–52.

7

Forms of equality

Ferenc Feher and Agnes Heller[1]

I

A spectre haunts the industrialized world—the spectre of egalitarianism. Demands to equalize the first and third worlds or to reduce needs to bring about social equality are articulated by movements and theories which keep 'social equality' on the agenda. But, as we will try to show, a consistently implemented egalitarianism is a myth. All attempts to realize it as a general principle of social organization in a context of even minimal industrialization lead to a decline of wealth. Yet, recurring egalitarian tendencies constitute an *indispensable* social monitoring system. They always point to concrete inequalities that threaten to become permanent and therefore must be opposed. That is why theories and movements that point out inequality and seek to eliminate it must be recognized as socially valuable.

To characterize egalitarianism as a social movement incorporating specific principles, it is necessary to study the main types of human equality. These fall into two basic types: equality with respect to ownership of property and equality in the evaluation of men as individuals.

Equality in ownership

One interpretation of this calls for the equal distribution of social goods—that is, an 'equal share' of property, an equal distribution of the land, or equal ownership of the means of production. This view is generally connected with obsolescent conditions of production or agrarian societies, especially if the equal distribution of social goods also means equal divisions. But this concept of equality can also refer to equality of needs or to an equal level of the satisfaction of needs. Usually, when this demand claims to be a general principle of social organization, it is tied to a play for the simultaneous redistribution of property. But when it is directed only at small groups, it may refer

[1] Translated from the German by David J. Parent; first published in *Telos*.

solely to consumption. Lastly, this conception can mean equality in the allocation and control of social goods. This can mean that all have control over their own, equally apportioned, property, or that all have an equal say in matters of politics, management, and so on.[2]

But the demand for equal property is never made where the economy has not yet developed into an independent sphere, that is, where reciprocity is subordinate to kinship or social custom, where the latter serves as the 'natural' means for the equalization of goods, and where redistribution is carried out through personal, face-to-face relations which guarantee equality. In short, this demand can never arise where redistribution and reciprocity remain on the level of a quasi-natural homeostasis.[3] Rather, this demand appears only in a limited form under conditions of undeveloped commodity production, where the goal of relative equality of wealth is to create and preserve the material basis for equality in making political decisions.

In general, the concept of and demand for equal ownership are responses to the generalization of commodity production and the independence of the economy from other social areas. These demands thus appear when the system of redistribution through kinship bonds and social customs breaks down. Equal exchange in the self-regulating market then becomes the sole form of reciprocity or symmetry in the economic sphere, that is, when the main task of the new, profit-oriented production and redistribution is to conserve existing inequalities resulting from the market and to create new inequalities. Thus, with developed commodity production, economic inequality becomes the basis of general social inequality. This results in a divergence between constantly developing needs—growing in both quantity and quality—and their satisfaction, and growing antagonisms between the 'haves' and the 'have-nots'. The classical form here is the relation between bourgeoisie and proletariat in nineteenth-century *laissez-faire* capitalism. Egalitarianism thus appears as a universal ideology wherever inequality becomes a recognized and accepted social condition (in other words, where there

---

[2] This latter programme holds that, simply because their property is equal, all individuals should have an equal vote in social matters. This sort of egalitarianism stems from the particular equilibrium of agricultural societies, based as they are on community property or land already divided into separate parcels. Consequently, this programme was the one most closely connected with movements aiming to equalize property ownership. But today, in the midst of hyper-industrialization, we are witnessing the revival of such demands for equal disposition over property—even in regard to its use.

[3] We have borrowed the concepts 'reciprocity' and 'redistribution' from Karl Polanyi. But we use them in a specific sense relating to conditions of developed commodity production and industrialization.

is inequality in property ownership, the satisfaction of needs, or the ability to make decisions).[4]

Equality of men as individuals

This concept of equality arose with the concept of humanity. In its original formulation, it is perhaps only the blurred reflex of the process by which mankind attains self-consciousness. In essence, it holds that we are all human beings and as such are equals. This idea first appeared in Christianity and was perfected with the proclamation of equality before the law. The basic principle here (never fully realized, but also never in principle denied) is the abstraction of person and deed from property and from social rank (from the place occupied in the division of labour).

[4] Here Polanyi and Sahlins do not mean by 'reciprocity', 'redistribution', and 'market mechanism' the different forms of economic transactions, but three basic types of economic organization. According to Sahlins: 'Pooling is socially a *within* relation, the collective action of a group. Reciprocity is a *between* relation, the action and reaction of two parties. Thus pooling is the complement of social unity and, in Polanyi's term, 'centricity'; whereas reciprocity is a social duality and 'symmetry'. Pooling stipulates a social centre where goods meet and hence flow outwards, and a social boundary too, within which persons (or subgroups) are cooperatively related. But reciprocity stipulates two sides, two distinct social-economic interests.' Sahlins, *Stone Age Economics* (Chicago and New York, 1972), pp. 188–9. According to Polanyi and Sahlins, societies can be regarded as organized on the basis of reciprocity if their economic, social and moral spheres are not fully differentiated, and if exchange is not based on market relations.

Of course, there are 'pure' economic systems—that is, built exclusively on reciprocity or redistribution—which exclude the competitive, price regulating market of buyers and sellers. But larger economic integrations cannot be pure: they entail economic transactions such as redistribution. Polanyi concurs with this: it is demonstrated precisely by him that the self-regulating market was only an economic utopia of the nineteenth century. Moreover, in the same work, his preference is given to a society in which market economy ceases to exist without the abolition of the market: 'Also the end of market society means in no way the absence of markets. These continue, in various fashions, to ensure the freedom of the consumer, to indicate the shifting of demand, to influence producer's income and to serve as an instrument of accounting, while ceasing altogether to be an organ of economic self-regulation.' *The Great Transformation* (Boston, 1967), p. 252. It is in this sense that we introduce the concept of redistribution into our argument as one of the regulative channels, but by no means the only one.

There is, however, a crucial similarity between the reciprocity of economic anthropology and the market mechanisms of buyers and sellers: both presuppose *symmetrical* relations (in contrast to redistribution), and include symmetrical, dual transactions. These relations always have an *economic* function, since they are social channels for the satisfaction of needs (primarily material ones). No modern, dynamic society is possible without symmetrical economic relations: they cannot be replaced by redistribution. Thus, we call all symmetrical economic transactions 'reciprocity', in contrast with asymmetrical redistribution, or 'centrality'. Only a social balance—albeit conflict-laden —of symmetrical and asymmetrical economic transactions can guarantee the functioning of an optimal economic decision-making model that satisfies the needs of individuals in modern society.

II

Ever since the revolutions of the eighteenth and nineteenth centuries seeking *liberté*, *egalité*, almost all social systems regard equality in some sense as a positive value. But there are two opposing models. One considers equality as a partial principle within prevailing inequality, while the other seeks to generalize equality as the basic social principle. The first model is characterized by the possibility of unlimited acquisition of property and the conscious acceptance of inequality. Supporters of this model see exchange in the self-regulating market as the only conceivable form of reciprocity, entailing inequality in needs and consumption and in the social hierarchy. Of course, various groups most affected by inequality and whose needs are least satisfied demand a more equitable distribution. Thus, today the ideologies of inequality increasingly employ a social game theory to investigate the role of such pressure groups within the model. Here, however, a more equitable redistribution is possible only in the area of consumption. Decision-making is not redistributed, and the 'will of all' has nothing to say about this. At best, it only chooses those who will.

Within this model of inequality, two forms of equality are generally recognized. First there is equality before the law, which has never been more than an ideal inasmuch as it is in constant conflict with the inequality of property. To remedy this contradiction, the independence of judicial power is usually built into the model as a partial guarantee. Ideally, the judicial arm is independent of the executive or legislative arm, but it can never avoid the underlying principle of inequality. Although within this model all constitutions guarantee men's equal rights, these rights can be realized only negatively—by forbidding certain actions. Anatole France's *aperçu* is more profound than first appears: equality negatively defined only increases actual inequality. Furthermore, all those eighteenth- and nineteenth-century liberal utopias that sought to complement the negative code of law with a positive and rewarding part turned out to be naive and unfulfillable because they lacked a supporting social mechanism.

The second type of equality within the capitalist model is that of equal opportunity. This is a relatively recent development and is connected with the increasing influence of pressure groups. This principle abstracts from the place occupied in the division of labour as well as from other factors, such as sex, race or religion. A prime example of this is the demand for equal opportunities for men and women. As a widespread social postulate—a kind of social 'domino theory' according to which the prevalent system of inequality can be broken at any point—the principle of equal opportunity is an excellent substitute for genuine equality. Although its role cannot be underestimated in as far as it challenges centuries-old inequalities, it is far more illusory than the idea of equality before the law, since it is *positively* formulated and as such contradicts the basic principle of property ownership and power influence. Its latent function, in fact, is to assure the optimal 'distribution' of individuals in the social hierarchy. The constant struggle between this principle of equal opportunity and the underlying inequality is part of the model and contributes to its functioning (for example, in the form of constant struggles for educational reforms, social and political opportunities, and so on).

The second basic model, that of egalitarianism, is opposed to the capitalist model and always comes about in response to it. Marx called this 'primitive communism,' the 'negative abolition of private property'. According to him, communism is

> 1. In its first form only a *generalization* and *consummation* of this relationship [i.e., private property]. As such it appears in a twofold form: on the one hand, the dominion of *material* property bulks so large that it wants to destroy everything which is not capable of being possessed by all as *private property*. It wants to do away *by force* with talent, etc. For it the sole purpose of life and existence is direct, physical *possession*. The task of the *labourer* is not done away with, but extended to all men. The relationship of private property persists as the relationship of the community to the world of things.... In negating the *personality* of man in every sphere, this type of communism is really nothing but the logical expression of private property, which is its negation. General *envy* constituting itself as a power is the disguise in which *greed* re-establishes itself and satisfies itself, only in *another* way. The thought of every piece of private property—inherent in each piece as such—is *at least* turned against all *wealthier* private property in the form of envy and the urge to reduce things to a common level, so that this envy and urge even constitute the essence of competition. Crude communism is only the culmination of this envy, of this levelling-down proceeding from the *preconceived* minimum. It has a *definite, limited* standard. How little this annulment of private property is really an appropriation is in fact proved by the abstract negation of the entire world of culture and civilization, the regression to the *unnatural* simplicity of the *poor and undemanding* man who has not only failed to go beyond private property, but in fact has not yet even reached it.[5]

The first model is distinctly capitalist. Property as ownership is the source and at the same time the limit of appropriation, in other words, appropriation is subsumed to ownership. This fusion is also accepted in the second model, that of primitive communism, as the 'negative abolition of private property'. The difference between the two models is not that unequal ownership is regarded by the latter as the source of unequal appropriation, but that it regards theoretically equal owner-

[5] Karl Marx, *The Economic and Philosophic Manuscripts of 1844*, ed. with an introduction by Dirk J. Struik, trans. Martin Miligan (New York, 1964), pp. 132–4.

ship as the source of likewise equal appropriation. As Marx described it, ownership as the essential expression of private property is 'universalized' and 'developed' in primitive communism.

Thus, the second model is characterized by the following traits: first, strong limitations on ownership. One way to do this is to divide a society's material forces into 'equal portions'. Today, however, this is purely utopian and, even in principle, incoherent (for example, how can raw materials and energy be divided into 'equal portions'?). Another way is through the state's confiscation of all property. As Marx concludes, the model of 'primitive communism' in its pure form can be either democratic (and thus mixed with self-deception), or despotic (as in the latter case).

The second characteristic of the primitive communism model is the equalization of needs. Since modern individuals are violently outraged by egalitarian conceptions (public opinion is so strong here that people are seldom candid on this subject), to evaluate this proposal, we must turn to the classics. In *Conspiration pour l'Egalité*, Buonarotti—one of the main historians of the Babeuf movement—speaks with naive candour:

> The natural equality that we envisage is this unity of *needs and feelings* which are born with us or develop by the first use we make of our senses and organs. The need to eat and reproduce; self-love; pity, the ability to feel, think, desire, communicate one's ideas and understand those of our fellow men, and to conform our actions to the rule; hatred of constraint and love of liberty exist *to about the same degree* among all healthy and well constituted men. *Such is the law of nature*, from which the same natural rights emanate for all men.[6]

The naiveté of this passage reveals social intentions more clearly than the scholarly epigone's complicated mental constructions. When Buonarotti—and, in retrospect, Babeuf—speak of the *uniformtiy* of needs and feelings (for example, 'to about the same degree'), it is clear that they apply purely quantitative criteria to essentially unquantifiable human expressions. Thus, the result is a social movement as impractical as it is radical. Instead of reviving the system of social inequality, it suggests that we ignore the heterogeneity of all our feelings and needs, and sacrifice personality—one of the most significant developments of human culture.

Ideologies of this type contrapose 'natural' to 'artificial' needs.[7]

[6] Buonarotti, *Conspiration pour l'Egalité* (reprinted, Paris, 1957) I, p. 29. Italics added.

[7] This polarity can take on quite different forms, according to various ideological points of departure: real needs versus those that are only imagined or which are aimed at prestige, natural needs versus luxuries, etc. Yet, they all lump cultural needs (especially those indispensable for creation and reception of advanced culture) into the category of imagined needs, luxuries, etc. As Marx put it, primitive communism 'wants to do away *by force* with talent, etc.', and is 'the abstract negation of the entire world of culture and civilization'.

This polarity is inevitable in all egalitarian ideologies that call for a levelling of needs, since, in order to do so, the 'right' structure of needs has to be determined. The reason is evident: where reciprocity and redistribution balance out in an almost natural fashion, there are no right or wrong needs, since there is no alternative to the status quo. The problem arises only with the generalization of commodity production, where the inequality of needs and consumption is already a fact, that is, wherever the prevalent structure can and should be confronted with an alternative.

Thus the two recurrent features of ideologies calling for the levelling of needs are, first, the 'right' structure of needs is always determined in contrast to something, and thus narrows the world of human wealth. Furthermore, this demand is always authoritarian since it abstracts from what people regard as their own needs, or else regards them as 'delusions' to be eliminated. Of course, a critique of the predominant structure of needs based on chosen values is by no means impossible or *ipso facto* authoritarian. But the levelling of all needs to a single exclusive model is inevitably tyrannical. What, then, are the functions of the egalitarian model and what are its chances of success?

The *democratic model of egalitarianism,* which seeks to divide ownership into 'equal parts', is utopian not only for industrial societies, but furthermore in all societies where redistribution centres cannot function independently of world commerce. Moreover, it is a *regressive* utopia since it would reduce and undermine the material resources of society. All redistribution centres would break down, together with mechanisms that regulate commodity exchange. It would bring about a system of *haphazard exchange* whose only real redistribution would be the redistribution of poverty. Again, this utopia is condemned as regressive from the viewpoint of our value preference based on Marx, from the preference of man rich in needs.

Before going further, it is necessary to establish whether Marx's *man rich in needs* is identical with *homo oeconomicus,* that is, whether his enrichment can be distinguished from the all-consuming, all-repressive development of human needs in bourgeois society. As an empirical historical product, *homo oeconomicus* arises along with *man rich in needs* as the promise of a free species. The growth of needs of *homo oeconomicus* is based on universal quantification. Its perfection is industrial production hypostasized to infinity. Its faith is in the transcendence of technological progress, in the 'future', in industrial production 'yet to be achieved'. *Man rich in needs* also opts for social dynamism, but for him it does not consist just in the increase of quantifiable needs. Although he sides with industrial development (accepting the continued development of the domination of nature, the growth in world trade, and so on), *man rich in needs* still subjugates the economic sphere to ecological limits and to the recognition that the birth of new, qualitative needs is also a new enrichment—one, moreover, that is opposed to linear growth.[8]

The *'despotic model' of egalitarianism* is enforced by the state as the 'representative of public interests'. It carries out the confiscation of the private ownership of everything simply by defining private property, or by setting the quantitative upper limit on ownership. Of course, it can always redefine these limits either in an authoritarian way or under the influence of pressure groups. In this model, all decisions are centralized in the state, which is not only the most important executive organ of redistribution but also its only centre. This is further guaranteed by the fact that the state not only has unlimited power to redistribute material goods and energy resources, but can also redistribute the work force. Symmetrical market relations vanish for the simple reason that the state has no partner. At the same time, the state regards all free activities as dysfunctional and eliminates them. Therefore, the elimination of symmetrical market mechanisms cannot be supplanted by the revival of reciprocity in the form of 'gifts', which is the form assumed by the redistribution carried out by the state. In this way, the authoritative character of the 'equalizing' centre is further strengthened.

This model—'despotic' in the Marxian sense—is an illusion and at the same time a destructive character trait in regard to our value preference. It is illusory in its belief that equality can be attained by fixing an upper limit on ownership. Since to achieve the reduction of needs the model requires an authoritarian state, over-centralization of redistribution, and the degradation of symmetrical mechanisms, a new inequality comes to permeate all of social life, in other words, that between those who distribute and those who are distributed. Marx has already indicated the destructive nature of this new inequality: it is the complete negation of personality by the 'representatives of the common interests' and the negation of the entire world of civilization and culture. While this model does not absolutely exclude dynamism, it does preclude the *qualitative needs* of personalities and a plurality of life-styles. Furthermore, even though this central determination of needs cannot bring about uniformity (for the simple reason that not all needs are quantifiable), it nonetheless brings about the impoverishment of the permitted life-styles.

But even the embittered confrontation between the capitalist and primitive communist models cannot transcend the bourgeois era.

---

[8] Our standpoint is radically different from that of the *homo oeconomicus* of bourgeois society and, insofar as it is evolutionary, also from Polanyi's, however much we may have drawn from him. Polanyi's anti-evolutionism is a result of his hatred of 'free market society' and of capitalism's quest for universality. We are evolutionists from a specifically Marxian standpoint that sees 'free market society' as the creator of world trade, and thus as the source of the possibility of *man rich in needs*.

Both subordinate appropriation to ownership or else incorporate the former into the latter. The first model represents the world of private property, while the other model represents the world of universalized private property, to use Marx's terms. In the former, ownership is both the source and the limit of the origin and satisfaction of needs and participation in decisions. In the latter, ownership is by allocation: a centrally determined amount of goods is 'allocated' for the disposition of individuals as consumers.

Both models seek to further the 'common interest', but in different ways. Marx's statement, that 'the general interest is precisely the generality of self-seeking interests',[9] applies to the first model. The 'general interest' is thus constituted in the struggle of particular forces and is nothing but the *generalization* of the strongest particular interest operating 'behind men's backs'. In the second model, if the general interest is centrally determined, those other interests and needs that crop up at various social points are denounced as particular (that is, excludable and negligible) when compared with the centrally determined ones. The majority of individuals does not participate in real decision-making processes in either model. Reified forces decide on personal needs and possible actions. Thus, both models become reified and alienated structures, though in different ways and for different reasons.

III

Is there an alternative, *third* model? Is it possible to transcend the first model by a non-egalitarian one which takes egalitarianism into account as a 'social monitoring system' and incorporates into its structure its 'negatively valid' truths? These are real questions which, like all theoretically responsible questions, are at the same time *postulates*. More precisely, the question is: *can the two factors of property—ownership and appropriation—be separated* in modern society? In other words, can the *process* of abolishing alienation begin in modern society while *preserving* social dynamism, considering the relativity of wealth and the constant recurrence of 'scarcity'?

A solution to this is possible only by clearing up two further questions. First of all, why and under what conditions do we, following Marx, regard ownership and appropriation as two different aspects of property? Second, why do we regard their separation and simultaneous social 'encounter' as the starting point for the abolition of alienation?[10]

[9] Karl Marx, *Grundrisse*, trans. Martin Nicolaus (London, 1973), p. 245.
[10] Our analysis of the various aspects of property parallels Andras Hegedüs's study, 'Adalékok a tulajdonviszonyok szociologiai elemzéséhez' (Contributions to the Sociological Investigation of Property Relations), *Magyar Filosofiai Szemle* 6 (1969).

As to the first question, we equate ownership with possession. As an abstraction, this means the ownership of one, or the ownership of some people, where all others are excluded from its use, from the satisfaction derived from it and from the disposition over it. Of course, this is only a theoretical abstraction, since the particular, exclusive satisfaction of needs, just as the exclusive disposition over them, goes beyond ownership in the direction of appropriation. Furthermore, it is abstract inasmuch as modern society creates a duality among all working people: they are both producers and consumers. Only in an abstract model can one picture a producer who completely satisfies his needs from what he exclusively owns (even though he might share this ownership with several others). Lastly, it is an abstraction since 'exclusive ownership' cannot be understood in the sense of one's omnipotence over property: in simple terms, the more complicated a society is, the more regulations it has and the less the individual can do as he wishes with what he owns. But whenever he can do something, *he alone can do it, and not someone else.* For this reason, ownership is exclusive.

Appropriation, the other aspect of property, entails the satisfaction of needs connected with production, a hand in decisions pertaining to production, distribution, and consumption, and the determination of their preconditions. Two groups of production-related needs must be distinguished. First, there is the need for activity, in other words, the need to express and realize one's personality, the development of one's abilities through work and socially vital activities. Secondly, there are the requirements for consumption of immediately produced goods, be they material or non-material (for example, cultural products, medical services,) whose precondition is production.

By definition, there can be no ownership without appropriation, for the very purpose of ownership is in appropriation. I only want to own something—and at the same time exclude others from this ownership —when the property secures a particular field of appropriation for me. But this does not mean that one's ownership is the source of all that one appropriates. On the contrary, the process of appropriation always goes beyond ownership.

The excellent feature of capitalist society is that in it, the amount of goods appropriated is completely determined by ownership, while the 'location' of the goods appropriated, when compared with previous societies, is least of all one's ownership. The specific feature of bourgeois private property is the unity of the contradiction between social production and individual expropriation. The limit to satisfaction of needs is determined by ownership; the more one owns, the more one can satisfy needs of activity *and* consumption. Furthermore, participation in decision-making also grows in direct proportion to ownership. You are what you have. Human conditions appear as conditions of things. At the same time, the need-satisfying quality of ownership is subordinated to social production; only at the point of possession can it be the source of need satisfaction. Thus, appropriation is a category of the conditions of property; and ownership and appropriation are separate aspects, even though their object is the same: that is, they are reciprocal determinations.

The answer to the second question, then, is that capitalism is the exemplary alienated society. In its fully developed forms, ownership not only determines the limit of appropriation, but also strives for its universal subjugation. This condition is enhanced by the fact that capitalism is a universal money society, 'free' of the bonds of caste or kinship systems. Consequently, the means exist for universal quantification—hence, the dominant striving to compare what is incommensurable and to reduce qualitative needs to quantitative ones. But the limit on ownership—that is, that it can only *strive* for universal subjugation of appropriation—is important.[11] The complete homogenization of the two basic aspects of property is thus revealed to be a myth believed by the supporters as well as the staunchest detractors of liberal capitalism.

Despite all these qualifications, the analyses of ownership are accurate: one *is* what one *has* and the needs that can be satisfied or the social conditions one can dispose over depend purely on wealth. Ownership dominated the appropriation process by transforming its entire environment into the universe of quantifiable needs, and by establishing ownership as the exclusive standard for disposition—again a quantitative principle. The simultaneous development of these two aspects creates the world of bourgeois private property.

The positive abolition of private property is not identical with the simple 'abolition of all ownership'. This socially nonsensical objective cannot be seriously entertained, even in its most extremely egalitarian form. Moreover, the development of *man rich in needs* presupposes the expansion of ownership of things used to satisfy needs, and the directions that this expansion may take can be blocked or rechannelled

---

[11] Two examples suffice to show the limits of homogenization. One is the revolt of the propertyless against the injustices of appropriation, from the Luddites to the labour union movements at the end of the nineteenth century. However one labels them— 'anarchist' or 'reformist'—it is difficult to deny that these movements have influenced the appropriation of surplus value since they have reduced the 'extension' of capitalist ownership, even when they did not question its 'propriety'. In so doing, however, they demonstrated the practical possibility of separating the two aspects right in the midst of the supposed universal homogenization. The second example, which was repeatedly analysed by Marx, is that, even at the height of *laissez-faire* capitalism, the bourgeoisie had to delegate a considerable degree of control, in part because the administration of ownership and the regulation of the process of appropriation seldom could be carried out by one person: the complete surveillance of the process of appropriation by the owner was usually only an ideal.

only as a result of a consensus reached through discussions and social conflicts.

The positive abolition of private property means that ownership will no longer be the focus of social dynamics; that appropriation gradually will be freed from the ownership that suppresses it; and that essential human forces will increasingly be realized in the process of appropriation as the origin and satisfaction of new, qualitative needs and as disposition over its objective preconditions and results or, in broader terms, appropriation as the mastery of the world's objective wealth. Thus, this process can be the real sphere of the human appropriation of the world, that is, of the positive abolition of private property, because here 'taking possession' is *not* necessarily an exclusive act but *presupposes* a similar activity by other men. Our model thus presupposes two parallel series: the increase in the amount of delimited, separate property (the expansion of needs), even though certain directions of expansion may be blocked, and the gradual 'emancipation' of appropriation from the domination of ownership. These two tendencies comprise the process of the positive abolition of private property. But is this model practical? In other words, is a responsible experiment to realize it in a modern, dynamic world possible? To answer this, we must re-examine the meaning of reciprocity and redistribution.

Modern society is a commodity-producing society; thus, the point of departure for a model purporting to be a 'third way' is the recognition of the existence of commodity exchange as an economic necessity. Commodity exchange, that is, the market, is the only form of symmetrical economic relations in existence.[12] It functions as the basis of calculation for all stable industrialized societies, in a twofold sense: first, it is this basis that provides the terms to assess social wealth. Its rival could only be a system of entirely arbitrary central decisions or a 'simulated market', a totally superfluous detour either to the market or to the above mentioned subjectivist model. Further, it is the market that allows a society to calculate scarcity and shortages where scarcity means the finiteness of natural energy resources at a given historical moment and the finiteness of working time available in a concrete social context. This means that it is impossible to abolish property as ownership in a concrete social dimension. The property holder appears in the market as an 'owner', the subject of reciprocity in exchange relation. All sorts of property can enter into symmetrical market relations—private, exclusively owned property, collective property (owned by a group of stock holders, or a workers-owned factory), nationalized enterprises with independent economic authority, and so on. In our model, the predominant place will be

---

[12] Much of what follows is derived from the unpublished manuscript of György Bence, Janos Kis and György Markus, *Is A Critical Economy Possible?*

occupied by the property held by democratic groups and by state property authorized to take independent economic initiative. Although we presuppose a society where these two forms of collective ownership prevail, we are still operating within a world of symmetrical market relations, since the market remains as the basis of economic calculation.

Thus, *ownership cannot cease to be a factor in determining appropriation*. The positive value of ownership in a *social* model is based on two factors which have proven to be lasting achievements of mankind, transcending the pre-capitalist and capitalist periods: the rational administration of property as the source of the rational satisfaction of needs, and the *direct* relation of decision-making to ownership. This applies not only in economics, such as the planning of personal accumulation and consumption, or in the affairs of a small community (for instance, the family), but also to 'personal life strategies'. It is easy to see how significant this is for the growth of all people and how far it extends beyond the sphere of ownership. The control learned in the disposition of ownership develops the abilities for rationally sharing in the process of appropriation as it becomes emancipated from ownership.

Appropriation is freed from ownership in yet another decisive respect, that is, in *redistribution*. The existence of need structures pointing beyond the scope of ownership is the precondition for appropriation as more than mere 'appropriation' of whatever consumer goods one may own. Here appropriation as redistribution is not only the redistribution of socially produced goods, but also the determination of overall social strategy—a constant redistribution of all of society's material and spiritual resources through a general consensus. The precondition for this is the equal possibility of deciding on redistribution for all. This is one constituent of the process of appropriation *not* connected with ownership or with symmetrical market relations. Equal participation in redistribution is not just the only rational significance of the equal opportunity to articulate needs emancipated from ownership, but is also the essential reinterpretation of the concept of property. What remains of the concept of ownership is the basic act of personal satisfaction of needs and the social basis of calculation constituted in the act of exchange.

As the process of appropriation (presupposing a new structure of needs) becomes predominant, the world's objective wealth, which is in principle appropriated by all in order to develop, becomes human property. But this can be achieved primarily by *communal* acts which, by definition, have no exclusive character.

What, then, is required so that redistribution becomes increasingly determined by appropriation and decreasingly by ownership? As already mentioned, the increased expansion of ownership—as the enrichment of needs—does not rule out limiting some possible directions of expansion. On a broad social level, this means placing limitations on those private groups and collective properties which, because of their monopoly situation, can disproportionately influence redistribution, thus subverting equality in decision-making. Thus, the old call for socialization and nationalization reappears within this model. But this call today is not followed by the traditional argument of planning versus anarchy. It is ridiculous to think that the liquidation of the basis for calculation carried out in the elimination of symmetrical market relations would in any way promote the cause of purposive rationality. Thus, two limits must be set on the realization of these preconditions. First, from the standpoint of purposive rationality, nationalization becomes mystified only when the amount of property has reached or exceeded the point where a centralized administration is the only viable economic alternative. The second limit is dictated by two principles of value rationality: one, there should be no income without work as a constant basis of self-preservation and two, the state's control of ownership must never become such that it would tend to destroy values in the previously described manner.

The second precondition for democratic redistribution is just the reformulation of the previous one in a different way. The development of a broad scale of ownership by groups, communities and the state which makes possible symmetrical market relations creates a situation where the state can and should be the administrative organ of redistribution, while still not extending over all social life. The state will be the 'representative of general interest' and not 'generality' itself. This model strives only for a dynamic equilibrium, in other words, the model does not know or recognize a panacea for every possible dysfunction. Yet, even assuming the purely democratic character of ownership groups, there is always the danger that the symmetrical market relations once again become dominant and the state loses influence as the administrative organ of redistribution.

Another precondition for equality in redistribution is equality in decision-making. But what does this mean?[13] First of all, subjects should have a growing competence in all areas (that is, all areas should equally be areas of decision). Second, individuals should have the opportunity to participate equally in decision-making. Within such a framework the idea of 'equal opportunity' is no substitute for equality, but is a real mechanism in equalization. To decide one must have the

[13] Here we need to mention recent untenable views of egalitarianism developed during the great social conflicts of the last decade. They can be briefly summarized as follows: since all men are equally competent to make the most varied decisions, hierarchic orders are conscious mystifications that can be abolished by the revolution. This disregard of the division of labour creates illusions that are still with us today.

ability and competence to decide. This can never be the equal competence of *all* men in *every* single question, but all men are competent
in *some* socially relevant question. Moreover, an individual's competence can grow. But for this to take place, individuals must be assured
equal opportunity, which means equality of the unequal. While
original differences in abilities can and should be diminished, they can
never be completely eliminated.

Finally, there is the question of equality of income. Today, those
who accept the egalitarian standpoint are concerned with the principle
of equal income. At first, this idea seems so plausible that all other
interpretations seem artificial or insincere. Why, then, do we reject it?

The idea of equality of income is popular because it is plausible;
it offers a quantifiable and clear criterion and fully corresponds to the
spirit of bourgeois society, which measures only in terms of ownership. Thus, it does not correspond to our model.

To clarify this point, it is helpful to discuss the relation of ownership and income in the two previous models. In the case of the first
model, the relation of income to ownership is clear. Income either
stems from ownership (as revenue) or from the sale of labour
power (as wage). In the despotic model of egalitarianism, however,
the central authority allots an equal income to the whole population
on the basis of its estimate of social wealth. When ownership is
distinguished from appropriation, however, it becomes evident that
both models separate property from income. In the first model, no
wage worker can ever directly influence the process of social appropriation, while in the second case the central authority converts the
whole society into an ensemble of wage workers. Even if a perfectly
equal distribution could be achieved, with the representatives of the
central authority receiving only as much as wage workers, a new
inequality would still result between those who determine income
and those whose incomes are determined. Only those completely
imbued with the bourgeois spirit can consider this inequality to be
secondary with regard to income inequality.

In our model, wage labour is abolished and collective owners themselves decide their income. Of course, there would be upper and
lower income limits reached through free discussion and social
decisions made by those concerned. The lower limit must enable the
satisfaction of all needs within the given cultural context so as to
allow individuals to participate freely in the appropriation process.
By this participation, he also satisfies a whole series of other needs
not expressible in quantitative terms. The upper limit on income
would prevent any one person from gaining power over others,
especially over entire groups of people.

At the same time, efforts to equalize income must not disregard
the actual plurality of needs. It is argued that, if needs are allowed

to develop unchecked, men will always want more, thus leading to extremes of wealth and poverty. Therefore, a central authority is necessary, since the fact that one person possesses more than another is already a cause of alienation. Despotic egalitarianism, which adheres proudly to the materialist standpoint, in fact represents the materialism of bourgeois society since it can think only in terms of quantitative needs: given a finite amount of goods, one person's needs can be satisfied only at the expense of another's. Despite the oppositional attitude, the spirit of ownership or of universalized private property prevails here, and the resulting alienation is the morality of collective envy. But if we envisage the future as a world where the free process of appropriation is the collective form of satisfying qualitatively different needs, and if we regard the qualitative needs that can be satisfied only collectively as fundamental from the viewpoint of the freely developing personality, then we must recognize the plurality of needs. The ethic of alienation should then itself be alienating for us as the spirit of collective envy, which we want to leave behind.

It is especially important to recognize the plurality of needs in work. Our model regards one's work as the basis for satisfying quantifiable needs and condemns parasitism. Moreover, the reproduction of social life always requires a certain amount of human labour which individuals must somehow divide among themselves. But here also we reject the pattern of despotic egalitarianism where not only is the same income ideally allotted to all members of society as wage labourers, but the quantity and quality of work are centrally determined as well. Labour becomes compulsory with no chance for an individual to select his or her life strategy. In this model, decisions are not the personal expression of free, communal individuals concerning their destiny, but are external and alien powers opposed to them. Of course, there will always be possible conflict so long as some have 'more' while others have 'less'. But the awareness of these conflicts and efforts to solve them are natural parts of the process of human self-liberation.

As the central question of industrialized society, the extension of decision-making in the area of production—that is, 'workers' democracy' or 'self-management'—is extremely important. Although in the industrial world everyone is affected by wrong directions in technological development, the warning signs for this and the need to redirect it can first be articulated by those closest to it. Of course, such a redirection has limits, but human control of technology is an integral part of the process of appropriation.

The *form* of participation in determining society's overall strategy of redistribution is, to use Habermas's terminology, 'undistorted communication'. Its regulative principle, the 'ideal speech situation'—that is, the open public character that plays so important a role in our model—is described by Habermas as follows:

An interchangeability of dialogue-roles is possible, and not just in principle. Furthermore, there is also an effective equality of opportunity in the perception of these roles, i.e., in the choice and performance of speech acts.... In the ideal speech situation, the only genuine speakers are those who have *equal opportunities to act* or to make use of representatives; for only reciprocal coordination in individual expression ... guarantees that subjects are candid with each other concerning what they really do and mean and, if necessary, can translate their extraverbal expressions into verbal ones. This mutuality of unimpaired self-depiction implies, further, a reciprocity of behaviour-expectations and excludes privileges in the sense of onesidedly binding norms of action.[14]

The public sphere analysed by Habermas and presupposed by our model is more than a formal principle. It speaks not only of the 'interchangeability of dialogue-roles', but also of the equality of the 'speakers' as active people and excludes 'onesidedly binding norms'. This principle of public life corresponds to our process of appropriation, which includes the free possibility of formal 'verbal acts', but which does not remain on the level of this formality, inasmuch as it is embodied in both institutionalized and spontaneous forms.

The last precondition for our model is that the total social learning process become an organic part of the process of appropriation. Today education is caught between those who see it essentially as the hierarchic training of specialists, and those who regard the whole hierarchy of technical knowledge as mere mystification created by the division of labour. Both approaches identify education and instruction with the accumulation of knowledge and they see schools as the only place where this can be done. We reject both. The concept of instruction as the training of specialists is functional, but it ultimately cripples men. Yet, to deny the need for technical knowledge and all social differences that this implies is illusory. The competence to make decisions is necessary for the expansion and equalization of the decision-making process. Consequently, education is not merely a preparation for social activities, but is achieved in the actual carrying-out of these activities, in the very process of making decisions. Without this, the new model of redistribution is impossible. Instruction is not merely the acquisition of knowledge, but prepares people to make decisions: *school cannot be its only setting.*

To guarantee appropriation, culture should gradually be withdrawn

---

[14] Jürgen Habermas, 'Vorbereitende Bemerkungen zu einer Theorie der kommunikativen Kompetenz', in Jürgen Habermas and Niklas Luhmann, *Theorie der Gesellschaft oder Sozialtechnologie* (Frankfurt, 1971), pp. 137–8. Here Habermas speaks of 'reciprocity' and 'symmetry' in reference to equality attained as a result of communication. This appears to contradict our account where communication is regarded as the underlying determination of the process of redistribution, *detached* from reciprocity. But the contradiction is only apparent, as will become clear later.

from the context of reciprocity underlying commodity exchange. Of course, it is impossible to be more specific than this: it is the task of undistorted value-building communication of the public sphere to decide what the commodity 'can' and 'wants' to provide for culture. But, at the same time, this is inadequate. Certainly, the infrastructure must also be withdrawn from market controls in order to create a 'cultured environment'. The gradual rollback of market regulation in the area of culture entails that, in determining the proportion of resources allocated to cultural development, no market interest can constitute the predominant viewpoint. Rather, only the promotion of a new type of appropriation process is relevant (that is, the development of *man rich in needs*). Within a framework of this type of redistribution, the proportion allocated to culture cannot be a function of ownership (in other words, all individuals must have 'equal opportunity').

The appropriation process outlined here does not call for the abolition of the market, but for the separation of its functions that *laissez-faire* capitalism sought to homogenize. We have already described the first of these functions (the market as the basis of calculation): its existence is necessary for society's purposive rationality, and it does not make sense to speak either of its expansion or contraction. As to the second function, we agree with Polanyi: the market as a general reference system will gradually recede, the autocracy of 'having' will be abolished, and Marx's great postulate—the subjugation of the economic sphere to the totality of the social life process—will be realized. Equality in this model gradually becomes identical with the equality of decision-making possibilities both in reference to ownership and in the sense of the gradual separation of appropriation from ownership.

While we reject any guarantees for our model, we still must take into consideration the question of its possibilities for realization. In our model, conflict is no evil, but one of the principles that makes the system workable—so long as it does not reach the point where it destroys the ability of the model to reproduce itself. The most important conflicts are between ownership and appropriation; between the 'solvent needs' articulated on the basis of calculation and the need-correcting principle of the public sphere in the decision-making process (a conflict that results either in the attempt to subject fundamental areas of the appropriation process to a narrow profit-centredness or in the threat posed by exalted utopian plans for 'undistorted communication' to the functioning of the calculation basis); and between institutionalized and non-institutionalized forms of the public sphere concerning limitations of property and investments. All these conflicts are reminders that our model is not overly optimistic.

The possibilities for the model can be located, first of all, in a social need (in the form of dysfunctions, conflicts, and so on) that the model addresses. Yet at the moment, there are social forces moving in just this direction. The best chance for our proposal, however, lies in the fact that, while it takes account of the existence of nation-states, it has *mankind* as its reference system. The universalization of the first model implies that the 'weak' are downtrodden by the 'strong', while the universalization of the second model means that the sphere of need determination is turned over to a world government, a chimera that *eliminates* all particular interest groups, need structures, and national cultural traditions: in short, it eliminates reciprocity and forcibly quantifies qualitative difference of needs.

Mankind as the frame of reference for our model is determined by a basic necessity: for economic planning to work, it requires that all of mankind's energy resources and means at its disposal be considered, at least if we want to preserve the dynamism of needs and production. From this stems the very possibility of our model.

All this shows that, with respect to the broadest degree of openness of mankind, the dynamics of the self-regulating market cannot be a universal reference system. Thus, the outlined model is no naive wish, but stems from real needs. Of course, we do not intend to formulate new economic fantasies: the world's energy sources and supplies are a fact that must be accepted. Consequently, symmetrical market relations will remain in force. But since the universalization of the market's self-regulation into a universal reference system threatens to break down and thus make all calculation impossible, another form of reciprocity will appear more and more frequently—gift-reciprocity. This will not be detached completely from symmetrical market relations since its limits are determined by interests embodied in the basis of calculation and because the continued existence of world trade is also an 'interest'. It can be easily imagined that a gift-reciprocity implemented in the interest of the 'stronger' party's expansion of following the goals of a new 'need-determining' world centre is degraded into a pseudo-gift.

But if gift-reciprocity develops true to form and becomes a main channel for world trade, it would bring about a situation independent of property ownership and determined by the above-described appropriation process. Thus, a new type of redistribution would be the precondition of gift-reciprocity and at the same time would be confirmed by it. For gift-reciprocity is a form of redistribution *sui generis*: it entails a redistribution of forces and wealth and, if the gift is not to degenerate into a pseudo-gift, such a question can only be decided in the 'ideal speech situation', that is, through the equal disposition over it by groups of people.

IV

So far, we have considered primarily the first form of the principle of equality—that related to property. This form, as the exchange of equal values elaborated in the Marx quotation, plays an important role in symmetrical market relations, but not the only one. Gift-reciprocity between the integrations is not equal, because it does not follow the principle of symmetrical market relations. A 'gift' that promotes the development of backward areas or that seeks to avoid ecological disaster is 'reciprocal' in the most elementary meaning of the word, since the recipient responds to this gift by participating in world trade or by being smoothly integrated in production processes, and so on—although this 'return service' cannot be qualitatively regulated. Here, for the first time, we encounter the social meaning of the concept 'incommensurability', while at the same time a rationally comprehensible meaning of equality develops in the area of disposition (decision-making). In the process of appropriation, only equality of decision has social significance.

The second form of the principle was characterized by its abstraction from ownership. This form is prevalent in the model of equality before the law. In the model we are proposing, the idea of legal equality retains absolutely its validity as the social scale of judgement. Nothing can replace its social function. Even so, there have been attempts to revise it or to replace it by a system of *ad hoc* decisions dictated by 'general interests' from whose viewpoint this model is too inflexible. Or else it has been seen as excessively formal compared with the multi-dimensional wealth and totality of human individuality, thus requiring replacement by an uncodifiable *moral propriety*. But these two principles, often interwoven, would only produce arbitrariness and consequently the violation of human equality. Whenever a social structure endorses a formal principle of equality, the standard of equality before the law is inevitable and irreplaceable. Hence, violations of the formal principle of equality before the law in the name of some *raison d'état* cannot be condoned, especially in our model, where the state is not the exclusive embodiment of the 'general interest' but merely its executive organ.

There is a growing network of communities based on the principle of equality abstracted from property—a network that creates a series of symmetrical reciprocal mechanisms, preserves equality, but also transcends it in the direction of incommensurability. These communities can grow out of radical needs generated in the production process, or out of new needs of those 'drop-outs' who turn their backs on production. Of course, this is not to say that there are no problems with these movements. One objection frequently raised against the 'drop-outs' seems to be particularly justified: the criticism that they deceive themselves in thinking that they have stepped outside industrial civilization, while vegetating in its midst and allowing themselves to be nourished by it, that they oppose industrialization, while using its technical advantages. Their anti-work theory and practice is especially dangerous, since it seeks to replace productive life and self-realization (including objectification) with an artificially induced permanent euphoria. Yet, despite these deformations, without the broad development of such movements (and the gradual eradication of the parasitical, destructive ideologies of some of them) it would be impossible to realize either the subject of our appropriation process or the subject of worldwide gift-reciprocity. Thus, it is not the generalizable (and pluralistic) new subject of these communities who is utopian, but the rigidly rationalist idea that dares to hypostasize a world condition out of the mere insight of people living private and isolated lives. This transformation presents a number of psychological dilemmas. But it is no more impossible than it was for the free citizen of antiquity to regard slaves or barbarians as his equals in the eyes of God, or no more impossible than the idea of universal equality before the law for men of feudal epochs. While historical analogies have limited value for future-oriented models, there is little doubt that the *new* regulation of human production can develop only in conjunction with the subordination of the economic sphere to the totality of social life processes and the development of new lifestyles.

What are the advantages of such a network of pluralistically developed communal life styles? Their pluralistic nature is determined by the various qualitative structures of needs and by the different relations which produced them. The basic principle of such communal life styles is suited from the start to developing many reciprocal-symmetrical situations that can encompass the whole of everyday life. Thus, it is unimportant whether these communities may be transitory and constitute only an educational phase or may turn out to be permanent life styles for certain groups of individuals; whether they grow out of the needs generated by the appropriation process or represent a transitory opposition to the world of production; whether they form 'ideal communities' or encompass the greatest part of vital activities. Even the *community as an end in itself* points beyond itself, precisely by its situation oriented away from interests that create gift-reciprocity. Furthermore, these communities are the best means of education for the ideal speech situation as the form of public life necessary for the new model of redistribution. A worldwide network of communal life styles is the precondition for public communication where rational discussion is the accepted norm. The development of the entire spectrum of qualitative-radical needs is thinkable only in communities of this type, not because these communities suppress quantitative needs, but because the pillars of this community—the associated individuals—will develop their personalities and the 'gifts' themselves will become fundamental qualitative needs.

These reciprocal-symmetrical communities differ from those resulting from the restructuring of life styles during previous historical periods, where it was undertaken as a society-constitutive endeavour in the direct sense of the word. It suffices here to refer to the role of friendship in the Greek *polis* or to the function of the intimate family circle in bourgeois public life as analysed by Habermas. Because of the complicated nature of modern society, these communities are not state-constitutive but citizen-constitutive. They contain one of the most important nuances of meaning for the principle of equality—the equality of personal contacts embodied in 'face-to-face' relations abstracted from property.

The last question for our model is this: if we expect the future to bring about this incommensurability based on equality but transcending it, have we really abstracted from property?

The answer is yes. The realization of incommensurability in the network of personal contacts is based on this abstraction. In a broader sense, however, this abstraction can always be only *relative*. The precondition for our model is the emancipation of appropriation from ownership. Therefore, it is more than a moral utopia.

But the process of the abolition of alienation is essentially a Kantian 'regulative practical idea', presupposing an infinite progression—in other words, a process whose limits we cannot conceive, owing to contemporary industrial civilization and our own value assumptions. The concept of infinite progression is consciously contrasted with Hegel's conception of the 'return of the world spirit', because the 'moment of returning home' as the clear and final ending of alienation is a crypto-theological concept—not for philosophical, but for sociological reasons. Our model is based on the ever possible conflict between ownership and appropriation, between reciprocity and redistribution. It recognizes no cure-all in the form of ideal institutional configurations and takes into account recurrent inequalities and the constant process of equalizing them in the gradual (and practically infinite) task of achieving equality in decision-making.

The aim of our model, then, is not *equality*, but constant *equalization* always restructured in social movements and institutions in response to concrete inequalities; not the abolition of ownership, but its purposive, value-rational restriction and the gradual emancipation of appropriation from ownership; not the reduction of needs nor the constant growth of the needs of *homo oeconomicus*, but the creation of a human being *rich in needs* whose needs-dynamic is not only or even primarily limited by scarcity, but who is directed to other, heterogeneous qualitative needs, to needs oriented toward the wealth of human contacts. No longer will the role of purposive-rationality be autocratically dominant and monopolistic, but purposive-rationality will be acceptable only together with informal, non-quantifiable principles of value rationality.

Suggested reading

Brian Barry: *The Liberal Theory of Justice*. Oxford, Clarendon Press, 1973.

Norman Daniels (ed.): *Reading Rawls*. Oxford, Blackwell, 1975.

F. E. Dowrick: *Justice according to the English Common Lawyer*. London, Butterworth, 1961.

Carl J. Friedrich and John W. Chapman (eds): *Justice – Nomos VI*. New York, Atherton Press, 1963.

Hans Kelsen: *What is Justice?* Berkeley, University of California Press, 1957.

H. L. A. Hart: *The Concept of Law*, especially chapters 8 and 9. Oxford, Clarendon Press, 1961.

Robert Nozick: *Anarchy, State and Utopia*. Oxford, Blackwell, 1975.

Ch. Perelman: *The Idea of Justice and the Problem of Argument*. London, Routledge, 1963.

John Rawls: *A Theory of Justice*. Cambridge, Mass., Harvard UP, 1971.

Julius Stone: *Human Law and Human Justice*. London, Stevens, 1965.

Contributors

Brian Barry is a Professor in the Departments of Political Science and Philosophy, and in the College, of the University of Chicago. He is a Fellow of the American Academy of Arts and Sciences. Born in London in 1936, he studied philosophy, politics and economics at Oxford and received the DPhil in 1965. He was the founding editor of the *British Journal of Political Science* and has served on the editorial boards of the *European Journal of Political Research*, the *American Political Science Review*, *Political Theory*, and *Government and Opposition*. In 1976–7, he was a Fellow at the Center for Advanced Study in the Behavioral Sciences, Stanford, California, where the first draft of the paper appearing in this volume was prepared. Professor Barry's books include *Political Argument* (1965), *Sociologists, Economists and Democracy* (1970), and *The Liberal Theory of Justice* (1973). He is also the editor of *Power and Political Theory: Some European Perspectives* (1976) and (with R. I. Sikora) *Obligations to Future Generations* (1978).

Ferenc Feher, a Marxist dissident who was forced to leave Hungary with his wife Agnes Heller in 1977, is Senior Research Fellow in the History of Ideas Unit in the Australian National University and is now working on a political biography of his friend and teacher, Georg Lukács. Born in Budapest in 1933, he was educated in history, philosophy and literary and social theory at the Eötvös Loránd University, Budapest, and wrote his doctoral dissertation, under the supervision of Lukács, on *The Poet of Antinomies: Dostoevsky and the Crisis of the Individual*. It was published in Hungary in 1972 and has been translated into Portuguese. Dr Feher is the editor of the four-volume German edition of Lukács's *Aesthetik* (1973) and co-author (with G. Lukács, A Heller and others) of *Individuum und Praxis* (1976), and (with A. Heller and G. Markus) of *Die Seele und das Leben* (1977), which has been translated into French and Italian.

Subjected to political harassment in Hungary in the 1950s and again from 1973 to 1977, he has published numerous articles on social and literary theory and Marxist philosophy.

Agnes Heller, a leading member of the 'Budapest School' of critical Marxism inspired by Georg Lukács, emigrated from Hungary in 1977 and is now Reader in Sociology at La Trobe University, Melbourne. Born in Hungary in 1929, she was educated at Eötvös Loránd University, Budapest, and took her doctorate with a thesis on 'Chernyshevshski and the Theory of Rational Egoism'. From 1953 to 1958 she was Associate Professor in that university's Department of Philosophy, in which Lukács was Professor; from 1962 until 1972, when she was deprived of her post, she was Chief Research Fellow in the Institute of Sociology of the Hungarian Academy of Sciences. Dr Heller was the first editor-in-chief of the Hungarian review of philosophy, *Magyar Filozófiai Szemle*, in 1956 and is now a member of the advisory board of the review *Praxis* (Zagreb) and of the editorial boards of *Aut-Aut* (Milan) and *Social Praxis* (Toronto). She has been a Visiting Professor in the Free University of Berlin and given guest lectures in American and German universities. Her books, originally published in Hungarian and translated into a number of European languages, include *Chernyshevski and the Problem of Rational Egoism* (1965), *Social Role and Prejudice* (1961), *The Ethics of Aristotle* (1966), *Renaissance Man* (1968), *Value and History* (1968), *Ethics* (1969) and *Everyday Life* (1970). Her most recent books are *The Theory of Needs in Marx*, first published in Italian in 1974 and in English, French and German in 1976, and *The Critique of Fromm's Theory of Aggression* (Italian, 1977).

Eugene Kamenka is Professor of the History of Ideas in the Institute of Advanced Studies of the Australian National University and has been (in 1973, 1974 and 1976) Visiting Professor in the Faculty of Law in the University of Sydney. He is a Fellow of the Academy of the Social Sciences in Australia and Fellow and Secretary of the Australian Academy of the Humanities. Born in Cologne in 1928, Professor Kamenka was educated in Australia in the Sydney Technical High School, the University of Sydney and the Australian National University. He has worked and taught in Israel, England, Germany, the United States, Canada, the USSR and Singapore. His books include *The Ethical Foundations of Marxism* (1962), *Marxism and Ethics* (1969) and *The Philosophy of Ludwig Feuerbach* (1970); he has edited *A World in Revolution?* (1970), *Paradigm for Revolution? The Paris Commune 1871–1971* (1972), *Nationalism – The Nature and Evolution of an Idea* (1973), and with R. S. Neale, *Feudalism, Capitalism and Beyond* (1975). He is general editor of this series,

'Ideas and Ideologies', in which he has co-edited and contributed to *Law and Society: the Crisis in Legal Ideals, Human Rights, Bureaucracy: the Career of a Concept* and *Intellectuals and Revolution: Socialism and the Experience of 1848.* His most recent volume is *The Portable Karl Marx* (1980).

Wiesław Lang is Professor of Legal Theory and Head of the Department of the General Theory of State and Law in the Institute of Law and Government of the Nicolas Copernicus University in Toruń, Poland. He was born in Lwów, Poland (now USSR), in 1928 and graduated from the Faculty of Law of the Jagiellonian University in Cracow, where he completed a doctorate and became Adjoint Professor in 1965. He has studied Scandinavian legal philosophy as Ford Foundation Fellow in Denmark, Sweden and Norway under the tutorship of Professor Alf Ross and worked in the United States on contemporary American legal philosophy as a Fellow of the American Council of Learned Societies. In 1977 he delivered a series of lectures on legal philosophy in the Department of Jurisprudence in the University of Sydney. Professor Lang's books include *Obowizywanie prawa (The Validity of Law,* 1962), *Struktura kontroli prawnej organów państwowych Polskiej Rzeczypospolitej Ludowej (The Structure of Legal Control of State Organs of the Polish People's Republic,* 1963) and *Teoria Prawa (The Theory of Law,* 1972). He is a member of the Legislative Council—the consultative body advising the Polish government in matters of legislation—and of the editorial committee of *Państwo i Prawo,* the monthly law review edited by the Institute of State and Law of the Polish Academy of Sciences.

J. A. Passmore is Professor of Philosophy in the Institute of Advanced Studies of the Australian National University, former Vice-President of the Institut Internationale de Philosophie, past President and Fellow of the Australian Academy of Humanities, Fellow of the Academy of the Social Sciences in Australia, Corresponding Member of the British Academy and a Foreign Honorary Member of the Royal Danish Academy and of the American Academy of Arts and Sciences. He was Visiting Fellow in All Souls College, Oxford, in 1970 and again in 1978. Born in Sydney in 1914, he was educated at the University of Sydney, where he lectured in philosophy before taking the Chair in the University of Otago, New Zealand and then moving to the Australian National University. His books include *Ralph Cudworth* (1951), *Hume's Intentions* (1952), *A Hundred Years of Philosophy* (1957), *Philosophical Reasoning* (1961), *Joseph Priestley* (1965), *The Perfectibility of Man* (1970), *Man's Responsibility to Nature* (1974), the 1976 Mason Welch Gross Lectures at Rutgers University, *Science and its Critics* (1978), and *The Philosophy of Teaching* (1979).

Julius Stone, who held the Challis Chair of International Law and Jurisprudence in the University of Sydney from 1942 to 1972, is now an Emeritus Professor of the University, Professor of Law in the University of New South Wales and Distinguished Professor of Jurisprudence and International Law in the University of California's Hastings College of the Law. Born in Leeds, Yorkshire, in 1907, he was educated at the Universities of Leeds, Oxford and Harvard, and holds doctorates in law from all three universities. He began full-time teaching as Assistant Professor in the Harvard University Law School from 1932 to 1936, when Roscoe Pound was Dean, and returned to it as Visiting Bemis Professor in 1956–57. He has been a Fellow of the Center for Advanced Studies in the Behaviorial Sciences, Stanford, California, and of the Woodrow Wilson Center of the Smithsonian Institution, and Visiting Professor in centres of learning that include Columbia and Stanford Universities, the University of California at Berkeley and the Hague Academy of International Law. He has received the World Law Award of the Washington Peace Through Law Conference (1965) and is a Foreign Member of the Royal Netherlands Academy (Division of Letters) and a Fellow of the Australian Academy of the Humanities and of the Academy of the Social Sciences in Australia. His 26 books and numerous articles in the fields of jurisprudence and international law include *Law and the Modern State* (1939), *The Atlantic Charter: New Worlds for Old* (1943), *The Province and Function of Law* (1946), *Law and Society* (3 vols, with J. P. Simpson, 1949–50), *Legal Controls of International Conflict* (1954), *Aggression and World Order* (1958), *Legal Education and Public Responsibility* (1959), *Law and the Social Sciences in the Second Half Century* (1964), *Legal System and Lawyers' Reasonings* (1964), *Human Law and Human Justice* (1965), *Social Dimensions of Law and Justice* (1965), and *Approaches to the Notion of International Justice* (1970). His *Legal Controls of International Conflict* won the American Society of International Law Award in 1956.

Alice Erh-Soon Tay is Professor of Jurisprudence in the University of Sydney. She was born in Singapore in 1934 and educated at Raffles Girls' School, Singapore, Lincoln's Inn and the Australian National University, where she took her doctorate with a thesis on 'The Concept of Possession in the Common Law'. She has practised in criminal law and lectured in law in the (then) University of Malaya in Singapore and the Australian National University, and been a visiting research worker and Visiting Professor, on various occasions, in the United States, the USSR and the Federal Republic of Germany. She is the author of articles on common law, jurisprudence, comparative law, Soviet law and Chinese law, and of several contributions to the *Encyclopedia of Soviet Law*, besides being co-author, with her husband, Eugene Kamenka, of a forthcoming study, *Marxism and the Theory of Law*. In this series, she has co-edited and contributed to *Law and Society* and *Human Rights* and contributed to *Bureaucracy*; she is also co-editor (with E. Kamenka) of *Law-Making in Australia* (1979). She is an Executive Member of the International Association for Philosophy of Law and Social Philosophy and served as President of the Association's Extraordinary World Congress held in Sydney and Canberra in 1977.

Index